When Your *Heart* Cries Out to God

When Your *Heart* Cries Out to God

Harold Sala

HARVEST HOUSE PUBLISHERS
EUGENE, OREGON

Unless otherwise indicated, all Scripture quotations are taken from the HOLY BIBLE, NEW INTERNATIONAL VERSION®. NIV®. Copyright © 1973, 1978, 1984 by the International Bible Society. Used by permission of Zondervan. All rights reserved.

Verses marked KJV are taken from the King James Version of the Bible.

Verses marked NKJV are taken from the New King James Version. Copyright ©1982 by Thomas Nelson, Inc. Used by permission. All rights reserved.

Verses marked NASB are taken from the New American Standard Bible®, © 1960, 1962, 1963, 1968, 1971, 1972, 1973, 1975, 1977, 1995 by The Lockman Foundation. Used by permission. (www.Lockman.org)

Verses marked TLB are taken from *The Living Bible,* Copyright ©1971. Used by permission of Tyndale House Publishers, Inc., Wheaton, IL 60189 USA. All rights reserved.

Verses marked MSG are taken from The Message. Copyright © by Eugene H. Peterson 1993, 1994, 1995, 1996, 2000, 2001, 2002. Used by permission of NavPress Publishing Group.

Verses marked ESV are from The Holy Bible, English Standard Version, copyright © 2001 by Crossway Bibles, a division of Good News Publishers. Used by permission. All rights reserved.

Cover by Left Coast Design, Portland, Oregon

Cover photo © iStockphoto.com; Author photo by vasquezstudios.com

WHEN YOUR HEART CRIES OUT TO GOD
Formerly published as *Guidelines for Finding Your Way*

Published by Harvest House Publishers
Eugene, Oregon 97402
www.harvesthousepublishers.com

Library of Congress Cataloging-inPublication Data

Sala, Harold J.
When your heart cries out to God / Harold Sala.
p.cm.
ISBN 978-0-7369-2572-3 (pbk.)
1. Christian life. I. Title
BV4501.3.S247 2009
248.4—dc22

2008036843

Printed in the United States of America

09 10 11 12 13 14 15 16 17 / BP-NI / 10 9 8 7 6 5 4 3 2 1

Affectionately dedicated to the wonderful men and women—
both staff and volunteers—
in the United States and the Philippines who have labored alongside me.
Without them neither this book nor the ministry of Guidelines International
could have become a reality.

Acknowledgments

I want to express my appreciation to my daughter Nancy Deushane for her insightful assistance in grouping the book's selections; to Margaret Duffield and Louise Calvert, who spent many hours editing the manuscript and made significant contributions to the flow of ideas; and to my administrative assistant, Luisa Ampil, who patiently edited and processed the materials, which were initially written for my radio program, *Guidelines—A Five Minute Commentary on Living.* I'm also grateful for the partnership with Harvest House Publishers, who has been a great enabler and encourager. My special thanks goes to Paul Gossard for his insightful comments and superb editing, making this book more readable. Thanks to all of you!

Contents

Chapter 6—When You Worry

Chapter 7—When You Need Courage

Chapter 8–When You Are Afraid

Chapter 9—When You Hope

Chapter 10—When You Are Angry

Chapter 11—When You Are Depressed

Foreword

Anyone can find a negative or cynical perspective in times of turmoil and trouble. They're everywhere, from the doomsday headlines to the water-cooler conversations about ever-shrinking retirement accounts. Throw in a daily dose of war and terrorism, a *20/20* broadcast about economic downturn, a trip or two to the doctor, a birthday, and you have a prescription for full-blown pessimism and depression.

Dr. Harold Sala has dedicated his life of ministry to countering our culture of negativity with the only message of hope and encouragement that is lasting: the hope we find in Jesus Christ.

Harold is neither a pop psychologist nor a motivational speaker, giving out sugary, feel-good messages that fail the real-life tests we encounter. He is a professor and a student of God's Word—where he directs his readers for hope.

This book, *When Your Heart Cries Out to God,* is intended to be a source of encouragement covering a vast number of topics with short, insightful comments designed to challenge your thinking, confront your doubts, push back your cynicism and pessimism, and encourage you to look up and believe God as you make your way through the minefields of life.

Could you use some practical insight from the Bible in the areas of worry and self-discipline? Do you have family members who could use an encouraging word from Harold on anger, fear, or faith? Do you have a neighbor or a co-worker who struggles with loneliness, health issues, or discouragement? These thoughtful chapters can be just the right message, at just the right time. I think you will be blessed, as Kay and I have been, by Harold's uplifting insights.

Dr. Rick Warren
Author of *The Purpose-Driven Life*
Senior Pastor, Saddleback Church
Lake Forest, California

Look Up to God

In the early hours of February 3, 1943, the USS *Dorchester,* a troop carrier, was plowing through the frigid, icy seas off the coast of Greenland. Aboard that overloaded ship were 902 men who were on their way to join American forces fighting in Europe. The *Dorchester,* traveling at half speed because of ice floes, was an easy target for a German submarine. Unexpectedly and suddenly, the restless sleep of the men crammed in their bunks was shattered, when a torpedo sliced through the dark waters and slammed into the bulkhead with a tremendous blast.

Immediately the gaping hole in the side of the vessel allowed it to start taking on water. Panic ensued. There were neither enough life rafts or life jackets for the men. On board that ship were four chaplains: two Protestants, a Catholic, and a Jew. Seeing there were insufficient life jackets, the four chaplains took off theirs and gave them to men whose lives had been spared. As the ship began to list, these four held hands in a heroic show of unity and prayed as the ship went to its icy grave only 27 minutes after the torpedo struck.

Only 230 of the 902 aboard that ship lived to tell about the dark night of disaster, but when the survivors were rescued, they told the story of the four chaplains and what they had done. Every newspaper in the Western world carried the story and eulogized their self-sacrificing deed.

But as Paul Harvey says, "It's the story behind the story" that makes this even more meaningful. One of those chaplains, Lieutenant Clark Poling, was the son of well-known Christian leader Dr. Daniel Poling, the editor of *The Christian Century* magazine. Back when Clark had been a college student, Dr. Poling had received a telephone call saying, "Dad, I'm coming home. Don't tell Mom but meet my train at..." and he told him when he was arriving.

If you had been the father who got such a telephone call, what would you have thought? You would probably have asked yourself, *What is so important that he has to come home and talk and doesn't want his mother to know about it? Is there a girl involved? What's wrong?*

The dad met the train, and the two of them drove to the church office, where they went in, closed the door, and sat down. The dad then said, "Okay, son, what is it you want to talk about?"

A sober young man looked at his father and said, "Dad, what do you know about God? I've got to know for myself!" What Dr. Poling told him was important—tremendously important. (You'll find his answer in the epilogue. Don't peek now!)

There are seasons to the journey of life from the moment you come into the world to the time when, if you have accepted the gift of salvation through Jesus Christ, God calls you home to heaven. And our needs, which are different from time to time, prompt our hearts to cry out to God—sometimes in pain, sometimes in need, sometimes in fear, sometimes because we want to know Him better, and sometimes in praise and worship.

When Your Heart Cries Out to God is intended to be a source of encouragement throughout the changing seasons of life. In this book you will find selections on 25 topics relating to life's challenges.

Of course, you can use the table of contents and go directly to the section that will help you through a particular need; however, I encourage you to read one selection each weekday (five a week), along with the "resource reading" for a snapshot from Scripture. You may want to highlight thoughts or make notations in the margins of the book or in a journal to help you in the future as you face particular needs.

May God encourage your heart as you find your way through life, learning that God is sufficient for every need, for every crisis, for every day from the cradle to the time you cross the Jordan and enter into the presence of the Lord!

Harold J. Sala

One Thing You Still Lack

When Jesus heard this, he said to him, "You still lack one thing. Sell everything you have and give to the poor, and you will have treasure in heaven. Then come, follow me."
LUKE 18:22

Insight: God gave you a spiritual nature, and no matter how much you have in life, until you connect with Him there will always be an ingredient missing from your life.

Anyone who has ever visited ancient Jericho can testify to the reality that in the summer it can be unbearably hot. Locals are convinced that hell itself is only ten degrees hotter than Jericho. There is an old aphorism that in China only mad dogs and Englishmen go out in the noonday sun, and that surely applies to Jericho as well, which is why a remarkable drama unfolded as Jesus approached the city on His way to Jerusalem.

So vivid was this happening in the life of Jesus that three of Jesus' biographers—Matthew, Mark, and Luke—wrote about it. The story itself is simple enough. A young man, having heard that Jesus was passing by, came running and knelt before Him (Mark 10:17), voicing a question that was perplexing to him.

There is an element of urgency in this encounter. The man had made no appointment. Neither did he bother to consider whether his interview was convenient for Jesus. He simply knew that this was his opportunity to get something off his chest, and he had to take advantage of the moment.

There is also an element of drama in the situation as well. All three of the Gospel writers point out that this man was wealthy. People with lots of money do not run. They snap their fingers and give orders, and others do the running for them. Furthermore, there is an element of desperation as well. Men with money are used to people deferring to them—but humiliating himself before Jesus, the young man kneels in the dusty road. Looking up into the face of Jesus, he asks, "Good teacher, what must I do to inherit eternal life?"

In the event you have never studied the Gospels (meaning Matthew,

Mark, Luke, and John), you need to know that each one represents a different viewpoint. Mark is called the Gospel of Action. Reflecting a Roman viewpoint, Mark goes to the heart of things. He does not waste words. Mark points out something that his colleagues Matthew and Luke omit. At this point Mark says, "Jesus looked at him and loved him" (Mark 10:21). For "looked," two Greek words could have been used. The first means to observe casually. But the other word—the one Mark used—means to gaze intently at someone. So Jesus looked intently into the face of this troubled young man who knelt before Him and loved him, knowing full well that the great wealth he had would be a stumbling block.

"You still lack one thing," He said, adding, "Sell everything you have and give to the poor, and you will have treasure in heaven. Then come, follow me" (Luke 18:22).

So he immediately disposed of his wealth, forsook his easy lifestyle, and became a disciple, right? Wrong. The record says he walked away full of sorrow because he was very rich.

What's the issue? It's simple: Who or what comes first in your life? Your money, your power, your position, or your God? Earlier Jesus had said, "Seek first his kingdom and his righteousness, and all these things will be given to you as well" (Matthew 6:33).

Andrew, my grandson, had just turned seven when he shocked his mother by saying, "Mother, I'm afraid I'm going to go to hell!"

"Why?" asked Bonnie, somewhat perplexed.

"Because I'm afraid I love my little blue bucket and shovel [a birthday gift] more than God!"

Whether it is your pride, your wealth, or your little blue bucket that stands between you and obedience to the will of God, Jesus wants to come first. "Come and follow Me," is still the invitation Jesus Christ makes to those who ask, "What must I do to inherit eternal life?"

Resource reading: Luke 18:18-30

A Rich Man and the Kingdom of God

Jesus said to his disciples, "I tell you the truth, it is hard for a rich man to enter the kingdom of heaven. Again I tell you, it is easier for a camel to go through the eye of a needle than for a rich man to enter the kingdom of God."

MATTHEW 19:23-24

Insight: There is a deep longing in the heart of every person to know God. Your thirst to know Him was put there so He might satisfy it.

Truth is always stranger than fiction, and nothing is more entertaining than real life. That's the way it was when a young man encountered Jesus as He was approaching Jericho on His way to Jerusalem. The whole incident was touching but awkward. Hearing that Christ was passing his way, the young man ran and knelt before Jesus.

In response to his question about what he needed to do to inherit eternal life, Jesus told him that he still lacked one thing. What was it?

First, we know it was not adequate resources. Matthew, Mark, and Luke all describe him as having "great wealth." So money was not lacking. A Jewish proverb says that when you are rich, you are handsome and you sing well too! John Paul Getty, once among the richest in the entire world, used to say that when you know how much money you have, you aren't very rich. This young man probably was included in that group of elite people. But with all his money, he did not find happiness. He had the mark of desperation as he ran and knelt before Jesus.

The second thing he did not lack was education and culture. This was obvious from his speech and his deportment. Money can buy an education, but it cannot buy happiness—something that Amy Vanderbilt learned. This woman, whose very name was synonymous with etiquette and culture, had all the advantages a good family can give. Her grandfather Cornelius had established the university that bore the family name, yet she was miserable and unhappy. Her marriage was troubled, and her health was challenged by hypertension. We will never know whether her fall from the window of her townhouse on East 8th Street in New York was accidental, caused possibly by dizziness resulting from medication, or suicidal; but what we do know is that money, culture, and opportunities are no guarantee of lasting happiness in life.

The third thing this young man did not lack was influence and achievement. Luke, who himself was a medical doctor, described this young man as "a ruler," meaning a leader of a synagogue, an important position that carried with it respect, authority, and influence. J. Robert Oppenheimer, the German-born Nobel Prize–winning scientist, had influence, achievement, and recognition. He was known as the Father of the Atomic Bomb, yet he died frustrated and unfulfilled. Speaking of his successes he said, "They leave on the tongue only the taste of ashes."

Finally, this young man did not lack moral goodness. Frankly, he was the kind of man you would like for a neighbor—by his own account he was not a murderer, adulterer, or liar, and he honored his parents and loved others around him. Yet Jesus told him that he lacked one thing: What was it? Going to the bottom line, Jesus told him that what he lacked was a personal relationship with God, which Jesus had come to bring. Lacking this, the young man lacked everything. "Go, sell everything you have and give to the poor...then come, follow me," Jesus told him.

Did he do it? No, he turned and walked away sorrowfully because his wealth meant more to him than having a relationship with God.

Lest you misunderstand, the point is not that success is wrong in itself. What is wrong is anything that crowds God out of your life, anything that leaves no room for Him to be your Lord and reason for existing. Today a lot of us have the same struggle. The push for success, the desire to get ahead, the need to gain power or influence—these are all-consuming and thus become lord of our lives. Well did Jesus point out "a man's life does not consist in the abundance of his possessions" (Luke 12:15).

Take time to read the account of this young man's conversation with Jesus found in Luke 18. You may see yourself mirrored in his image.

Resource reading: Matthew 19:16-26

Becoming a Christian

God...gave His one and only Son.
JOHN 3:16

Insight: Many people consider themselves Christians in a cultural context, but there is a deep relationship that Jesus Christ made possible whereby you can have a personal encounter with God and know you belong to Him.

"According to your understanding, who is Jesus Christ?" In response to this question, two-thirds of some 10,000 college students said they believed Jesus Christ is the Son of God. Yet when these same students were asked how they could become Christians, 90 percent said they did not know.[1] What those students expressed is quite true of many people. Salvation is not a matter of knowing facts—it is a matter of acting on them. What counts is not knowledge but action.

A certain amount of knowledge, though, is prerequisite to action. Who is this One called Jesus? What is the relationship of His life and teaching to us today? Is He really who He claimed to be?

The biblical and secular records tell us that Jesus was born in the little town of Bethlehem, a few miles from Jerusalem. The physician Luke writes that Jesus was born of a virgin without a human father. Should Christ have been an ordinary human, this fact would be pretty hard to accept. The virgin birth of Christ was no afterthought in an attempt to glorify His life.

For centuries, the prophets had been foretelling such a birth. Seven hundred years before Christ was born, the prophet Isaiah stated this fact (Isaiah 7:14). In 1947, a scroll containing the text of the Old Testament book of Isaiah was found near the Dead Sea. Carbon dating places the writing of this scroll, which foretold Christ's coming, at about 200 BC. Placed in the cave about AD 70 to 73, that manuscript had become a piece of fulfilled history.

At the age of 30, Christ began His ministry. From the beginning, it was obvious that He was different. He spoke with authority, not as the rest of the teachers of His day. His viewpoint was different too. He spoke as one who commanded the course of the universe. People brought the sick and diseased to Him, and He healed them without exception. He never paused to consider if it could be done. He made no clinical analysis—He simply spoke the word and the healing took place. He commanded, and it happened. In short, He claimed to be God. Actually it was for this He was eventually crucified. But even in His death, He was different.

When He died and was buried, the Roman governor Pilate gave the order to make His tomb as secure as possible. The Roman army put soldiers there to guard it; the religious leaders of His day made it as secure as could be. Unbelief has tried to seal it for 2,000 years, yet the tomb has remained empty. Jesus Christ rose from the grave after three days. He told His disciples ahead of time that He would (Matthew 12:38-40).

Two-thirds of the 10,000 college students interviewed accepted these facts at face value, and I believe you do as well, but only 10 percent were sure about how these facts relate to becoming a Christian. Christ Himself made it clear what a person must do to become a Christian. He said, "Whoever hears my word and believes him who sent me has eternal life and will not be condemned; he has crossed over from death to life" (John 5:24). John said, "To all who received him, to those who believed in his name, he gave the right to become children of God" (John 1:12).

To become a Christian you must believe that Christ, God's Son, died in your place to pay the penalty of death for sin, which you earned and cannot pay (Romans 6:23). Becoming a Christian is not a matter of joining a church or doing this or that. It is accepting the fact that Christ became sin for you—in a real and personal manner. It involves your willingness to believe that, as God's Son, He identified Himself with your sin. It is accepting the fact that God treated Him at Calvary like you should have been treated—so that for all eternity you can be treated as Christ should have been treated. As the apostle Paul put it, "God made him who had no sin to be sin for us, so that in him we might become the righteousness of God" (2 Corinthians 5:21).

Resource reading: John 3

Letting the Image of God Shine Through

In the same way, count yourselves dead to sin but alive to God in Christ Jesus.
ROMANS 6:11

Insight: Silver bears the mark of its artisan. God's child also bears His mark, His image, which the world knows and recognizes.

It's a sobering thought to realize that the world judges God by what they see of Him in the lives of His children—in my life and in yours. We look at our lives and recognize that instead of mirroring His love, justice, character, and peace, we often reflect a distorted picture of God, one fogged over by our human failure. "Not good enough!" cries our incriminating conscience. Then in failure we feel like turning away.

We know that the world should not judge God by what they see in our imperfect lives. We would like to shout, "Don't look at me! I'm just human! Look beyond me and see the living God who raised His Son from the dead!" but we do not have that opportunity.

C.S. Lewis contended that a Christian should never be judged by what his or her life *is,* but by how it *would have been* had the person never come to Christ. He's right, but the fact remains, we either make the world want what we've got or give them a good reason to walk away thinking, *If that's Christianity, why bother!* As the salt of the earth, our lives should make people thirst for the living God.

In a time when slavery was accepted, Paul wrote that Christ freed us from the slavery of sin so we willingly became "slaves to God" (Romans 6:22). Even the lives of slaves were a witness for God. When Paul wrote to Titus, he instructed him that slaves were to be subject to their masters. They were to strive to please them and not to talk back. They were to be honest, not stealing from their masters, proving they could be fully trusted "so that in every way they will make the teaching about God our Savior attractive" (Titus 2:10).

Here are questions that make this topic personal: Why does so little of God's true nature come through my life? Why do I manage to mess things up so others see little difference between my life and that of a non-Christian who makes no pretense of having encountered the living God?

Paul offers solutions to these problems. Following his comments about making the teaching about God our Savior attractive to unbelievers, he says that the grace of God teaches us to say no to ungodliness and worldly passions and to live "self-controlled, upright and godly lives in this present age" (Titus 2:12).

A recent news story from Russia told how a new manager took over a farm and promised the workers salaries almost four times what they had been making, provided they promised not to steal from their employer. Some refused to do so, thereby tacitly acknowledging they were stealing more than four times the amount of their salaries.

Honesty and integrity—keeping your word, doing what you say you will do, being punctual, and working eight hours for eight hours of pay—are part of what make your faith look authentic in the eyes of a skeptical world.

God will invade our lives to the degree that we open our hearts and say, "Lord, take control!" Jesus said that no person can serve two masters. When we seek to be masters of our own lives, living according the dictates of our emotions and calling on God only when we are in deep trouble, the world isn't much impressed. They do the same thing.

When a little boy was knocked down by an angry crowd in a subway train, a businessman stopped, picked up the boy's backpack, and helped him to his feet. Surprised, the little boy looked into the man's face and asked, "Is you Jesus?" When we do God's deeds, the spontaneous message is that people have seen Him. The world judges God by what they see of Him in our lives.

Resource reading: 2 Corinthians 2

Born Again

Jesus declared, "I tell you the truth, no one can see the kingdom of God unless he is born again."
JOHN 3:3

Insight: The term *born again* has been so widely applied that it has lost some of its poignancy, yet this is the term the Bible uses to describe having a relationship with God through His Son, Jesus Christ.

Dear Dr. Sala," wrote a listener. "I'm 26 years of age, and at this point in my life, I have such an empty feeling. I'm a member of a Baptist church (which I haven't been to for at least a month). I'm trying to reach for something, but I don't know what! I'm spiritually weak. Is there a time in our lives when we become stumped—you don't know which way to go? If you are able to answer these questions, please reply."

A second letter struck a kindred note. A friend wrote, "I have asked God to save me, but my faith is very weak when I get worried. Then it is as if I don't believe in God. I am afraid my faith is so small God has not saved me. With this little faith, can God save me? As long as I have problems, I can't believe. Please help me!"

Perhaps you can relate to the heart cries of these two friends. Way down in your heart you would like to believe...but so many things have happened, you have begun to wonder if something is wrong with you or whether faith works for you at all. Hold on, friend. This section is just for you. Only God knows how many folks live with doubts in their heart. Questions such as these abound:

- Is my faith strong enough?
- Why can't I get on top of my temptation?
- Why doesn't God speak to me as He does to other people?

The bottom line, of course, is that the doubts and questions rob you of your peace and the assurance of your salvation. You do not know whether God will receive you at all should you die and knock at heaven's gate.

Based on what my two friends told me, I have more confidence that

God has heard them than they do. You know why? I have greater confidence in the promises of God and know the Word better. But how much do you have to know to have assurance you are on good terms with God?

First, settle some issues once and for all, issues like this: Would God lie to you? Will He keep His word? Did He really mean what He said when the prophets of old recorded His Word? Simple questions but vitally important ones. Long ago Moses wrote, "God is not a man, that he should lie, nor a son of man, that he should change his mind. Does he speak and then not act? Does he promise and not fulfill?" (Numbers 23:19).

The New Testament says, "If you confess with your mouth, 'Jesus is Lord' and believe in your heart that God raised him from the dead, you will be saved" (Romans 10:9). Did you believe in your heart and verbally confess Christ as your Savior? If you did, then God will honor His Word. You can know you are His child. John wrote, "He who has the Son has life; he who does not have the Son of God does not have life" (1 John 5:12).

But how do you explain the doubts and questions? In some cases, we depend on feelings rather than the facts from God's Word. Our emotions are an unstable barometer of reality, and we cannot depend on them. Sometimes Satan does use doubts and questions to convince us that salvation may work for others but not for us. At other times we ask, "How could I really be God's child and have the problems I have?" We fail to understand that God promises to take us *through* the deep waters but not always to deliver us *from* them. You can know that you are born again, and you can have that knowledge today.

Resource reading: Romans 10:1-13

The God of Peace

Whatever you have learned or received or heard from me, or seen in me—put it into practice. And the God of peace will be with you.

PHILIPPIANS 4:9

Insight: One of the most critical differences between the God of the Bible and pagan gods is that the God of the Book is a peace-loving Father, not an angry deity whose wrath must be assuaged.

A comedian making light of God's instruction to Noah mimics Noah's response to God's call, saying, "What do you want, God? I didn't do nuthin'!" That was supposed to be humor, but it underlines a pretty common belief that God will not bother you if you do not bother Him. Sadly enough, individuals who prefer to live independently of their Maker and live in rebellion against Him are the real losers, not because of God's wrath but because of the blessings they are denied.

Only those who know God come to an understanding of how great His love and compassion are toward those who fear Him and walk in the light of His Word. I've been thinking of some of the qualifying phrases that describe God's nature. For example, Jeremiah records the words of God Himself: "I am the LORD, the God of all mankind." Then He asks the rhetorical question, "Is anything too hard for me?" (Jeremiah 32:27). Knowing that nothing is too hard for God is comforting when we have needs and knock on heaven's door in prayer.

But what most speaks to my heart are three phrases found in the New Testament that describe God: *the God of peace, the God of all comfort,* and *the God of hope.* For the next few moments focus on these three great qualities: peace in the midst of the storm, comfort in times of trouble, and the hope of eternal life.

The first phrase—the God of peace—is found five times in the New Testament. In Paul's letters to the churches at Rome, Philippi, and Thessalonica, places where he had ministered, he refers to God as the God of peace. The writer of Hebrews ends his letter with this blessing:

the Lord has laid on him the iniquity of us all" (Isaiah 53:6). Without a shepherd, sheep quickly wander and go astray. That's why the shepherd is so important. Left on their own, sheep are vulnerable to predators and enemies of all descriptions.

We're sheep. That's why *we* need a shepherd.

The Bible describes this wandering or going astray as a deliberate act of spiritual rebellion of the heart, as missing the mark (using the analogy of an archer whose aim falls short of the target). The Bible calls it sin. The middle letter—I—best characterizes what sin is all about: *my* will, not God's will.

Making peace with God begins when you acknowledge you have gone astray. This should not be too difficult. Deep down in your heart you know your own sin and waywardness. The second thing you must do is to recognize the voice of the shepherd and claim Him as your Lord and Savior. Jesus, using this very analogy, said, "I am the good shepherd" (John 10:11). He also said, "I am the way and the truth and the life" (John 14:6).

Now, a word of warning. There are a lot of false shepherds: individuals, philosophies, even religions that claim to take you to God. But only one shepherd proved He is the Son of God by dying and rising again on the third day—proof that Jesus was and is the Great Shepherd, the One sent from God.

The final step in making peace with God is to claim His Son as your Shepherd and Savior and begin to follow Him. Too easy? Some think so, but I have learned that when you follow the Shepherd, you will get to know Him. When you know Him, you will love Him. When you love Him, you will obey Him and keep His commandments.

It takes about as long to make peace with God as it does to swallow your pride and ask directions when you are lost. For those who are stubborn, it is easier for a camel to pass through the eye of a needle. For those who are childlike and humble, it's as easy as reaching for an outstretched hand when you have fallen.

Resource reading: Matthew 11

Enjoying the Peace of God

I, even I, am he who blots out
your transgressions, for my own sake,
and remembers your sins no more.
ISAIAH 43:25

Insight: God sent His Son with a white flag to bring about a deep and lasting peace not only with those who are rebels, but also with those who *have simply gone astray and missed the way.*

John Ruskin, the English poet, wrote, "You may either win your peace or buy it: win it by resistance to evil; buy it by compromise with evil." I think Ruskin would agree with the premise that you can find peace only one of two ways: either live in a castle or fortress so secure, so strong, and so impenetrable that no one—even God Himself—could ever come within, or else make peace with your enemies.

The first option is not a real possibility, but the second is.

"Dear Dr. Sala," wrote a friend of Guidelines. "More than anything else I would like to know that I have peace with God."

I have been producing Guidelines for Living, carried on radio and TV and printed in newspapers, since 1963. In these intervening years, only God knows how many have responded, pouring out their hearts, often revealing intimate details of their lives. Many write and tell about the unrest and discontent of broken relationships with God: the young woman who feels estranged from God since she aborted her unborn child, the man who walked out on his wife and children for another woman, the teenager who feels cheap and distraught over continuing sexual escapades, the elderly lady who fears her activities as a youth will keep her from heaven. All of these individuals want to make peace with God but are not sure how to do it. How do you make peace with God?

In war, both sides of the conflict draw lines and build fortifications with a no-man's-land in between. Sometimes we build fortifications in our lives and wall out the sunlight of God's love. We raise the drawbridge and hurl our angry thoughts and words against God, who we think is our enemy. He's not.

A long time ago, God sent His Son, unarmed, to make peace with us. He walked across that vast no-man's-land—that dark valley that separates us from God, that separates mortal from immortal—into our world. The Son was born in Bethlehem. He made it clear that His Father is not an angry enemy, trying to get us. Jesus said, "Peace I leave with you; my peace I give you. I do not give to you as the world gives. Do not let your hearts be troubled and do not be afraid" (John 14:27).

First, you must understand that God wants you to have peace with Him. God's Son came to show you how to find His peace, to drive away the darkness of fear and the bitterness of loneliness.

What caused separation from God initially? Long ago Isaiah wrote, "We all, like sheep, have gone astray…Your iniquities have separated you from your God." This broke the peace and created our loneliness. "Your sins have hidden his face from you, so that he will not hear" (Isaiah 53:6; 59:2).

The second step to peace with God is to understand that God made Christ to be sin for you so you might be accepted, without guilt, in God's sight. This enables God to forgive your sins, your rebellion, your wrongdoing. But forgiveness is not automatic. You've got to ask for it, confessing your sin. That's your part, and it's the equivalent of running up the white flag and calling a truce to the war.

Then what happens? God says, "I, even I, am he who blots out your transgressions, for my own sake, and remembers your sins no more" (Isaiah 43:25). That's good news, friend. When you know that God has forgiven you, His peace fills your heart. Then you may also need to forgive someone else, perhaps even yourself.

Resource reading: 2 Peter 2

The Way That Leads to Peace

When a man's ways please the
LORD, he makes even his enemies
to be at peace with him.
PROVERBS 16:7 NKJV

Insight: The most difficult part of finding peace is getting started. Cumbered with pride or blinded by anger or unwilling to be thought weak, we hesitate to take the first step that leads to lasting peace.

One of the Church Fathers, Clement of Alexandria, used an interesting expression. He wrote of "the way of peace" or "the path that leads to peace." Though the expression is not found in the Bible, there are literally hundreds of expressions in that grand book that tell us God's intention is for us to live in peace.

Would you personally like to make peace with someone? With a husband, an aged father, or an individual in the workplace who has mistreated you? For years you have lived with the thought of revenge, but now you are not so sure that all the hostility, the loneliness, and the pain are worth it. Besides, you have a nagging feeling in your gut telling you that not only was the other person wrong, but that you also are wrong.

The way that leads to peace. What is it? If peace is your goal, there are four steps, or guidelines, for you to pursue.

Guideline 1: The way that leads to peace is marked by the commitment of two parties who want peace. There are three things you cannot do: climb a fence that leans toward you, kiss a person who leans away from you, and make peace with someone who refuses to come to the table and talk. That's why Paul wrote, "If it is possible, as far as it depends on you, live at peace with everyone" (Romans 12:18).

Often though, when you run up the white flag and indicate that you want peace, the enemy—though not willing to be the first to bend—is more than glad to meet you at the peace table.

James Ramsay MacDonald was the prime minister of England between the two world wars. At one point he had a discussion about peace with a fellow government official, who thought MacDonald was idealistic and unreal. MacDonald argued for peace, while the official, who was a specialist on foreign affairs, was unimpressed.

"The desire for peace does not necessarily ensure it," said the antagonist.

"Quite true," countered MacDonald, but quickly added, "Neither does the desire for food satisfy your hunger, but at least it gets you started toward a restaurant."

Guideline 2: The way that leads to peace is marked by the willingness of two individuals to give up their anger and—yes—negotiate. Frankly, some enjoy being angry. It gives them a reason to justify their baseness and rottenness. Besides, they find it much easier to sling mud or stones or bullets than to admit they too might have been wrong. At some point, the way that leads to peace demands you forget about the issue of who was right and who was wrong. You must consider the benefits of peace to be more worthwhile than the perverse satisfaction of having justification for your anger.

Guideline 3: The way that leads to peace is marked by the refusal to continue the battle. It's difficult to have a war when nobody wants to fight. There's an old story, well documented by a variety of sources, which illustrates the point. On Christmas Eve in the year 1914, German and British soldiers were in trenches facing each other. Since this was the first Christmas Eve of the war, neither side was sure if they would fight on Christmas or desist for the day. Finally, British soldiers raised signs in German: *Merry Christmas.* Then carols were sung on both sides. Eventually soldiers met in no-man's-land to exchange candy and cigarettes. Not until reinforcements were sent in, who had not witnessed that event, did fighting begin anew.

Guideline 4: The path to peace is marked by goodwill. The path may not be well-worn, but wise are those who travel it.

Resource reading: Isaiah 26:1-5

Peace in Our World

The LORD *is good, a refuge in times of trouble. He cares for those who trust in him.*
NAHUM 1:7

Insight: Regardless of conflict or turmoil in our world, you can have a heart ruled by peace. Your attitude is a choice, not a circumstance imposed on you.

Nobel Prizes are awarded each year by the king of Sweden to individuals who have made outstanding contributions to humankind in six fields: physics, chemistry, physiology and medicine, literature, economics, and peace. Alfred Nobel, in his will, directed that his large estate should be used in this manner. Who was Alfred Nobel, and why did he choose to give away his wealth in this manner?

Nobel was born in Stockholm, the son of an inventor. He received his early education in nearby St. Petersburg and his training as an engineer in the United States. When he returned to his native Sweden, he began to experiment with nitroglycerin in his father's factory. Before this time, there had been no way to handle this substance without extreme danger, and many people died trying to use it. Nobel, however, combined nitroglycerin with an absorbent substance, producing a product that could be used with relative safety—dynamite.

He set up factories all over the world and eventually became one of the world's richest men. But for the rest of his life, he was plagued by poor health and haunted by the realization that his invention, through military uses, brought death and injury to many thousands of people. It had never been his intention to use dynamite for war, but for peace. To assuage his guilt, Nobel set up a fund of about $9 million—an immense amount of money in that day—with the intention of using the interest to reward outstanding contributors to the betterment of humanity.

The Nobel Peace Prize was given for the first time in the year 1901. This coveted prize has been awarded to a wide array of individuals, such as Jean Henri Dunant, the Swiss founder of the Red Cross, Albert Schweitzer,

Martin Luther King Jr., and Mother Teresa. Every recipient receives both a medal and a monetary gift.

Alfred Nobel died in 1896, long before two major wars tore our world apart and before the splitting of the atom, which meant the entire world could be destroyed by nuclear weapons. But there is one thing for sure: Nobel understood the importance of having peace rule our world, our lives, our neighborhoods, and our homes.

Personal peace is one of today's most sought commodities, and scores of individuals seek it in different ways. However, it is an individual, personal, internal matter.

Long ago, Peter the fisherman, who was one of the inner circle of Jesus Christ, wrote that we should make every effort to be found spotless, blameless, and at peace with God. Have you discovered that when people are at peace with God, they usually are at peace with others and with themselves? It is impossible to be really at peace with God while you are at war with your spouse or a child or a friend.

Peace does not necessarily mean the cessation of difficulties or problems. Rather, peace is serenity in the face of the storm and the confident understanding that God will take you through the conflict.

Years ago a certain art school held a contest, with a prize to be awarded for the drawing or painting that best depicted peace. The winning entry was a painting of a great storm ravaging a large tree, and on one of the branches was a small bird's nest. The mother bird had spread her wings over her young and, sitting quietly, gave them the protection that saved their lives.

That, friend, can be a picture of God's care for you in the face of the storm. The prophet of old was right when he wrote, "The LORD is good, a refuge in times of trouble. He cares for those who trust in him" (Nahum 1:7). It's still true.

Resource reading: Isaiah 26:1-5

The Need for Love

God demonstrates his own love for us in this:
While we were still sinners, Christ died for us.
ROMANS 5:8

Insight: Love is a decision, a commitment to care, which must be nourished and fed daily.

Our need to be loved was established by God Himself, and it was He who also made provision for that great need to be met in our families. Do you remember the familiar words of the apostle Paul to the Corinthians: "And now abide faith, hope, and love, but the greatest of these is love"? No matter how great the need for love, it seems that our capacity to love each other has been seriously diminished in the world of quick fixes and fractured, broken relationships.

Have you ever asked yourself, *What has happened to our ability to love?* Has it been gassed by the pernicious fumes that have polluted our environment? Or has it simply been pushed aside by our selfish desire for gratification? Have we so confused love with sex that we no longer understand what it is? I asked myself that question as I picked up the paper and read of a three-year-old who was seriously injured in an automobile accident.

This little boy was paralyzed from the neck down, but what was more distressing was that his mother told reporters she did not intend to visit him in the hospital. She no longer wanted to be bothered with a crippled son. There is a good ending to this story, though. Dr. Gary Gieseke, the neurosurgeon who treated the three-year-old, told his wife about the boy, who had no visitors in the hospital. She started visiting him every afternoon and eventually fell in love with him. She and the doctor finally adopted the boy and gave him the love he needed.

Countless thousands of children are crippled emotionally and psychologically by a lack of parental love. Talk to a counselor in a juvenile detention home or prison, and you will discover that almost all the juvenile offenders have one thing in common—they came from a home where love was missing. The home is the great classroom where a child first learns what love is by responding to it as an infant. As a child, he observes it in the lives of his parents and in his own way begins to practice it.

We hear a lot about parents who have no love for each other, but what of the parent who honestly confesses to have no love for a child? Is it not natural for a mother to love her child? (Before you answer that, think for a moment. First, it is perfectly normal for every parent to have days when God's precious jewels are only semiprecious. It may be one of those days when you are tired and your nerves are on edge. Every time you try to get your face washed, a three-year-old bangs on the door loud enough to wake the dead. You hear a little voice say, "Mommy, Mommy" every 30 seconds for most of your waking day. In an unguarded moment you may think, *I just cannot stand my kids. I would do anything to get away from them.* Every mother has that need periodically, but the need does not mean you do not love your child. Not for a moment!)

Yet some parents have no love for their children. How else do we explain the bizarre happenings that have filled our papers in recent times, as parents—for only-God-knows reasons—have killed their own offspring. There are people who have lost their love for each other and for their children because their hearts are hardened and they have lost their capacity to love.

Has your ability to love been stifled by the cares of living, hardened by the push to get ahead? Then, friend, it's time to get your priorities straightened out, which begins with the source of love: God Himself. "God is love," wrote the apostle John. "The one who does not love does not know God" (1 John 4:8 NASB). When you allow God to touch your life, one of the first results is a new capacity to let love flow through you. It's the only solution to a tough issue.

Resource reading: Romans 5:1-11

Keeping Love Alive

Guard yourself in your spirit, and do not break faith with the wife of your youth.
MALACHI 2:15

Insight: Love is an unconditional commitment to an imperfect person to meet the needs of that person in a sacrificial way.

Henry Ford, the industrialist who put the world on wheels, was asked after 50 years of married life how he managed to stay happily married. His reply: "I've treated marriage like I've made automobiles—just stick to one model." It's regrettable that he did not follow his own advice.

Even so, more than a few who do "stick to one model" find that happiness in marriage eludes them. They have worn the same wedding ring for twenty or thirty years, yet most of those years have been marked by strife and unhappiness. Their commitment may be strong enough to keep them married but not strong enough to resolve the issues that keep them from being happy.

Do you ever ask the question, "What happens between the time a couple stands at a marriage altar with eyes glowing and hearts burning with happiness, and the time they stand before a judge to ask for an annulment or a divorce?"

"Is marriage the sole cause of divorce?" reads the slogan on a sweatshirt I saw recently.

Sometimes the blow that shatters a relationship comes like a bomb you did not expect, but more often it is like a slowly growing cancer that infests your relationship and calluses your feelings. That must have been what happened to the person who described marriage as "a condition in which a woman never gets what she expects and a man never expects what he gets."

Instead of holy wedlock, marriage becomes unholy deadlock. While divorce is not the will of God for His children, neither is it the will of God for us to be in relationships that harbor anger, bitterness, and distrust. Both are wrong—in different ways.

"It just can't be the will of God for me to remain in an unhappy relationship," people tell me. While they are partly right—it isn't God's will for two people to harbor bitterness and anger—they are far off course in thinking that changing partners will change the emotional temperature of their lives.

What happens when a marriage goes wrong? Love has begun to wither and die. We've taken each other's love for granted, and the resulting abuse produces a wilderness in our lives.

Years ago, Irving Berlin tenderly wrote, "I'll be loving you, always, with a love that's true, always." Not only are those words sentimental and slushy, they are also untrue. God only knows how many times I have asked couples, "Do you love each other?" And I hear the mumbled response, "I used to, but I don't know if I love him [or her] any more after what has happened."

After 50 years of marriage, an old gentleman was asked the secret of his good marriage. He reached into his pocket and pulled out an old watch. "This is it," he said. What did an old watch have to do with marital happiness? "When Sarah and I got married, her dad took me aside and gave me a package saying, 'This is all you need to know about marriage.'" Holding up the watch he said, "This was inside it." Pressing the stem of the old watch, the cover flew open and engraved on the inside cover of the watch, now 50 years old, were the words, *Say something nice to Sarah every day!* "That," he said, "has been the secret of our happiness."

How do you keep love alive? By not presuming on each other, by acts of kindness, by remembering love is a fire that must be rekindled every day.

A closing thought: You can start over, but you never start again. You can change partners, but you never go back to the genesis of a relationship and start from there. Think about it.

Resource reading: Proverbs 31

Loving God and Your Neighbor As Yourself

Do not seek revenge or bear a grudge against one of your people, but love your neighbor as yourself. I am the LORD.

LEVITICUS 19:18

Insight: You cannot love your neighbor as you should until you have met the God of love described in the Bible.

Facing the building in Jerusalem in which the Knesset, the Israeli Parliament, meets is a beautiful menorah, a gift from Britain to Israel. It was created by the well-known sculptor Benno Elkan and is covered with images that tell the story of Israel's long and colorful history. A menorah, a seven-branched candelabra, represents the fullness of God.

One of the seven branches of Elkan's menorah shows a rabbi with a pupil standing on one foot before him. The rabbi was Hillel, one of the greatest in Jewish history. But what's the story behind the student standing on one foot? According to tradition, which Elkan beautifully illustrated, the unnamed student had challenged Hillel's teaching, asking if the rabbi could teach him the law while he stood on one foot. And Rabbi Hillel replied, "Do not unto your neighbor what you would not have him do unto you."

The Jewish leaders taught first that the people should "love the LORD your God with all your heart and with all your soul and with all your strength" (Deuteronomy 6:5). Not only did the people of Moses' day struggle with that one—we struggle with it today, if we honestly admit how many things push God toward the sidelines in our lives.

The Jews also believed that loving your neighbor was the second great commandment upon which the law rested. When Jesus was challenged by the question, "Which is the greatest commandment in the Law?" he answered, "Love the Lord your God with all your heart and with all your soul and with all your mind." He then added, "This is the first and greatest commandment. And the second is like it: 'Love your neighbor as yourself,'" explaining, "All the Law and the Prophets hang on these two commandments" (Matthew 22:36-40).

For a moment, ponder what Jesus is saying. He is asserting that everything found in the books of Genesis, Exodus, Leviticus, Numbers, and Deuteronomy, along with all of the writings of the prophets, including Isaiah, Jeremiah, Ezekiel, Daniel, and the 12 called minor prophets—all of them put together can be summed up in two powerful truths: loving God with all your being and loving your neighbor as yourself.

While loving God this way is not easy, it is less offensive than loving the neighbor (not mine, of course!) living next door who puts his garbage in your trash can, who throws away your mail when it is delivered to his mailbox, who plays loud music when you want to sleep, who lets his dog bark in the middle of the night, and who—let's face it—is not very lovable.

There is one thing for sure: You will never love your neighbor as yourself until you have first learned to love God with all of your heart. Paul explained that the love of God is shed abroad in our hearts by His Spirit who is given to us (Romans 5:5).

So how do we learn to love God? First, by finding out who He is. You must know Him before you will ever love Him, and once you have come to know Him and His great love and compassion for you, your heart will cry out, "Yes, Lord, I do love You and want to serve You." Then His great love will flow through you, reaching your spouse, your neighbor whom you neither know nor like, and those whom you work with.

Loving God is the key. May God help us to know Him and to love Him so we can love our neighbors.

Resource reading: Matthew 22:34-45

The Tremendous Power of Love

God so loved the world that he gave his one and only Son, that whoever believes in him shall not perish but have eternal life.
John 3:16

Insight: Giving and receiving love is a basic emotional need that cannot be met apart from interaction with others.

Erich Fromm, an often-quoted psychologist, believed that loneliness and the inability to love are the underlying causes of both psychiatric and emotional disorders. Scores of social scientists have aptly demonstrated that love is absolutely essential to life itself. People cannot be well-rounded individuals if they are unable to relate successfully to others and have not discovered the power of love.

"There comes a time in the development of every person," says Joshua Liebman in his book *Peace of Mind,* "when he must love his neighbor or become a twisted, stunted personality."

Such a person ended up in a women's prison in Paris. She was lonely, afraid, angry, and bitter, and she resisted every attempt of people to break through the defensive barrier she had built around herself.

But a little woman who worked among the prisoners knew love is more powerful than the hatred this prisoner grew up with. As the woman visited the prison, she would speak to the prisoner, who hurled back bitter epithets and demanded to be left alone. Nonetheless, the visitor kept on offering gospel tracts and telling the prisoner that God loved her no matter how far she had strayed from His presence. The response was a snarl: "*Nobody* loves me. Don't talk to me!" For several years every attempt to bridge the barrier was met with rebuff, but in the meantime the woman prayed that God would give her an opportunity to express love. Then without planning or even thinking about it, she gained the opportunity with a spontaneity that had the breath of heaven.

On that particular day, the woman began her round, passing through the jail as she normally did each week. When she passed the bunk of this hardened and hateful woman, she stopped and kissed the prisoner on the forehead. At first she reeled back and drew up her arm in anger, as though she was going to strike the one who had planted a kiss on her forehead. Looking up into the face of her undeserved friend, she began to weep and then sob almost uncontrollably. "Why did you kiss me?" she asked. "Nobody has kissed me for many years. Kick me, strike me, use me, and leave me—but kiss me, no." You can chalk up one more victory for the healing power of love.

Individuals who have grown up in homes with little or no love find it difficult to give and to receive love. You may be one of them. Nonetheless, every person alive responds to the power of love. Some individuals, slightly irregular in shape and personality, find it hard to accept love. There may be one such person in your life, but do not give up. Love is the antidote to the problems of the world.

I've often thought of that woman in the Paris prison, and I see my old nature in her story. As a loving God reaches down to me in love, my old self wants to pull away, thinking, *I don't need your help or love!* Paul understood, for he wrote, "But God demonstrates his own love for us in this: while we were still sinners, Christ died for us" (Romans 5:8). That's the acid test—a demonstration of love so costly that it required the life of God's Son.

What's the bottom line? First, do not give up striving to reach out in love when your attempts to love are rebuffed; and second, when people attempt to show love to you, realize that their love meets a need not only in your life but in theirs as well. That's the way God made us!

Resource reading: Luke 15:11-31

The Quest for Real Love

Set me as a seal upon thine heart,
as a seal upon thine arm: for love is
strong as death; jealousy is cruel as the
grave: the coals thereof are coals of fire,
which hath a most vehement flame.
SONG OF SOLOMON 8:6 KJV

Insight: Love is the most powerful force in the entire world.

Shortly before his death, John Paul Getty, once said to be the richest man in the world, said that he would gladly give all of his millions for the love of a woman. Had he first given away his millions, he would then have found out if he was loved for his money or for what he was—something he never learned. Sometimes people go through life searching for love, never quite finding it. Like the vision that is always on the horizon but never within their grasp, real love eludes them.

The ancient king of Israel, Solomon, could have related to what Getty said, because his life was an ongoing series of relationships, most of which never satisfied. Many of his marriages were merely political or social contracts, without the commitment of love; however, Solomon did understand what love is.

He is credited with having written one of the most unusual of the 66 books of the Bible, the Song of Solomon, a poetic rendition of the quest for real love. In this lovely and graphic story, you see both the picture of two lovers committed to each other and the larger image of God's love for His people, Israel.

As he comes to the end of this beautiful love story, Solomon makes two requests of his lover: "Place me like a seal over your heart," and place me "like a seal on your arm" (Song of Solomon 8:6). Your heart is personal and inward. Your arm is visible and public. He wanted both personal intimacy and public commitment.

Tyrannical dictators have tried to force public identification for their own purposes, but their people, having no love for their rulers, have ended that commitment as soon as they could. During the Third Reich, Jews were forced to wear yellow armbands with the Star of David, thereby identifying them as Jews. In Soviet prisons, prisoners were tattooed with their prison numbers on their knuckles for the entire world to see. But, as would be expected, the people removed or covered them as soon as they had opportunity.

Solomon says that love has to be both personal and public so there is outward recognition of the inward affection you have for someone. He then makes three interesting observations about love:

First he says, "Love is as strong as death" (8:6). Frankly, I would have used another image, rather than that of death. I would have said that love is as strong as a raging river or greater than a majestic mountain or stronger than a lion—but no, Solomon uses the image of cruel death, which shows no favoritism and eventually claims us all.

Then he says, "It burns like blazing fire, like a mighty flame. Many waters cannot quench love; rivers cannot wash it away" (8:6-7). Yes, with this our hearts agree. True love always wins out, says the poet.

Solomon adds a final thought: "If one were to give all the wealth of his house for love, it would be utterly scorned" (8:7). Countless thousands of wealthy men and women like John Paul Getty have said, "I'm never sure whether someone loves me for what I am or for my money."

Money can never buy the smile of a child, the love of a spouse, or the peace that comes by knowing you are right with God.

Are you still searching for love, or have you found it? Love is a decision, a commitment to care. It is both public and private, both intimate and observable by anyone who looks at your life.

An old aphorism says, "The best things in life are free!" and certainly love would fall into that category. Love makes the world go 'round, say some, and while others disagree, one thing is for sure: Love makes the ride worthwhile. It's still true. Solomon would agree.

Resource reading: 1 Corinthians 13

Closing the Door

Anyone, then, who knows the good he ought to do and doesn't do it, sins.
JAMES 4:17

Insight: The longer you wait to learn discipline, the more difficult it is.

How often have you heard the line, "He just couldn't say no!" or "She knew better than that. That's not how she was raised!" What's the problem? In many cases, it's a lack of discipline that leads people into situations they know to be wrong.

Often I sit down with couples whose marriages are failing. One spouse will turn in anger to the other and hurl the words, "Why did you do that?" The feeble response is often, "I don't know. I just couldn't help myself!"

Needed is discipline—or more specifically, self-discipline, the kind that has feet connected to a backbone that motivates you to close the door on the refrigerator or walk away from temptation, the kind that gives you the strength to hit the button on the TV controller or click the mouse on your computer when you have strayed into areas that Paul calls "secret and shameful" (2 Corinthians 4:2).

My experience with people leads me to conclude that most people who find themselves in moral quicksand are not blind to what they are doing. True, they are not thinking through the consequences, but they simply do not have the self-discipline necessary to turn an about-face and close the door on temptation.

What are the consequences of self-indulgence as opposed to self-discipline? A broken home, shattered confidence when a mate no longer trusts, loss of self-respect, and perhaps God's hand of discipline.

You are free to make whatever decisions and choices you please, but you cannot control the consequences of those choices. For those who are God's children, not only does life yield harsh discipline, but God gives it as well. "Hey," you may say, "I thought God was a loving God." He is. That's exactly why He disciplines His children.

The New Testament writer of the book of Hebrews reminds us,

> You have forgotten that word of encouragement that addresses you as sons: "My son, do not make light of the Lord's discipline, and do not lose heart when he rebukes you, because the Lord disciplines those he loves, and he punishes everyone he accepts as a son" (Hebrews 12:5-6).

"Better to be pruned to grow," said John Trapp, "than cut up to burn." It's still true.

Hitting the wall can be a good thing. Sometimes a swift kick in the pants is what you need to help you realize you need to change. God uses discipline to get your attention, to help you realize that continuing on the path you are on leads to disaster. Charles Spurgeon wrote, "I bear my willing witness that I owe more to the fire, and the hammer, and the file, than to anything else in the Lord's workshop."

Changing your attitude is the first step, what the Bible calls repentance. It's the deep-seated emotion that makes you realize you have been playing with fire, and it's time to change *fast*.

The second step is changing your actions. It's important to realize that the decision to do right brings with it God's help, which you have lacked until then. God will not do it for you, but knowing that He's able to give you the resolve you lack and His strength for your weakness makes it much easier for you to do right—even when it is painful. "For God did not give us a spirit of timidity, but a spirit of power, of love and of self-discipline," as Paul wrote to Timothy (2 Timothy 1:7). Stop and think about that advice. Who gives us power, love, and self-discipline? God does. Have you asked Him for these?

Self-discipline not only closes the door on temptation, but it also brings rich dividends spiritually. Remember, you can choose to do whatever you like, but with every choice come consequences—both negative and positive—which you neither choose nor avoid.

Resource reading: Hebrews 12:1-12

Steps to Self-Discipline

For Christ's sake, I delight in weaknesses, in insults, in hardships, in persecutions, in difficulties. For when I am weak, then I am strong.
2 CORINTHIANS 12:10

Insight: Developing goals that are in line with God's purpose for your life and learning discipline to accomplish them is not only pleasing to your heavenly Father but will also give you a great sense of self-worth and accomplishment.

When he was a child, he was never disciplined. "Love is all a child needs," his mother had said, adding, "When he's older, he'll learn what he should do." In grade school, he fought with his classmates and talked back to his teacher. In high school he brought beer to school, which resulted in his suspension. In college he was caught cheating on exams, but no official action was taken. He could not hold a job because he could not get himself out of bed in the morning. When he married, he could not say no to credit card debt or other women who were available. He failed in marriage, in business, and in life.

Is there a common thread to patterns of failure in the lives of millions of people? There is—a lack of discipline. It is everybody's problem in an age of indolence, fast food, quick fixes, and relationships without commitment or meaning.

A lot of people—perhaps even you—are not caught in the dangerous whirlpool of this problem. But in their hearts they know they need more discipline—the kind that makes you eat healthier, get up when you need to, make sure your kids learn good habits, and stop spending money when it's gone. Sounds good, right? The following guidelines can help you develop self-discipline.

Guideline 1: Take the little steps first. When that voice within says, "This one time won't matter!" you've got to take quick, decisive action. Eating three chocolates that weigh only ounces can put pounds on you in places that cause you to sit on the beach in a T-shirt instead of a swimsuit.

Instead of indulging in a rich dessert, opt for a piece of licorice. Punctuality is also a matter of discipline. When you are late, you are saying, "All of you at this meeting are not as important as I am, so you can wait for me." Set two alarm clocks. Put one alarm across the room. Practicing discipline in the small things produces results in big things. It sets the pace for future gains.

Guideline 2: Be accountable to someone. The strength of small groups—Alcoholics Anonymous, Weight Watchers, a weekly prayer group—is accountability. That means you have to be willing to let someone look you in the eye and ask tough questions. Have you stayed on your diet this week? What did you read in your quiet time this morning? Were you on time every day this week? Those are tough jabs but necessary ones.

Guideline 3: Understand that developing self-discipline is in accord with what God wants you to do. Goals that are in line with God's purpose for your life also bring God's strength and help for your weakness. To the Corinthians Paul wrote, "For Christ's sake, I delight in weaknesses, in insults, in hardships, in persecutions, in difficulties. For when I am weak, then I am strong" (2 Corinthians 12:10). This means you can find strength through prayer and find hope that life can be better. Paul succinctly personalized this principle in Philippians 4:13: "I can do all things through Christ who strengthens me" (NKJV).

Guideline 4: When you fail, start again...and again. If your first trip to the driving range does not allow you to compare favorably with Tiger Woods, take some lessons and keep hitting the ball, but don't give up after a few hooks and slices.

One of the greatest needs in our personal lives today is the need for discipline. It can be the key to success and help you accomplish the will of God for your life.

Resource reading: Philippians 4

Obedience in Discipline

Demas, because he loved this world, has deserted me and has gone to Thessalonica. Crescens has gone to Galatia, and Titus to Dalmatia.
2 TIMOTHY 4:10

Insight: Because the mind-set of our culture is to indulge ourselves rather than to discipline ourselves, learning discipline is difficult, but the rewards are sweet.

Discipline and obedience are two sides of the same coin, and frankly, there are not many coins bearing the stamp of these two qualities in our pockets and purses these days. True, we like the fruit of both. Women admire the slim figure that has been gained through rigorous exercise and careful dieting, and men certainly wish they had the rippling muscles of a weight lifter or the prowess of a linebacker. Instead, their bulging waistlines testify to the reality that they cannot say no to junk food, and if they do exercise, they certainly park as close to the gym or fitness center as possible. Convenience, you know.

The word *obedience* seems to smack of dependence, of losing your independence or not thinking for yourself, or certainly of not being in control. Anything that causes us to lose control seems to stick in the craw of any member of the human race. It always has, but in the last generation, knuckling under—whether to be at school on time, to work the required number of hours, to pay taxes honestly, or to have nothing kept secret from a spouse—has been difficult, if not impossible, for most of us.

Certainly, we admire those who do have discipline in their lives—the Olympian who trains for years, rising early when it is cold and dark to go to a cold ice arena or gym; the arctic explorer who pushes the envelope of survival, braving the bitter edge of endurance; the mountain climber who pushes toward the top, his oxygen depleted and his muscles burning with fatigue; and the struggling merchant who refuses to quit and eventually makes good. Yes, we all want to be like that. Who wouldn't like to see his face on the cover of *Sports Illustrated* or her figure on the cover of *Fitness*?

So why aren't there more who make it to the top? The price is just too great. The path of obedience is drudgery. It's painful instead of joyful, and the discipline necessary to achieve is lacking. True, we'll take the shortcut if that will work. Bring on the steroids to build muscle, the pill to lose weight, or the investment to succeed financially. History is full of wannabes, the ones who wanted to be the first to arrive using whatever means they could—cheating on their records, fixing the log book, using deceitful measurements, bribing officials.

Victory gotten with purloined currency is shallow and tentative, and the possibility of discovery always hangs over the head of the cheater and liar. Athletes who are forced to return the gold carry the stigma with them forever, no matter how many gainfully won medals they may acquire.

Here's something else to think about. God expects no less than the world does when it comes to winning or reaching the top. The same miasma of thinking that has infected us in the past few decades also creates spiritual pygmies who know the language and wear the costume fairly well but lack the stamina and courage to go the distance. Explaining that his fair-weather companions had quit and gone home, Paul wrote to Timothy, "Demas, because he loved this world, has deserted me and has gone to Thessalonica. Crescens has gone to Galatia, and Titus to Dalmatia" (see 2 Timothy 4:10). Paul, on the other hand, commended Timothy to the Philippians, saying, "I have no one else like him, who takes a genuine interest in your welfare. For everyone looks out for his own interests, not those of Jesus Christ" (Philippians 2:20-21).

God's standard is unchanging. Never forget that discipline and obedience are inseparable for anyone who gets to the top.

Resource reading: 2 Timothy 4

Learning Discipline in an Undisciplined World

I beat my body and make it my slave so that after I have preached to others, I myself will not be disqualified for the prize.

1 CORINTHIANS 9:27

Insight: When you learn to discipline yourself, life moves progressively toward accomplishments you otherwise could not achieve.

With the possible exception of waking up and finding that you are married, nothing is more of a shocker than waking up to discover you are in the Marines for a four-year hitch. Your mom is no longer around to make your bed, pamper you, do your washing and ironing, or call the school with a fabricated excuse when you are too lazy to do your report.

Instead, you encounter a drill sergeant who is tougher than nails, meaner than a junkyard dog, and more overbearing than anything you have ever encountered. He convinces you he can break your neck and would consider it a pleasure to do so if you don't jump and bark "Sir!" at the appropriate times.

Why is the sudden infusion of discipline in a young person's life more shocking than a bad drug trip or a plunge into ice water during the dead of winter? Because, simply put, many young people have grown up in a pampered, indulged world where others do everything for them. They neither knew discipline nor understand what obedience is about.

Though you probably would not say so out loud, I may have just described you. How do you develop discipline in your studies, in your business, in your physical appetites, and in your relationship to God? Frankly, you will never succeed in any endeavor—whether it is your marriage or your business—unless you learn discipline.

Or perhaps you thought your mother was the meanest in the world when she insisted you do things for yourself, things that other kids never had to do. You hated it, but you had no choice. She was teaching you discipline. When you grow up experiencing it, you can eventually discipline yourself. Many people in today's culture, however, grew up with few limits, no curfews, and rare denials.

Self-discipline is gained at a great cost.

First, there must be a motive for discipline. Why bother? Writing to the Corinthians, Paul puts the motive for discipline in the context of the athlete who wants to win a prize. The Corinthians understood that word picture. "I beat my body and make it my slave so that after I have preached to others, I myself will not be disqualified for the prize" (1 Corinthians 9:27). No cheating. No shortcuts.

The next step certifies the obvious—practice and gradual progress. It's important. Not knowing or understanding this, a lot of people try something, find it difficult, and quit. The key to successful discipline is a series of incremental steps toward the top. You do not go to a gym, put on 200-pound weights, and start lifting them on the first day.

A young man told how his grandfather, a blacksmith, could lift bags of potatoes weighing 100 pounds, a bag in each hand as he held them at arm's length. "Granddad was not always like that," he quickly added. "He worked up to it. He started with 5-pound sacks, then 10-pound sacks. Eventually, he progressed to 25-pound sacks, and then 50-pound sacks. Finally, he could lift a 100-pound sack in each hand. Then," said the boy, "he started putting potatoes in the sacks."

Try discipline in the small areas of your life—returning phone calls, being punctual to meetings, doing what you tell your kids you will do, getting up when the alarm goes off, carrying out the trash today instead of procrastinating.

He who is faithful in the small tasks eventually will have the strength and discipline to succeed at the greater ones. The path to the top is a succession of small, inconsequential steps that eventually rise above the levels where others turn back.

Resource reading: 1 Corinthians 9:24-27

Discipline from Within and from Without

Although he was a son, he learned obedience from what he suffered.
HEBREWS 5:8

Insight: No great accomplishment has ever been made apart from self-discipline, the kind that often demands saying no to things you would rather do. It means knowing when to curb appetites and desires to accomplish what you would probably avoid otherwise.

In the military you accept the discipline of obedience when you enlist, swearing allegiance to your country, flag, and those authorized to represent them. You learn to stand tall, throw back your shoulders, and bark, "Yes, sir!" on cue. Failure to comply means paying a price: scrubbing the barracks floor with a toothbrush, running five miles in your bare feet, standing at attention in the broiling sun, or getting tossed into the stockade. That's the way it is. People learn fast, if they survive.

There's another kind of discipline, also, the kind that takes doctors out on a call in the middle of the night, that keeps a scholar up nights studying far into the early hours of the morning, and that motivates mothers to respond to the cries of their babies. The first is imposed by others; the second is imposed by one's self.

What's the difference? Military discipline leaves a mark on a person—no one would deny that—but when the four-year hitch in the military is over, often the rigid discipline is left behind. Self-discipline, though, is a lifestyle, a motivation from within, a mind-set dictated by conscience or desire, not fear or force. It feeds on duty or the desire to accomplish something worthwhile and lasting.

In the military the important thing is to obey orders. You do not need to see the whole picture. That's not your responsibility. You are accountable only for complying. You have confidence that your immediate superior knows what he or she is doing. Without asking, "Do you really know what you are doing?" you respond, "Yes, sir!" and get to it.

Now before I take this any further, may I ask, "Which type of obedience does a Christian face when it comes to obeying God?" Is the discipline of the Christian life a voluntary one? Or does God force you to knuckle under, much as does a drill sergeant? Before you answer, consider these ideas:

First, remember, you have a will of your own. God does not force you to walk the path of obedience or leave the world behind to take up your cross. Jesus stands at the crossroads and says simply, "Follow Me!" It's your decision, your choice.

Some instructions have to be taken by faith—instructions we accept because we believe God knows what is best for His children. We trust and obey. That's what faith is all about. Yet consider this: When God says, "Do this and live!" He means just that. Some directives are not on a "this would be nice if you did it" basis.

In reading through the books of Exodus, Leviticus, Numbers, and Deuteronomy recently, I've been impressed with how God repeatedly asked His children for just one thing: obedience to Him. Compliance was difficult and often fragmentary. At times, they refused, assuming they knew better than God what needed to be done, and for this there was a price to pay. God never said, "I guess we'll forget about it this time. Poor child. You didn't think I meant what I said." There are consequences—good or bad—for every choice and action.

A final thought: Jesus Himself faced difficult tasks. Hebrews says He learned obedience through His suffering. He gave us a model and taught us that obedience to what God asks will never be a disappointment. Once you are convinced that God does know the future and what is best for His children, learning to walk in simple obedience becomes a joy, not a chore. Think about it.

Resource reading: Proverbs 3:1-12

Suffering—Why?

Yea, though I walk through the valley
of the shadow of death, I will fear no evil;
for You are with me.

PSALM 23:4 NKJV

Insight: No person would choose to suffer, but those who have suffered often would not trade what they have learned and experienced in exchange for an easier way out.

Have you ever experienced a time when everything was going just right and then suddenly, for no apparent reason, the tables turned and everything went wrong? Perhaps you were involved in an auto accident on the day your insurance expired or the day you found you were unemployed. Perhaps you awakened in a hospital and realized you would have days or weeks of serious illness ahead of you. Whenever misfortune strikes, the question usually rises, "Why? Why did it have to happen? Why did God let it happen to me?" The human heart always seeks to find answers to the difficulties that come in life.

For more than 2000 years, the Bible, God's sacred Word, has served as a guide to life. It is life's textbook, and it has stood the test of time. One of the oldest books in the Bible is the book of Job, and it seems only fitting that this book should deal with one of the oldest problems of humanity—the problem of suffering. Job faced a crisis of suffering, with no apparent reason for his calamity. At first he searched for an answer and found none. It seemed as though he walked alone through a dark valley. But in time, Job came to realize that just as fire refines the gold, suffering burns up the dross and leaves us richer, stronger, and wiser.

The Bible does give us insights into the dark hours of suffering. Sometimes God allows us to walk through the valley of suffering or difficulty so we slow down long enough to take stock of our lives. Instead of being laid up by illness, the time becomes "called aside for stillness." Hours of convalescing give us the time we need to get away from the problems we face and think through them. It is in the hour of need that faith becomes practical. All too often, we respond to the resonate tones of a pipe organ, the thrill of praise music, or the encouragement of close friends, but when these are gone, we face life alone and our faith is put to the test.

Jesus came to make a difference in the hearts of men and women 24 hours a day, 7 days a week. He is not an abstract quality of goodness or a superhuman who cannot relate to what we are facing. He knew what it was to hunger and thirst, to face the suffering of physical discomfort, the loneliness of being forsaken by His friends, and even the agony of facing death alone. While it is true that He lived a sinless life, He was still human—very human.

Paul tells us about Jesus, "God made him who had no sin to be sin for us, so that in him we might become the righteousness of God" (2 Corinthians 5:21). He then broke the power of death and rose from the grave so He might live in the hearts of men. It may well be that you are now walking through a particular hour of darkness in order that you might experience the undergirding, sustaining presence of God you would otherwise have never known. Well has it been said that our extremity is but God's opportunity.

King George VI of England faced life with a speech impediment. He spoke deliberately and sometimes with great difficulty. In a particularly dark hour during World War 2, he went before the British Parliament and spoke these words, which have inspired faith and courage in countless millions: "I would rather walk in the dark with God than walk in the light with men." What spirit! Walking with God is at times lonely. Many, however, are just not interested in placing their hands in His nail-scarred hands. Those who do choose to walk with God find a deep peace that lets them face the uncertainty of the future. Nahum 1:7 says, "The Lord is good, a refuge in times of trouble. He cares for those who trust in him." Have you made the wonderful discovery of taking refuge in the Lord and trusting Him when trouble knocks at your door?

Do not hesitate to turn to Him for grace and strength—there really is no other way. When we turn to Him, we can say with David of old, "Yea, though I walk through the valley of the shadow of death, I will fear no evil; for You are with me."

Resource reading: Psalm 23

Your Response to Trials

Five times I received from the Jews the forty lashes minus one. Three times I was beaten with rods, once I was stoned, three times I was shipwrecked, I spent a night and a day in the open sea.
2 CORINTHIANS 11:24-25

Insight: Difficulties never leave you where they found you; either they drive you to your knees where you find strength or they push you away from God.

One of the strange things about trials is that when they knock at your front door or sneak through the back door of your life, you never quite expect them. You know other people face them, but you have been spared. When you do go into combat with them, you also feel that nobody else has ever faced the same intensity of testing nor do they understand what you are going through.

The Greek word translated *testing* has two meanings: a trial that comes from without or a temptation or solicitation to do wrong that comes from within.

Long ago, Paul warned against presumptuousness—thinking that you are immune from trials—and he went on to assure us that when we face periods of difficulty, God will take us through. You find those words of counsel in 1 Corinthians 10:12-13:

> If you think you are standing firm, be careful that you don't fall! No temptation has seized you except what is common to man. And God is faithful; he will not let you be tempted beyond what you can bear. But when you are tempted, he will also provide a way out so that you can stand up under it.

Throughout the New Testament, you will find a common theme: Periods of testing come to all of God's children. The only questions are *when* and *what kind* they will be. Tests are not an indication you have been abandoned by God or selected for an attack from Satan. They are the result of living in a broken world, a world hostile to the values of God's children.

Peter addressed the issue when he wrote to suffering brothers and sisters in Rome. He indicates our response should be threefold: First, we should rejoice because, no matter how strange the logic is, we share in the suffering and the glory of Jesus Christ. Second, we should commit ourselves to the loving care of our heavenly Father. And third, we should continue doing what we know is right, no matter what others do. Let's take a closer look at his advice.

"Dear friends," writes Peter, "do not be surprised at the painful trial you are suffering, as though something strange were happening to you. But rejoice that you participate in the sufferings of Christ, so that you may be overjoyed when his glory is revealed" (1 Peter 4:12-13). After rejoicing, Peter says (in my words), "Run up your flag and commit yourself to the Father!" There are times when we tell the truth but still are accused of lying (*misinformation* is now the more acceptable word). We are abiding by our consciences. Even friends misunderstand us, and they think we have sold out and are compromising.

Peter says, "Commit yourself to the Father who knows your heart and who will write the last chapter." Then he says, "Don't give up and quit!" In other words, he challenges us to continue doing the right thing. Here are his words: "Those who suffer according to God's will should commit themselves to their faithful Creator and continue to do good" (1 Peter 4:19).

When you are falsely accused and misunderstood, you are forced to look within and ask yourself, *Who am I doing this for—the glory of God or the plaudits and gratitude of other people? Have I chosen to please men or God?* After you work through that, you have a motive to keep on doing the right thing.

"If you suffer as a Christian," writes Peter, "do not be ashamed, but praise God that you bear that name" (1 Peter 4:16). What name? The name *Christian!* Today that name is still used, in the same way it was when first applied to believers, as a term of derision and scorn. Though trite answers never satisfy the deep questions of the heart, there are reasons—reasons we may never fully understand until we reach heaven.

Resource reading: 2 Corinthians 10:1-6

Suffering and the Promises of God

I needed clothes and you clothed me, I was sick and you looked after me, I was in prison and you came to visit me.
MATTHEW 25:36

Insight: God promised to be with you in times of difficulty, not to exempt you from them.

There is a common perception in the world today that faith in Jesus Christ will exempt us from the trials and hardships of life, especially those that diminish good health, happiness, and prosperity. When we buy into this concept and discover that our prayers do not always turn back the hostility of a world that thinks Christians are bigoted and strange, we become disappointed and disillusioned.

In his book *Who Switched the Price Tags?* Tony Campolo tells of an incident when a prankster broke into a store and switched around the price tags on the merchandise. Likewise, someone has messed with God's message and has switched the price tags when it comes to telling people that suffering is part of the package. Thus, many will not appreciate what we stand for and believe.

Peter addresses this issue in the first letter that bears his name, and he says that the believer's response is not fighting fire with fire but rather rejoicing because the Spirit of glory and of Christ rests on you. Jesus said we are to rejoice when people persecute us and say all manner of evil against us, because they persecuted the prophets before as well.

A hostile world is out there, but the issue is, how do you respond? Do you fight fire with fire? Or do you rise above the trials and difficulties with strength that others do not have?

Peter advised us,

> To this you were called, because Christ suffered for you, leaving you an example, that you should follow in his steps... When they hurled their insults at him, he did not retaliate; when he suffered, he made no threats. Instead he trusted himself to him who judges justly (1 Peter 2:21,23).

When times of difficulty come for you, promises accompany them—something we need to remember.

First, times of difficulty are accompanied by *the promise of His presence.* Jesus said, "In this world you will have trouble. But take heart! I have overcome the world" (John 16:33). He also promised, "I am with you always" (Matthew 28:20). Would you not be more comfortable about a surgery if you knew that the hand of the doctor is in the hand of a living Savior who guides it?

Furthermore, the trials that come to us also come with *the promise of His protection.* Peter writes that we are "shielded by God's power until the coming of the salvation that is ready to be revealed in the last time. In this you greatly rejoice, though now for a little while you may have had to suffer grief in all kinds of trials" (1 Peter 1:5-6). *Father-filtered* is the way one person expressed the belief that nothing can get through to us apart from the will and protection of our Father—which means He goes with us through the fiery trial.

There is also *the promise of His purging or cleansing.* In spite of the fact that we would rather avoid times of difficulty, good always comes out of them. Peter writes about our faith being as gold, which is put into the furnace and refined. He goes on to say our faith will never perish, even though gold will.

Amy Carmichael used to tell of the village goldsmith who would take ore and melt it in a clay pot over the fire, occasionally raking off the impurities. "How do you know when the ore is ready?" she asked. His reply: "When I can see the reflection of my face in it." So is it with the trials that produce the reflection of our Father's face in our lives.

Most of us would just as soon skip the fire, but it is all part of the process that God uses to refine us and to demonstrate His power in our lives. The fiery trial produces the presence and purity of God in our lives, which the world can never understand.

Resource reading: Jeremiah 31:1-14

When Persecution Stalks You

Blessed are you when people insult you, persecute you and falsely say all kinds of evil against you because of me. Rejoice and be glad, because great is your reward in heaven, for in the same way they persecuted the prophets who were before you.

MATTHEW 5:11-12

Insight: Rejoice when you suffer? Jesus says yes. You are then in the company of some of the finest people who ever walked on Planet Earth.

There is a job opening in your company, and you have both the experience and education necessary. It looks like a sure thing. However, another person gets the job. You are told it was a management decision, but a friend of yours in management says that colleagues resent that you do not drink with the other employees.

You are a doctor, and because of your Christian convictions you refuse to participate in certain billing practices you view as dishonest. Your colleagues shun you and make comments behind your back that are untrue as well as derogatory.

It's the real world! Right—but it is also a form of hostility that believers have endured for a long time. As early as AD 65, no more than a generation from the birth of the early church, Peter addresses this issue. But in his day, persecution went far beyond verbal insults.

Tacitus, the Roman historian, tells us that the emperor Nero inaugurated an era of persecution that continued, in varying degrees, until the conversion of Constantine. Nero, a depraved and corrupted Caesar, had Christians sewed into the skins of wild animals and then attacked by his hunting dogs for sport. Others were burned to death in the imperial gardens, their bodies having been covered with pitch and oil.

It was open season on Christians. Why? What had Christians done to the pagans of Rome? There were some reasons, shallow as they may be.

1. The innate goodness of the believers annoyed individuals, whose consciences were pricked by their belief system. Christians were monotheistic and worshipped one God. Furthermore, they came

home at night to the same husband or wife. Homosexuality, which was common in early Rome along with infidelity, was denounced. The fact that many of the Caesars were openly homosexual only made the distaste that Rome had for this sect of Judaism (as it was first viewed) more pronounced.

2. Rome further disliked the fact that Christianity appealed primarily to the working class, since the rich often resent the poor. Compound that with the anti-Semitic prejudice (because of the Jewish roots of Christianity) for a genuine case of hostility.
3. The dogmatism of Christianity also rankled the sweepingly pantheistic Romans, who held to hundreds of deities, all of whom were idols or myths. But Christians denounced idols and affirmed that Jesus Christ is Lord of lords and God of gods. Smug arrogance was the way Rome viewed it.

   In Rome, there was a structure of groups known as guilds, similar to unions today, and each of these held to a patron god; but Christians would not participate in the rituals or ceremonies invoking the blessing of the pagan gods. Neither would they wear amulets or charms for good luck. They stood out as being different, and different they were.

   Eventually, rumors surfaced that Christians actually ate the flesh of people and drank their blood in a strange love feast, which was accompanied by orgies. Naturally, individuals chose to believe the rumors rather than investigate the facts.
4. Rome resented the fact that Christians were militantly evangelistic and took advantage of every opportunity to proselytize people from all faiths. Unwilling to let Christianity be just another religion, Christians insisted there was no other way to gain favor with God apart from believing in Jesus Christ.
5. Christians held dogmatically to a belief in the death and resurrection of Jesus Christ, who spoke of a final judgment when all men would give account for their sins.

Take these five together and you've woven a fabric of hostility that still surrounds believers today who are in the world but not of the world.

Resource reading: 1 Peter 5

When You Suffer

Do not be afraid of what you are about to suffer. I tell you, the devil will put some of you in prison to test you, and you will suffer persecution for ten days. Be faithful, even to the point of death, and I will give you the crown of life.

REVELATION 2:10

Insight: While the world is no friend to grace, the presence of God who extends grace to his children sustains us in dark hours.

On a warm summer day in AD 64, fire broke out in the poor quarters of Rome near the Colosseum. In those days the streets of the city were narrow and used primarily for foot traffic. Many buildings in that area had been built of wood, and in the dry heat of summer, they burned quickly. In only hours there was a conflagration unlike anything Rome had ever seen. The Temple of Luna was consumed, along with the Shrine of Vesta. Hundreds, then thousands, of people became homeless.

When people tried to extinguish the blaze, they were forcibly restrained by the imperial soldiers. This led to the belief that the emperor Nero, who had a fixation with buildings that bore his name, was really responsible for the fire. In a nearby tower, he watched and gloated. For three days the city was ablaze. In the evening as the sky glowed with the burning inferno, it is said that Nero played his fiddle with glee on the balcony of the imperial palace.

When a public outcry arose, Nero needed a scapegoat, and so, says history, the Christians of Rome were his perfect choice. First of all, the growing Christian population was not liked. Large numbers of Jews, whose success in the business world was resented, had converted to Christianity. Furthermore, dislike for Christians was fueled by rumors, such as the belief that Christians were cannibals who ate flesh and drank blood in their religious rites—which we know as communion today.

The madness of prejudice quickly turned into the fire of persecution, and people who had lived relatively peaceful lives were suddenly victims of malicious cruelty they had never before known.

Within months, the apostle Peter, who had known something of prejudice and persecution himself, picked up his pen and wrote to help those who were suddenly confronted with pain and suffering they did not deserve or expect. He wrote,

> Dear friends, do not be surprised at the painful trial you are suffering, as though something strange were happening to you. But rejoice that you participate in the sufferings of Christ (1 Peter 4:12-13).

Another version translates the phrase "painful trial" as "fiery ordeal," which accurately describes what they were going through. Literally, the word means "the process of burning." Men and women who were peaceful and law-abiding suddenly had become targets of hostility, which must have been a mystery to them. The admission *Christianus sum* (I am a Christian) made them victims of hatred and violence that was immune from prosecution in the Roman courts.

What believers were going through then is still being repeated today. In the 1 Peter 4 passage, which you ought to become familiar with, Peter talks about two kinds of suffering. First, he says, "if you are insulted," which translates to emotional suffering, and then he says, "if you suffer as a Christian," which translates to actual physical suffering.

Why should you be the brunt of unkind words or prejudice because of what you believe? There are times when your basic goodness is a prick to the conscience of an unbeliever. Peter advises us to not be surprised when this happens. Would not logic demand that if something is to be no surprise, we should be aware of its possibility, if not outright expect it? Jesus said, "If the world hates you, keep in mind that it hated me first" (John 15:18). Paul wrote, "Everyone who wants to live a godly life in Christ Jesus will be persecuted" (2 Timothy 3:12).

"Rejoice," says Peter, for you share in the suffering of Christ—just make sure your suffering is not for wrong things you have done.

Resource reading: 1 Peter 4

It's My Nature to Worry

Don't worry about anything; instead,
pray about everything; tell God your needs,
and don't forget to thank him for his answers.
PHILIPPIANS 4:6 TLB

Insight: While worry is considered to be an acceptable pastime for many of God's children, it saps today of purpose and meaning and puts a dark cloud over tomorrow.

Is worry wrong? Who would deny that there is plenty to worry about—the state of the economy, security, health, the Middle East, marriage, children, cancer, the environment, and a long, long list of other concerns. But can we help worrying any more than we can help what happens to our good looks after age 50?

"It's my nature to worry—that's the way God made me! I just can't help it," some say. Myself, I admit I am not always known by the smoothness of my brow. I've taken a second, hard look at this issue as the result of reading a manuscript written by a friend of mine, a Christian physician, who contends that some people can no more help worrying than they can help aging. He believes they have a biological propensity to worry, just as some have a tendency toward poor eyesight or a receding hairline. The tendency to worry comes from parents, he stresses. While I admit that some people may have more of a biological tendency toward worry than others, can we go so far as to say the practice is acceptable before God by putting the blame on our genetic codes, which effectively lets us off the hook?

We have to confront several passages of Scripture clearly pointing out that worry is contrary to God's plan and purpose for our lives. First, Jesus had a lot to say about this subject during the Sermon on the Mount (Matthew 5–7), when He talked about the birds of the air who are fed by our heavenly Father and then chided His hearers about worrying over their clothes and what they would eat. It's obvious Jesus considered worry to be wrong because of the power of His heavenly Father to provide for His children.

Paul does not mince words, either: "Do not be anxious about anything, but in everything, by prayer and petition, with thanksgiving, present your requests to God" (Philippians 4:6). A paraphrase states it simply: "Don't worry about anything." Many people think statements like this are a benchmark or a goal, something lofty and idealistic but not possible in today's world. Yet what troubles me about this notion is that God never expects the impossible of His children.

This means, then, if God says I should not worry, there must be an antidote to the whole problem. I confess that on occasion I do worry because of threatening situations I don't like and can't do anything about, bringing the whole issue of control into the picture. When I'm fully in control, I can do something, even though it may be very little, to change a situation.

When I'm not in control, however, the question goes beyond my control to God's. Is He in control of what I can't handle? "Of course," you say. But worry in effect says, "God, if You are really there, I'm not sure You are big enough to handle this, so I'd better spend my time thinking about what I'm going to do if You fail."

Is there a solution to this problem we all indulge in? Yes. We learn to put into His hands what we cannot change, and we learn more about His nature and character, which give us confidence He is able to take care of the storms in life.

For a starter, I'd suggest you read Isaiah 40, which is about God's great power of creation, and then read Proverbs 3:5-6 about trusting Him, ignoring the signs that cause us to worry, and acknowledging Him in all we do. Remind yourself that He who created our world neither slumbers or sleeps. Then turn out the light and go to sleep. He'll take the night shift and the day shift to follow. He never fails.

Resource reading: Matthew 6:25-34

If I Can Just Get Through This Problem

I have told you these things, so that in me you may have peace. In this world you will have trouble. But take heart! I have overcome the world.

JOHN 16:33

Insight: You are the person who makes the decision to worry about problems or to trust the Lord to take you through your difficult times.

If I can just get through this problem, I'm sure everything will be okay. Ever think that? So you grit your teeth and, sure enough, you get through that problem, only to find several more have cropped up on the horizon. It's something like pedaling a bicycle. Going uphill is so slow and takes so much energy, while the downhill run is short and turns into another uphill climb quickly.

Long ago Jesus said, "In this world you will have trouble" (John 16:33). In saying that, Jesus was merely making a statement of how things are and will be until He comes to establish His kingdom.

The Chinese character for *crisis* is a combination of two characters that stand for *danger* and *opportunity.* Interesting! Both are involved when you are confronted with a problem.

"If I can just get through this problem..." Now, there's nothing wrong in getting through that one problem before you tackle the next one, but getting through the immediate one will not be the end of challenges.

The word we translate as *worry* or *anxiety* in the New Testament is an interesting one. Paul used it when he described his care or concern for the churches, a legitimate area of concern, but he also used the word when he talked about not being overwhelmed by the immediate problem, but rather praying about it and committing it to the Lord (Philippians 4:6).

That particular Greek word for *worry* comes from a verb meaning "to be drawn in different directions," or to be distracted to the point of being worked up over a situation. Do you ever find yourself in the position of having your head and your heart tell you different things? Your head says, "That problem confronting you is a big one!" and your heart says, "God is bigger than this problem. I can trust Him." You are drawn or pulled two different ways. The end result—you worry.

When I am confronted with a situation such as I have just described, I've learned that *I* decide the worry result—giving in to what my head says and worrying, or yielding to the inner witness of the Spirit in my heart that says, "Trust God!"

Paul Tournier, the Swiss psychiatrist who touched a generation with his commonsense observations, says that the most powerful and unused gift from God is choice, an observation that comes from God's Word, the Bible. In this whole matter, it is you—not circumstances or fate or the enemies of your soul—who does the choosing. *You* do! The choice is to worry or trust. Commit or vacillate. Progress or regress. Make decisions or have decisions made for you. Walk with the Lord or walk alone in the dark.

"In this world you will have trouble," said Jesus, but He did not stop there. If He had, the future would be pretty bleak. He continued: "But take heart! I have overcome the world" (John 16:33). Those words tell us that He not only walks with us as we take the upward climb, but He's on the other side to welcome us as well.

"If I can just get through this problem!" Frankly, that's not the proper point of focus. Rather, concentrate on finding His strength and power and learning from the experience you are working through right now.

In his book *Why Us?* Warren Wiersbe told of a blind acquaintance who was struggling with some tough issues. She turned to him and said, "Pray that I won't waste all of this suffering!" She was a woman who saw God's purpose in the upward climb. So can you, friend, no matter where you are on the incline of life.

Resource reading: 2 Corinthians 6:1-10

Why Worry?

Do not worry about tomorrow, for tomorrow will worry about itself. Each day has enough trouble of its own.
MATTHEW 6:34

Insight: Worry, like a stream that cuts through rock, erodes your peace of mind and turns good nights of sleep into restless nights of tossing and turning.

When Lyndon Johnson was once asked how he was getting along, he replied "Fine!" He explained that he had adopted a formula given to him by an old woman many years before. She said, "When I walks, I walks slow. When I sits, I sits loose. When I sees a worry coming on me, I just lies down and goes to sleep." Everyone has concerns to worry about. We worry about the weather, about taxes, about the world situation, and about government. We worry that someone will start another war—a big one. Single folks worry about getting married, and a lot of married folks worry about staying that way.

Have you considered the fact that worry is a senseless and futile pastime that only drains your life of energy and siphons your productivity? Yes, you know that—yet you worry. A panel of psychologists concluded that 40 percent of the things people worry about never happen. Then 30 percent of worry, they say, is about past events. It doesn't help one bit to worry about such things as yesterday's test score, our performance at last week's party, old grievances, or last year's opportunities. Further down, 12 percent of our worries are about our health. And 10 percent of the things we worry about are trifling items that really do not make a lot of difference. That leaves only 8 percent of our worries that psychologists would classify as legitimate areas of concern.

If these observations are true—and they seem quite logical—then we worry an awful lot about things we cannot control. "Worry," said George Lyons, "is the interest paid by those who borrow trouble."

One of the interesting, if not ironical, things about worry is that believers indulge in it just about as much as those who believe there is no God at all. If there is no God involved in the personal affairs of your life, it would be a good idea to worry a little bit every day—just to keep you on your toes, to keep you from going to sleep at the switch. But if there is a sovereign God who directs the affairs of His children and is in charge of your life, then you had better put your faith into practice by saying, "All right, God, please take over the night shift because I am going to sleep."

Do you *really* believe "all things work together for good to those who love God, to those who are the called according to His purpose" (Romans 8:28 NKJV)? In his opening remarks to the Ephesians Paul wrote of "the plan of him who works out everything in conformity with the purpose of His will" (Ephesians 1:11).

Can I anticipate your thoughts? You are not concerned about God's keeping the earth from colliding with another planet and brushing a few billion people off into space, but you do worry about the consequences of your own mistakes...what you did that you should not have done or what you should have said that you did not say.

In the end, do you not think that God is big enough and gracious enough to keep you and protect you from the tragic consequences of your own failures?

Are you fighting worry? Go out and look at the starry host of heaven and ask if He who put the stars in the sky is not great enough to meet you and help you through your difficulty. As Jesus said, "Every day has trouble enough of its own," so focus on today and leave tomorrow in His hands.

Resource reading: Luke 12:22-34

Do Not Worry; Do Not Be Afraid

Do not let your hearts be troubled
and do not be afraid.
JOHN 14:27

Insight: Jesus promised his followers "my peace," the kind that does not panic in the face of storm—God's kind of peace, which is still available today.

Jesus was meeting with His disciples behind closed doors in an upper room, which hid Him from public scrutiny—at least for the moment. His words flowed from His heart. He said with great confidence, "Stop letting your hearts be troubled!" Verbs in the Greek language, unlike English verbs, tell whether an action is ongoing, repeated, or one-time and the word Jesus used in the above passage indicated that the worry and concern in the disciples' hearts had begun a long while before and were continuing. But He says, "Stop worrying."

The Greek word usually translated "to be troubled" means to be disturbed or upset. It can also mean "to be terrified, or frightened." Used of water, the word meant "to stir something up." If you put two ingredients in a jar and shake it vigorously, you would use the same word. Simply put, the word is used of someone who is upset by a situation. The disciples who met with Jesus in that upper room had plenty of reason to be disturbed. Earlier in the week Jesus had drawn the anger of the religious community when He went into the temple and dumped over the tables of the money changers. They were angry and considered Him an enemy.

Moments before His command to stop worrying, Jesus had taken off His outer garments, draped Himself in a towel, and washed the feet of the disciples. Looking into their eyes, He had announced that one of them was a traitor who would deny Him. Peter, confirming the side he was on, announced that he would never deny his Lord, yet Jesus predicted Peter would deny Him three times before the cock would crow.

I'm convinced, however, that as Jesus looked at the twelve and said, "Don't worry; don't be afraid," He was looking beyond those who sat around that table. He saw the young couple whose child would be born with Down Syndrome. He saw the man whose wife of ten years would succumb to cancer, leaving a bewildered, confused husband with two small children. He saw the widow whose husband was buried shortly after he had retired and who had thought that, at last, they could travel and enjoy life.

What troubles you today? Is it a matter of indifference to God, or does what Jesus said speak to the need of your heart? Can you apply what Jesus said—"Stop worrying; stop being afraid"—to *your* life?

Jesus then gave them reason for confidence: "You believe in God; believe in Me." It was true! They did believe in God. From the days of Abraham, Isaac, and Jacob, their forebears had believed in God. It's no different today. Jews, Muslims, Hindus, and Christians all believe in God. What politician won't end his speech with a hearty, "God bless our great country"? But, said Jesus, "Believe also in Me."

If the historical record is true in stating explicitly that Jesus lived, died, and rose again, then He is alive today and can do something about the circumstances that distress you. Far too often we struggle with issues as though there were no God, as though Christ had never stilled the troubled waters and said, "Peace, be still!"

How often we toss and turn at night and struggle with depression by day because those words have not penetrated our hearts. He still says, "Stop worrying. Stop being upset and agitated over the circumstances of your life. Believe in Me!"

The faith factor can make all the difference in your life. Listen, and in the quietness of your prayer closet, you will still hear the echo of Jesus' words, and He will bring peace to your heart.

Resource reading: John 14:1-14

Worry or Concern?

...Casting all your care upon Him;
for He cares for you.
1 Peter 5:7 NKJV

Insight: There are legitimate concerns in life that are not truly worries—however, concern turns to worry when you refuse to believe God has a solution.

When abandoned cars had to be removed from the side of a nearby roadway, the highway department published the following notice in our local newspaper: "Westbound lanes of the highway will be closed between 9 AM and 3 PM while abandoned *cares* are pulled from the slopes below." Forget about abandoned cars! These days you cannot even toss your cares out the window.

As I chuckled at the misprint, I couldn't help thinking of what Peter wrote long ago about "casting all your care upon Him, for He cares for you" (1 Peter 5:7 NKJV). The fact is, a lot of people are holding on to their cares for all they are worth. *Will I make the grade? Will I get that job? Will she go out with me? Will we be able to keep our marriage together? Will I run out of money before I die?*

With the economy in a downhill slide and with personal relationships under pressure, people are deeply concerned about the future. Are you one of them? Have you discovered, however, that worry really works? Sure it does—haven't you noticed that what you worry about hardly ever happens?

I'm thinking of a person who was a chronic worrier. When he was enjoying good business, he worried it would change. When business was poor, he worried he would lose his business. When he got a good contract, he worried his competitor would steal his customer. Finally, he took the advice of a friend and went to a counselor. Immediately his outlook changed. When a friend inquired why he no longer worried, he said, "I hired this doctor to do my worrying for me."

"Really?"

"Yeah!"

"How much did you have to pay him for that?"

When the man mentioned a large sum of money, the friend said, "You know you don't have that kind of money. How do you expect to pay him?"

The businessman replied, "That's for him to worry about!"

We chuckle because we'd like to do just that, but we think we can't. Our cares keep us awake nights, they make our nerves taut, and they keep us on edge. Must we simply live with them, or is there help?

Much of our worry focuses on what may happen but hasn't yet happened, and on how people respond to us. *Do people like me? Do they think I am pretty? Will my company get the business?* To suggest that worry is futile and pointless does not stop us from participating in the practice.

When we understand that what happens to us as God's children is neither accidental nor capricious, this takes the pressure off and eliminates much of the concern we describe as worry. When we believe nothing happens to us apart from that which God allows, we can get loose of the cares that hold us captive on the roadway of life.

When I face days that I would just as soon skip, like Mondays with their staff meetings and interruptions, I have to remind myself that God is in control of the hassle, the pressure, the interruptions, and the circumstances that create cares in my life. This is not to suggest that you disregard your health or the safety of your family or your future. But it is to say that if God is God and you are His child, what is of such great concern that you should crease your brow with care? If nothing can separate us from the love of God—neither death nor life, neither angels nor demons, neither the present nor the future, neither height nor depth—who or what then should cause us to worry? Think about it...and leave those abandoned cares on the side of the road.

Resource reading: 1 Peter 5

The Need for Courage Today

David ran and stood over him. He took hold of the Philistine's sword and drew it from the scabbard. After he killed him, he cut off his head with the sword. When the Philistines saw that their hero was dead, they turned and ran.

1 Samuel 17:51

Insight: Having convictions—a strong sense of right and wrong—is the stuff that courage is made of.

The late Aleksandr Solzhenitsyn, who was banned from his native Russia, believed that one of the clearest indications of the spiritual and moral decadence confronting us today is the lack of courage, both in our personal lives and in government. Said the Nobel laureate writer, "A decline in courage may be the most striking feature which an outside observer notices in the West in our days. The Western world has lost its civil courage…in each country, each government, each political party and, of course, in the United Nations."

The longer I think about Solzhenitsyn's comments, the more convinced I am that courage is in short supply today. Notice the number of individuals who test the winds before expressing opinions, or the people in even your own office who hesitate to stick their necks out, or the friends who turn and walk away from social situations rather than having the courage to stay and ride out the storm. Seldom today do you find people who are willing to risk their reputations by making a decision on their own and then backing it up.

In times of war or chaos, a few people stand out as men and women of intense courage—usually individuals who were rather common, ordinary people in civilian life but who, in times of danger, throw themselves into the thick of battle without thought of what may happen to them personally. Courage is what prompted a quiet, unassuming woman, passing by a burning house and hearing the screams of a child inside, to shove past firemen and dash inside to rescue the child. "What courage," we say.

Or, what of the 80-year-old woman who passed by a darkened alley and heard the screams of a woman being molested? Without thought of personal safety, the elderly lady turned into the alley and began beating the attacker with her cane. You guessed it. The attacker was captured. When people asked, "Weren't you afraid you might be hurt?" she replied, "I'm tired of people hurting other people, and I felt I had to do something."

Have you ever pondered the question that I have often asked: "What is it that makes an individual act heroically? What is the ingredient that some seem to have, whereas others quickly walk by the darkened alley, not wanting to be involved?"

Our English word *courage* comes from the French word that means "heart." And when people manifest courage, I am convinced that it is the immediate response, even an unthought response, that comes from convictions in the heart about matters of right and wrong. People of intense courage, regardless of where or when, are usually individuals who have black-and-white ideas of right and wrong, truth and falsehood, justice and injustice. Could it be that Solzhenitsyn was right about our being soft on courage today because we have lost our sense of right and wrong? We have taken the path of least resistance. We have turned from the God of the Bible to our own ideas. When every man does what is right in his own eyes, few care enough to stick their necks out for other people.

I'm convinced that courage is not dead. I see it, among other places, in the lives of men and women who could turn and walk away from difficult family situations but choose to stay because they are intent on doing the right thing. What about courage in *your* personal life?

Resource reading: 1 Samuel 17

Finding Courage to Do the Common Task

Go, gather together all the Jews who are in Susa, and fast for me. Do not eat or drink for three days, night or day. I and my maids will fast as you do. When this is done, I will go to the king, even though it is against the law. And if I perish, I perish.

ESTHER 4:16

Insight: It often takes more courage to get up and face the day—to do every day what has to be done, be it fix breakfast and get the kids ready for school or make hard decisions at work—than to face danger.

In my file is an anonymous quote that says, "It takes more courage to be faithful in routine things than to risk one's life in a moment of spectacular danger." Do you believe that? It's one thing to dash into a burning building to snatch a child from the jaws of death, but it is another thing to stand by your sick spouse month after month or face the routine of a job you do not like.

My problems are overwhelming! I just can't cope anymore. I wish I had the courage to quit or to walk out and try something different. Statements such as those are typical of the letters that come to me day after day telling of difficult situations confronting people who grope for the courage to face circumstances they did not choose and have no power to change.

Dr. Rollo May, in his book *The Courage to Create,* contends that courage is not the opposite of discouragement or despair. He says, "Courage is, rather, the capacity to move ahead *in spite of despair.*" I am convinced that it is at this very point of giving up where you must find courage, drawing from resources you do not have. It is right here that the grace of God can provide the courage you lack.

Naturally, when we think of men and women of courage, we think of some of the great heroes of the Bible. We think of Daniel, who faced the lions rather than surrender his convictions. We remember a lad by the name of David, who faced the giant Goliath. And, of course, we recall the courage of Esther, who risked her life for her people, saying, "If I perish, I perish." But at times, instead of inspiring us, those examples only depress us. "I'm not Esther," you say. Or, "Look, I'm just me, and I don't have the kind of stuff that heroes are made of."

Our problems are not our biggest difficulty. What matters most is our reaction to them. If we believe that all the strength we will ever have is the resources within ourselves, then we probably will despair. I would. If, however, we believe that when we are at the end of our resources—which can happen quickly—we can find the strength and power of God to sustain and to do what we cannot do alone, then we can press on and trust Him. That kind of courage, friend, is born of the conviction that God is enough. When we believe that, we can press on no matter what confronts us. It is this kind of courage that enables the single parent to face the future. It is this strength that allows us to face one day at a time and keep moving forward.

Over 500 years ago, Thomas à Kempis struggled with this issue and concluded,

> It is good for us to have trials and troubles at times, for they often remind us that we are on probation and ought not to hope in any worldly thing...When a man of good will is afflicted...he realizes clearly that his greatest need is God, without whom he can do no good.

More courage is demonstrated by being faithful in routine tasks than by risking one's life in a moment of spectacular danger. The great unsung heroes of courage are the everyday people who keep on in spite of great difficulties.

John F. Kennedy, whose PT boat was rammed and sunk by a Japanese destroyer, which resulted in serious injuries for him, wrote, "Without belittling the courage with which men have died, we should not forget those acts of courage with which men...have lived."

You may well be one of them. Take heart!

Resource reading: Esther 8–9

Facing Life with Courage

When you pass through the waters, I will be with you; and when you pass through the rivers, they will not sweep over you. When you walk through the fire, you will not be burned; the flames will not set you ablaze. For I am the LORD, your God, the Holy One of Israel, your Savior.

ISAIAH 43:2-3

Insight: When common men and women are motivated by courage to do uncommon acts of valor, we call them heroes.

William Carey, a pioneer of the modern missionary movement, left his native England and went to India. In due time, he established himself and began to translate the Bible into the language of the people with whom he worked. Before the days of linguists and computers, translation was a long, slow process. Eventually a printer joined him, and after years of effort, Bibles were printed and the process of distribution began. One day, however, Carey returned from a time of ministry to find that a fire had broken out and completely destroyed the building that housed his offices and press. Far more damaging was the loss of his manuscripts, grammars, and dictionaries, which had all gone up in flames as well. Nothing short of death could have struck such a blow.

When a colleague tearfully related what had happened, did Carey react violently, slamming his fist on the table in anger? No, it didn't happen like that at all. "Without a word of despair, impatience or anger," writes a biographer, "he knelt and thanked God that he still had the strength to do the work all over again!" Instead of feeling sorry for himself or lamenting the tragedy of so many wasted hours, Carey went to work and eventually did a better job than he had done the first time.

Carey had apparently not spent much time struggling with the question, "Why do bad things happen to good people?" In his book, *Why Us?* Warren Wiersbe says, "Each of us has a personal 'statement of faith,' and it is revealed by the questions we ask." If Carey struggled with the issue of why God allowed that disaster, there is no record of it.

Many today seem to be infected with an ideology that, in essence, contends that God owes His children something and that, because of who we are, bad things should not happen to us. Naturally, I want to think that because I am a believer in Jesus Christ, I am going to enjoy health, wealth, and prosperity, yet that contention flies in the face of reality. Life does not work that way, nor does Scripture support that contention.

Your statement of faith is revealed by the questions you ask of God. Long ago He spoke through Isaiah the prophet, saying, "Fear not, for I have redeemed you; I have called you by name; you are mine." A comforting promise, right? But then God continues, "When you pass through the waters, I will be with you; and when you pass through the rivers, they will not sweep over you. When you walk through the fire, you will not be burned; the flames will not set you ablaze. For I am the LORD, your God" (Isaiah 43:2-3).

Notice that God did not say, "I'll deliver you from all rivers and valleys and difficulties," but, "when you face them, I will be with you." The word *when* contains no contingencies. Eventually, everybody faces a valley, which is not necessarily punishment or satanic attack, but may be just the result of living in a sinful world.

One time, when I was working in our Guidelines studio, I sustained a cut on my forehead that required 34 stitches to close. The same day my wife totaled our car in an accident that could have been fatal. Romans 8:28 says, "*We know* that in all things God works for the good of those who love him." It does not say, *We think* or *we understand* or *we feel.* We know! And in that confidence we must rest.

Resource reading: Isaiah 43:1-13

Why We Do Not Lose Heart

Since through God's mercy we have this ministry, we do not lose heart.
2 CORINTHIANS 4:1

Insight: Staying focused on your goal and being renewed in spirit daily are the keys to finishing on track.

Of the 13 letters that came from the pen of Paul, the great theologian of the New Testament formerly known as Saul of Tarsus, none is more personal and intimate than the letter in our Bibles known as 2 Corinthians.

In this letter, Paul opens his heart with a vulnerability that reveals all the stress marks of living on the edge. He admits, "We are hard pressed on every side, but not crushed; perplexed, but not in despair; persecuted, but not abandoned; struck down, but not destroyed" (2 Corinthians 4:8-9). His is not the attitude of "Poor me!" or "Look how much I have suffered!"

Paul truthfully points out that life is not always easy:

> Five times I received from the Jews the forty lashes minus one. Three times I was beaten with rods, once I was stoned, three times I was shipwrecked, I spent a night and a day in the open sea, I have been constantly on the move. I have been in danger from rivers, in danger from bandits, in danger from my own countrymen, in danger from Gentiles; in danger in the city, in danger in the country, in danger at sea; and in danger from false brothers (2 Corinthians 11:24-26).

How much does it take to stop a person dead in his tracks? Whatever the answer, it took more than that to cause Paul to quit. Did this man have deep experience with God's strength? If he did, are there some insights that can help us when we feel driven into the corner by the circumstances of life?

In the same letter, Paul uses the phrase "we do not lose heart" twice (2 Corinthians 4:1,16). The expression "to lose heart" is an interesting one. Used only one other time in the New Testament, it defines what discouragement is—losing heart. The same word was used in another first-century manuscript to describe the feeling of a woman in labor when she despairs of ever bringing forth the child.

Webster defines discouragement as that which causes one to weaken, to give up, to despair. What causes people to lose heart today? Three things, which can be described as 1) physical causes, 2) emotional causes, and 3) spiritual causes. Let's consider each category.

First, whenever a person struggles with health issues—with physical weariness or sickness that persists—that individual may lose heart, wondering, *Will I ever get well?* Then, when we become disappointed—find ourselves in a failing marriage, admit our finances are in shambles, or face a hopeless situation—we begin to lose heart. Finally, at times Satan opposes us, the children of God who are striving to do right, which causes us to wonder whether the effort is worth it...and we begin to lose heart.

What's the solution? In this passage where Paul says he does not lose heart, he gives us an answer that can be summed up in two words, *renewal* and *perspective:*

> We do not lose heart. Though outwardly we are wasting away, yet inwardly we are being renewed day by day. For our light and momentary troubles are achieving for us an eternal glory that far outweighs them all. So we fix our eyes not on what is seen, but on what is unseen. For what is seen is temporary, but what is unseen is eternal (2 Corinthians 4:16-18).

Renewal, the great secret that God has taught us through the seasons, means having time in the Word, time alone with God, time to regain strength and perspective—which helps us keep the main things of life the main thing. This is the only solution, the only way you can say with Paul, "We do not lose heart."

Resource reading: 2 Corinthians 4:1-6

We Do Not Lose Heart

We do not lose heart. Though outwardly we are wasting away, yet inwardly we are being renewed day by day. For our light and momentary troubles are achieving for us an eternal glory that far outweighs them all.

2 CORINTHIANS 4:16-17

Insight: God is no respecter of persons, which means the strength and renewal that Paul received is available to you. God gives His resources for victorious living as much today as in the first century.

You think you have problems? I suspect you would not trade your challenges for those confronting the apostle Paul. When he wrote in his second letter to the Corinthians, "We are hard pressed on every side, but not crushed; perplexed, but not in despair; persecuted, but not abandoned; struck down, but not destroyed" (2 Corinthians 4:8), he was facing things that would have sent the average person either into deep depression or flight. But Paul not only took it in stride, he actually seemed to grow with it.

How could he be under tremendous pressure, struck down, crushed, and perplexed, and yet stay on top of things? Paul knew about trials, not only through personal experience, but also through the study of God's word as a rabbi. What did Paul know that we do not? Read carefully. The following five truths can sustain you during a dark situation.

Paul knew that trials accomplish the purpose of God. He knew firsthand that life is a battle, but he also knew God was with him in his daily trials. Peter wrote, "Dear friends, do not be surprised at the painful trial you are suffering, as though something strange were happening to you. But rejoice that you participate in the sufferings of Christ, so that you may be overjoyed when his glory is revealed" (1 Peter 4:12-13). God had not forsaken Paul, though the enemy had come against him full-strength.

Paul had confidence that God would sustain him in times of great difficulty. Think back to Isaiah 43, where God says *when* we go through the waters He will be with us. *When* we go through the flood it will not drown us, and *when* we face the fire we will not be burned. It is a foregone conclusion that, as Jesus told the disciples, in the world we will face persecution.

Paul could face trouble because he knew we are residents of a kingdom that cannot be shaken, an invisible kingdom that cannot be destroyed. Hebrews 12:28 says, "Since we are receiving a kingdom that cannot be shaken, let us be thankful, and so worship God acceptably with reverence and awe."

Paul knew that God would have the last word. Sometimes it looks as though evil has triumphed in the world. Never did things look more bleak and dark than during the Nazi Holocaust, yet eventually the evil was defeated and truth prevailed.

Paul knew that we have a home in heaven. He wrote, "Our citizenship is in heaven. And we eagerly await a Savior from there, the Lord Jesus Christ" (Philippians 3:20).

Paul Shao's mother was an American missionary, his father a Chinese doctor. During the Cultural Revolution in China, the entire family became a target of persecution. For nine long months Paul was kept in total darkness. Eventually he was allowed to leave China. He later wrote to a friend that what he missed the most were the quiet, intimate moments he had with Jesus Christ during solitary confinement.

How can you lose heart when you know that the Shepherd of your soul walks with you no matter where you are, no matter what you face?

Resource reading: 1 Peter 4

The Fearless Factor

Do not be afraid, little flock,
for your Father has been pleased
to give you the kingdom.
LUKE 12:32

Insight: Fearlessness is not recklessness when you know that God is with you. It is the confident assurance that you are going God's way and, therefore, you trust Him for the unknown.

For four years, Bernadette Grey was editor-in-chief of a women's magazine. Her work-related responsibilities kept her in contact with some of the world's most successful businesswomen. In one memorable editorial she analyzed four factors that led to success among her colleagues. She mentioned optimism, uniqueness, a strong work ethic, and fearlessness.

While her four factors relate to successful executives who are women, they apply equally to every person who succeeds. The fourth factor—fearlessness—is especially intriguing. Though an individual who is afraid of failure almost always fails, yet fearlessness is not bold brashness and ignoring the possibility of failure.

There are two ways you can be fearless: You can have a daring and audacious disregard for reality, or you can have great inner strength that assesses the failure factor yet confidently moves ahead. Individuals who disregard reality are usually not fearless, but brazen. They often crash and burn. Those with inner strength, however, move forward with confidence.

Recently, I plowed through two biographies, which consumed more than a few hours of reading on airplanes. One was of General Douglas MacArthur, the liberator of the Philippines and the man who did more to shape the future of Japan after World War 2 than any other person. MacArthur, according to his biographer, William Manchester, read his Bible and prayed every day. The second was on the life of the British Prime Minister Winston Churchill, a contemporary of MacArthur. As pugnacious and sometimes as belligerent as a bulldog, Churchill believed that God hated and fought against the tyrannies of Hitler and Stalin. He hated Stalin almost as much as Hitler.

Both of these men faced tremendous dangers, personally and collectively. Both had responsibility for vast numbers of people on their shoulders, and both of them knew full well the great consequences of making wrong decisions. Incidentally, both of them on occasion exercised poor judgment and—yes—failed at their tasks. The thing that made them successful, though, is they had enough inner strength so that when a decision had to be made, they considered all the factors and moved ahead without fear.

The fearlessness of these courageous leaders came from an inner conviction that they were instruments in God's hands. Perfect? No! They made mistakes and plenty of them, but they were confident God would see them through.

Is this something you can do, or is this a quality of only truly great men and women? Okay, you aren't leading an army or a nation. You, however, may be boss in your family or a person who is trying to do a good job for your company. Can you as an individual also be fearless, even when the doctor says, "You've got melanoma," or your accountant says, "If you know how to pray, you had better pray for a miracle"? Can you be fearless when the circumstances of life seem to bully you?

Fearlessness does not depend on your strength. Knowing that God is in control—and that somehow, someway He will see you through—lets you move into the future without fear.

Safety is not the absence of danger as much as it is the presence of the Lord. In the Upper Room, Jesus told the disciples, "Stop worrying; stop being afraid."

How about it? Fearlessness always relates to the future, and when you get there, God will already be there. Make sure you acknowledge that it is He, not you, who brought you through the storm. He still says the same thing to you today: "Trust Me. I'll be there for you as My child."

Resource reading: Psalm 46

Guidelines for Overcoming Fear, Part 1

God has not given us a spirit of fear, but of power and of love and of a sound mind.
2 TIMOTHY 1:7 NKJV

Insight: Whistling in the dark may work to build courage in old movies; however, in real life, taking small courageous steps helps you overcome fear.

While many of our worries relate to the past, it is certain that fear relates to the future. Notice something, if you would. Most of our fears are generated from two dark caves: 1) what you have not experienced and, therefore, what is outside the reality of your known world; and 2) ignorance, or what you do not understand, which becomes a threat to you in one way or another. I have found the latter is especially the case when we get older.

The big need today is not to catalog fear, categorize it, dissect it, rationalize it, or glorify it. The great need is to know how to overcome fear, to find God's power in defeating it, and to turn it into a tool that works *for* us instead of *against* us.

Before I give you several guidelines that will help you fight fear, I'd like to impress upon you a powerful statement found in the New Testament. In 2 Timothy 1:7, Paul, a man who had faced tremendous threats to his personal well-being, who had been shipwrecked, and who almost lost his head to a Roman sword, wrote, "God has not given us a spirit of fear, but of power and of love and of a sound mind" (NKJV).

The word that Paul uses for fear means a debilitating, terrible kind of fear that makes you turn and run, that makes you a coward instead of a courageous person who faces the enemy—whatever or whomever it may be. With that in mind, here are three guidelines to help you overcome fear.

Guideline 1: Recognize and admit your fear. Some folks advocate the strong, silent approach—just ignore your fear and it will go away. Bluff your way, they say! You know, whistle in the dark and just pretend you are not afraid. It does not really work that way. Sure, I was afraid when I heard that a friend and her baby had been kidnapped. But I didn't panic. I knew why I was fearful. Sometimes we do not always know why we are fearful, though, which means we need a second guideline.

Guideline 2: Analyze your fear. Why are you afraid? Was Franklin Delano Roosevelt right when he said, "There is nothing to fear but fear itself"? Or was that only so much rhetoric without any basis in fact? Is there any real reason for you to be fearful? One of the most common fears relating to physical well-being is fear of cancer. A doctor friend of mine says that people are always coming to him with imagined symptoms of cancer. When he begins to talk with them and explores their family medical background, he learns that no one in their family has ever had cancer and that even a physical exam gives no evidence of cancer. Yet some people are not convinced. They are sure they have it! This fear is totally different from the fear of waking up one morning to find a lump you cannot explain. In that case, better move on quickly to the next guideline.

Guideline 3: Act upon your fear. Let's suppose that lump you discovered is cancerous. If you seek medical help immediately, in many situations the problem can be solved and then the concern is gone. But if you do not act upon your fear, if you just pretend the problem is not there, it could kill you.

Some folks worry about their kids and whether they will fly right when they grow up. Others worry about their beauty, which is sure to fade eventually. Some executives become consumed with fear of failure, when in reality they have performed more than adequately. To refuse to look fear in the face and seek a plan of action reduces us to frustration and perhaps even failure. There are some things no one in the entire world can do but you, and taking the first step to put fear to flight is one of them.

Resource reading: Psalm 91

Guidelines for Overcoming Fear, Part 2

Even though I walk through the valley of the shadow of death, I will fear no evil, for You are with me.
PSALM 23:4

Insight: The vast majority of things you fear will never come your way! It's a fact.

Sir Wilfred Grenfell was a great missionary doctor and statesman in Labrador. On one occasion this brave man was taking patients to the base hospital in his small hospital boat, when a storm threatened to drive his little vessel onto the rocks of the rugged shore. The boat was full of people who were sick and would not survive a shipwreck. Grenfell kept his course and safely got to port. "Were you afraid?" someone asked him later, and he replied, "The only thing I've ever really feared is the loss of courage and faith. If Jesus is the Master of your life, there is no room for fear." Grenfell knew the danger, but he trusted God and kept moving ahead.

Not all of us, however, are so fearless. In the previous section, I gave you three guidelines for handling fear. To those, add two more:

Guideline 4: Commit irresolvable fears to your heavenly Father. And what are irresolvable fears? They are the unknown quantities that can drive you up the wall, the great "what ifs" of life. What will I do if I lose my job? What if my child should use drugs? What if my mate is unfaithful to me? What if some madman should hit the button and plunge us into war? What if a star should fall on me some dark night? All of those fears could happen, but to dwell on them is irrational and only robs us of peace of mind. The what ifs are plaguing, gnawing fears that can ruin you.

I'm convinced God never intended us to bear some fears, and when we try to handle our load and His, we're not going to make it. An elderly Christian lady, after having read that God neither slumbers nor sleeps, shut off her light with the comment, "Why should both of us stay awake tonight?" Good reasoning. Someone with a flair for details counted 365 "fear nots" in the Bible, one for every day of the year.

For the Christian, the issue takes on a different dimension—the God element. Is there a God who is in control of my life, let alone the universe, or do the promises of Scripture mean absolutely nothing? *Like what promises?* you may be thinking. Like the precious verses found in Isaiah 43, in which God says when you go through the deep waters, He will be with you, and when you face the proverbial rivers that can drown you, He will be with you.

Those promises, friend, were not made just to spiritual giants such as Elijah or David or Billy Graham or the pastor of your church. Those promises have your name attached to them, provided you will accept them and believe them.

Guideline 5: Overcome fear by faith. Knowledge of the Bible is a powerful weapon for fighting fear. Have you really discovered what the Bible says about fear and overcoming it? Take a concordance and look up the word *fear.* You will learn it was one of the first emotions Adam and Eve experienced. You will read how David cried, "Yea, though I walk through the valley of the shadow of death, I will fear no evil; for You are with me" (Psalm 23:4 NKJV). You will find its antidote in the New Testament: " 'I will never leave you nor forsake you,' So we may boldly say: 'The Lord is my helper; I will not fear. What can man do to me?' " (Hebrews 13:5-6 NKJV). And perhaps the most important thing that you will learn is that you do not have to be afraid when you know God is with you.

Resource reading: Psalm 119:65-72

Guidelines for Overcoming Fear, Part 3

Do not fear, for I am with you; do not be dismayed, for I am your God. I will strengthen you and help you; I will uphold you with my righteous right hand.

ISAIAH 41:10

Insight: Even giants of the faith such as Corrie ten Boom experienced fear. None of us are exempt, but their examples of confronting fear and not turning in flight give us courage to press forward, even when we are scared and hesitant.

On her first trip into what was then the USSR, Corrie ten Boom carried a suitcase full of Bibles. At that time, she was more than 80 years of age. Yet she was spry and full of life. Having lived through the harrowing Ravensbruck concentration camp in World War 2, Corrie knew what it means to trust God day by day. As she stood in customs watching the Russian officials ransack the suitcases, her heart was filled with fear, and the very fact that she was afraid perplexed her. She reasoned, *God has never failed me, so I must trust Him now.* Quietly she prayed, "God, I believe it is in Jeremiah that You said, 'God watched over His Word.' Those Bibles are Your Word. Now I claim that, Lord. Watch over Your Word, my Bibles."

As she prayed, her fear disappeared. A customs agent approached her sternly asking, "Is that your red suitcase?"

"Yes, sir, a heavy one," Corrie replied.

"I am just through with my work. I will help you." And with that the man picked up her suitcase and carried it through customs and out to the car that was waiting for her.

What an experience!

The more you know about the nature and strength of our heavenly Father, the less prone you are to worry and to be afraid. Take a concordance and look up the word *fear;* now mark those passages with the word in your Bible. Read Isaiah 41:10-13 and Psalm 23. Read the words of God in Isaiah 41:13: "Do not fear; I will help you." When we understand something of God's strength and personal care, fear dissipates rapidly.

Years ago in Scotland, I visited a certain valley where John MacNeil, the famed preacher of the early 1700s, lived. I was told that when he was a lad, he had to work for a farmer who lived in another valley. At the end of the day, John would walk home in the dark through an area where thieves and robbers often attacked people. One night John was walking home when he heard footsteps. They were getting closer and closer. When John walked faster, the person following him walked even faster. As his heart filled with fear, John heard a booming voice behind him. "It is your father, John. Don't be afraid."

Bring your fear to the Father, and by faith let Him meet you. This is what drives out fear. Psalm 34:4 says, "I sought the LORD, and he answered me; he delivered me from all my fears." He will do the same for you as well. When God is in control, there is no need to be fearful.

There are two more guidelines to add to the arsenal of weapons you can use in neutralizing the strength of fear.

Guideline 6: Stand upon the promises of God's Word. This is why you need to memorize passages of God's book, promises you lock into your heart. They are yours forever. Remember Jesus used Scripture in confronting the devil when He was tempted. Take time to study what the Word says about fear, going beyond just grabbing a text here or there to comfort you.

Guideline 7: Remember the source of fear. God? No—fear comes from the enemy of our souls, Satan, who is a deceiver and a liar.

Fear often makes us take detours—we avoid people, we avoid situations, we avoid encounters with doctors, we even avoid ourselves. But faith puts fear to flight. It will work for you.

Resource reading: Isaiah 40:28–41:10

From Fear to Trust

Do not be afraid, Abram. I am your shield, your very great reward.
GENESIS 15:1

Insight: Fearing God—having a reverential appreciation for who He is—results in trusting Him. This allows His peace to fill your heart, because you have nothing to fear from Him.

A friend who hungers for God wrote to me that she struggles with the fear that her search for God will ultimately result in only disappointment. As I read her heart cry, I thought of the words of A.W. Tozer: "In this hour of all-but-universal darkness one cheering gleam appears: There are to be found increasing numbers of persons whose religious lives are marked by a growing hunger after God Himself."[2]

Do you, like this friend, struggle with the whole issue? Yes, you have a genuine hunger for God. You long to know Him, to walk with Him, to be used by Him, yet—and this is the quandary—you're held back by fear. You're hesitant to really turn loose, wondering if the end of the search will result in disappointment, rejection, or even greater uncertainty.

There are several steps to having a relationship with God.

Guideline 1: Get to know God, not a caricature of God. This means peeling away the layers of misconceptions and discovering who He is, what He likes and dislikes, and what He has done for His children.

Guideline 2: Overcome fear of God. Fear of God clusters around several issues. Perhaps you fear being rejected by God—turned away at the door as not being good enough, unable to please Him, unable to satisfy Him. You fear what God may expect of you. You fear embarking on a journey to find God but ending up disappointed, like someone who takes a long spiritual pilgrimage and then comes to the end with empty hands and heart.

Some fears are rational, and some are completely without foundation, but being told, "That's silly! There's nothing to fear," does not help. When you've been to the dentist and have experienced the searing and stabbing sensation as the drill hit a nerve in your tooth, you know pain, and you fear future drillings. Now, I can find plenty of people to testify that having a tooth drilled can be painful (at least, that's the way it used to be), but I've been working with people for more than 40 years, and I'm still waiting to find the first person who can honestly tell me, "God let me down!" or, "Jesus Christ was a big disappointment to me. It just didn't work!"

Is the fear of rejection a real one? Will God ask more of me than I can deliver—or should I say more than I *want* to deliver? In coping with that first fear, ask, "Have I personally experienced disappointment with God?" You also need to ask, "Have I unfairly blamed Him for what I or others were responsible for?"

I recommend you write in a journal and put your experiences down in black and white. Record your thoughts—what you pray for and what God does in your life. Jesus made a promise, a pointed one, when He said, "If anyone chooses to do God's will, he will find out whether my teaching comes from God or whether I speak on my own" (John 7:17).

A closing thought. A study of the phrases "Fear not" and "Don't be afraid" in the Bible shows they are almost always connected to God's presence, power, or performance. You find the words "Fear not, for I will..." or "Fear not, for I have..." or "Fear not, for I am..."—so ultimately the answer to your fear is confidence in the integrity of God Himself.

As the songwriter put it, "There's no disappointment in Jesus." Your search for God will be rewarded, and when you embark on the search with sincerity, it's usually a rather short one because He's there to find you! For whoever seeks, finds, and whoever finds is rewarded! God's promise is still valid: "You will seek me and find me when you seek me with all your heart" (Jeremiah 29:13).

Resource reading: Jeremiah 29:10-14

The Healing Power of Hope

Be strong and take heart, all you who hope in the LORD.
PSALM 31:24

Insight: What oxygen is to the lungs and food is to your body, hope is to your soul.

It happens every day in every major city of the world. A car is proceeding down the highway when another vehicle pulls directly into its path. There is the screech of tires as the driver jams on the brakes, but it is too late. The sickening thud is followed by the tearing of metal and the shattering of glass, punctuated with the screams of suffering. A broken, bruised body is pulled from the twisted wreckage, and soon an ambulance is racing toward the hospital with siren wailing and lights making eerie designs on building walls. The victim passes out and does not remember reaching the hospital, but upon arrival, a team of specialists go to work to save a life.

Moments later, the family arrives and begins the long vigil, awaiting news about the life hanging in the balance. Finally, the doctors walk out to talk with the family. Immediately, the family's first words burst out, "Doctor, is there hope? Is there hope?"

Centuries ago the writer of Scripture wrote that as long as a person is living there is hope. What oxygen is to the lungs and food is to the body, hope is to the soul. To the Corinthians Paul wrote, "And now abide faith, hope, love" (1 Corinthians 13:13 NKJV). If Paul were writing today—in the morning of the twenty-first century—do you suppose he would still say that hope remains?

Many are asking the question the coal miner asked when he was trapped by an accident. For him the day had begun as usual. The descent into the earth was routine, and the work started just like any other day, but that afternoon an explosion resulted in suffocating clouds of dust and overhead beams crumbling like match sticks. The miner was pinned by the debris, but he could still breathe. For hours he lay there, and finally he heard the picks and shovels of the men who were digging toward him.

Occasionally after that, they would stop their work and call the miner's name, straining their ears to hear the faintest sound. After one call, they did not hear a voice, but they did hear a sound—an intermittent knocking. "Shush!" They listened. "It's Morse code," one of them said. Sure enough, the miner although unable to speak, was tapping out the words, "Is… there…hope?"

Many today are gripped by a quiet despair, an uncertainty about the future, wondering if there is hope for our generation. Science and technology have united to produce the greatest arsenal of death-producing weapons the world has ever known. It never helps one to sleep better to realize that the atomic stockpile is great enough to kill every person on Earth several times over. To this concern add the problems of food shortages and a host of other difficulties. One geologist said that if the earth were completely hollow and filled with oil, we would still eventually run out of this black ooze unless we slowed our consumption of the resource.

Where shall we look for hope? Moscow? Beijing? Geneva? Bonn? Washington? Or shall we expect the United Nations to pass a resolution banning despair and pessimism? No, little hope trickles from the capitals of the world, but there is hope in a world considered hopeless by many.

Centuries ago, Jeremiah wrote, "Blessed is the man who trusts in the LORD, and whose hope is the LORD" (Jeremiah 17:7 NKJV). The Bible, reinforced by 5000 years of written secular history, declares that there is no hope in the heart of man apart from the hope that comes through faith in God.

Is it any wonder that the writers of Scripture talked about our Father as a certainty and a hope through whom life can be different? Faith becomes the doorway that provides hope for the future, and hope makes life worth living. Think about it.

Resource reading: Psalm 42

Hope in a Hopeless World

Why are you downcast, O my soul? Why so disturbed within me? Put your hope in God, for I will yet praise him, my Savior and my God.

PSALM 42:5-6

Insight: As long as life is present, your hope can reside in God. As long as God exists, your hope will not wither or die.

The brilliant writer Rudyard Kipling graphically wrote of the time "when Earth's last picture is painted," when we "lie down for an aeon or two." But personalizing what he described, will your life's last picture be one of peace or of despair? For many who have all but given up on hope for a better tomorrow, trapped in circumstances they do not like and did not choose, it may be dark and forbidding.

I'm thinking of the desperate plea that came from a talented young woman in her mid-twenties, a university graduate who is fluent in several languages. She wrote, "I don't understand what's going on inside me. I simply don't have the desire to go on living. I feel like I'm emotionally tired and exhausted. When I go to bed at night, I simply don't want to wake up the next morning because everything will be the same, no changes inside and outside. I don't know what's going on."

She's not alone, believe me. Thousands and thousands of youth today in every corner of the world are despairing of hope. Their numbers include businesspeople whose corporate failures bring shame and disgrace; others who take refuge in alcohol; retirees who say, "Is this all there is to life? Have I worked all my life only to end up with broken health, no friends, and nothing to live for?"

I call it the despair of hope. A wind of despair touches the lives of some of our brightest, most promising men and women.

I freely acknowledge that difficult, tough situations are not new. I think of Victor Frankl's writing about the importance of hope to those who were imprisoned during the horrors of the Nazi Holocaust in World War 2. And long before him, I think of God's children who, though placed in hopeless situations, kept their hope in God. Paul, imprisoned in Rome and facing execution, could still write, "Rejoice in the Lord always. I will say it again: Rejoice!"

Yet—and this is where we turn the corner—some face difficult situations and find hope, no matter how hopeless circumstances look. Abraham was like that. Paul, in writing about Abraham, said that he hoped against hope, holding on to the promise God had given him when the situation was impossible.

I will never forget a conversation I once had with Deborah Wang, known as Auntie Wang to her friends and family. When I met her, she was in her eighties and as frail as a cornstalk in the wind. Her husband, Wang Ming Dao, had been one of the architects of the house-church movement in the 1950s after China fell to Communism, and this little woman, who had never lifted a finger to hurt anyone, was guilty by association. Subsequently, she spent 20 long years in prison, and during that time, she saw her husband only three times.

Visiting this godly little woman in her tiny apartment in Shanghai, I got her to recount some of her experiences, and then asked, "Did you ever lose hope?"

The answer spoke far louder than her soft words, "No, never!" Her eyes spoke volumes. They said, "Oh my child, if you only knew how close and precious Jesus was during those years, you would not have asked such a foolish question."

One thing these people have learned for certain is that God is the God also of tough times, dark days, and difficult circumstances. They knew hope in a hopeless world. Have you learned that lesson?

Resource reading: Revelation 19:11-16

The God of All Hope

May the God of hope fill you with all joy and peace as you trust in him, so that you may overflow with hope by the power of the Holy Spirit.
ROMANS 15:13

Insight: The world may look hopeless, but the God of all hope brings a ray of light that grows stronger as you grow closer to Him.

Do not open! Gas being created!" were the terse words written in red felt-tip pen on a sign affixed to the door. Within, a 14-year-old Japanese schoolgirl had taken her life, following the directions of a Japanese Web site with instructions on mixing toilet-bowl cleaner with bath salts.[3]

For the tenth consecutive year, starting with 1998, the annual suicide rate in Japan has exceeded 30,000, which gives the country the highest rate among developed nations. Youths, seniors, and unemployed males are the largest groups among those people despairing of life…in a country where suicide is not socially rejected. The traditional religions of Buddhism and Shintoism are suicide-neutral, and so a failing economy and despair spur on the black horse of death.

Japan is not the only place where men and women are struggling with a lack of purpose in life. A Russian colleague of mine said that during one day in Russia, three eleven-year-old girls, in copycat fashion, separately took their lives. He said that among police in his country there are 1.2 suicides every day, and these do not include military units, where alcoholism and suicide rates are out of sight. He also said that in Russian prisons, suicide rates are so high that figures are no longer compiled.

What's happened? Why has despair of hope seemed to settle in over our globe like a dark, demonic vapor? Frankly, apart from the God of hope—the One who at Calvary demonstrated His love and care for us who live on Earth—there is not much hope that life will be better tomorrow.

We are running out of almost everything but people—oil, food, water, moral decency, encouragement, and gratitude. The AIDS virus has become a world epidemic. The United Nations has proved to be completely inept as a keeper of world peace. Atomic weapons are now aging and threaten to explode from decay or accident. Our environment is polluted. On the list goes.

Psychobiologist Curt Richter, doing research at the prestigious Johns Hopkins University, discovered that when rats were put into an absolutely hopeless situation, they simply gave up and died. The rats resembled thousands of prisoners in the concentration camps of Europe who, having despaired of hope, curled into a fetal position and refused food or water, thus ending their lives. But Richter discovered that when an element of hope was introduced, the rats endured even great difficulty and privation to survive.

We are not rats with minimal intelligence. We are offspring created by the hand of the Almighty, human beings, people of intelligence and spirituality. We are not animals. But without hope, we experience the same despair as laboratory animals.

Do you realize that as long as God lives, there is hope for your life? He hung the rainbow in the sky as a symbol of hope. God turned the darkest, most hopeless day that ever dawned into a victory—the day that the cross was planted on Golgotha as God's Son gave His life to bring you into fellowship with the Father. Just as the rats suddenly reversed their behavior when an element of hope was introduced, the introduction of Jesus Christ—who became flesh and blood; who said, "I am the resurrection and the Life"; who stood before an open tomb—is the ingredient that can turn your despair into hope. There is hope for today and hope for tomorrow when God lives and you are connected with Him.

I concede that our world looks hopeless, but we who believe in the certainty of resurrection must never forget that "no eye has seen, no ear has heard, no mind has conceived what God has prepared for those who love him" (1 Corinthians 2:9). Thank God for the hope that endures beyond the grave and lasts as long as an eternal God lives. No wonder Scripture calls Him the God of hope.

Resource reading: Hebrews 11:17-30

Riding Out the Storm

We have this hope as an anchor for the soul, firm and secure. It enters the inner sanctuary behind the curtain.

HEBREWS 6:19

Insight: Hope lets you ride out the storm when the ship of your life gets tossed about and you think you may not survive.

God made you in such a way that you can survive tremendous ordeals—illness, imprisonment, persecution, and privation. You can live without food and water far longer than you might think. You can handle a tremendous amount of stress, but there is one thing you cannot do without, and apart from this you quickly despair. It is hope! You can recover when illness has ravished your body. You can put your finances together again, and you can pick up the broken pieces of your world and go on after the bottom drops out, but when you are overcome by the despair of hope, you give up and die.

Have you ever been in a boat or a ship during a terrific storm, when you could not hitch a helicopter ride or take a submarine to avoid the waves? You were not about to give up and die, so you simply had to ride it out. Paul faced that situation when he was on his way to Rome and the ship was caught by a ferocious Mediterranean storm. You can read about it in Acts 27 of the New Testament. When bad came to worse, the sailors "dropped four anchors from the stern and prayed for daylight." Talk about a wing and a prayer.

For you who are fighting the despair of hope, there are four anchors that can keep you from the rocks and bring the dawn of hope.

Anchor 1: Hope in the person of God Himself. "Find rest, O my soul, in God alone; my hope comes from him" (Psalm 62:5). It makes a tremendous difference when you realize God is in control, that the circumstances of life—no matter how dark—are subject to His will and command, and that the storm can rage only as long as He allows it to rage. That's comforting, no matter how strong the wind.

Anchor 2: Hope in the Word of God. The psalmist wrote, "I wait for the Lord, my soul waits, and in his word I put my hope" (Psalm 130:5). He had learned that the winds seldom stop as quickly as they did on the Sea of Galilee when Jesus calmed the waters, saying, "Peace be still." When the sea is agitated and the winds are blowing, it takes some time for them to subside. "I wait for the Lord," he said. "In his word I put my hope."

One of my favorite hymns by Lidie Edmunds has this verse:

> My heart is leaning on the Word,
> The written Word of God.
> Salvation by my Savior's name,
> Salvation through His blood.

You can have confidence in the Word only when you become convinced that God's Word is true and, as Jesus said, cannot be broken. So you take it by faith and realize God will honor those marvelous promises His Word contains.

Anchor 3: Hope in the nature and goodness of the Lord. When you personally come to understand that God is good and that goodness flows from His essential nature, you also can accept the fact that He is not striving to punish you by allowing the winds to blow, but rather He's giving you an opportunity to discover how strong He is.

Anchor 4: Hope in the eternality of God. God lasts forever, and He provides an anchor that will hold us firmly through the temporary distresses of this life.

There is always a sunrise following the dark night. Remember, the sailors on board Paul's vessel put out four anchors and prayed for the daylight. The darker the night, the brighter the dawn.

Resource reading: Acts 27

The Blessing of Hope

Blessed is the man who trusts in the LORD, and whose hope is the LORD.

JEREMIAH 17:7 NKJV

Insight: The hope of Christians goes beyond government, movements, and politics. It sees God as the one behind governments, movements, and politics—and ultimately His Son will rule and reign, something that gives us hope for tomorrow.

The Greek philosopher Thales is credited with saying, "The most universal thing is hope, for hope stays with those who have nothing else." The ancient philosopher had a point. But for vast segments of the world's population—especially those who have nothing left but hope—even hope seems to be dying.

For millions of people in Africa and Eastern Europe, political conditions seem to drain the buoyancy of hope from their lives. War, famine, and disease leave in their wake suffering, despair, and untold agony. After Communism collapsed, the poverty and corruption left behind were to many a fiercer enemy. In the Middle East, millions of refugees ask themselves, *Will life ever return to normal?*

Whether it is the world's political situation, the economy, the environment, or the gloomy forecast for the future, there is a lot of despair on the landscape today. But in spite of it all, there is hope—though not necessarily coming from the council chambers of the United Nations, or the diplomatic envoys who shuttle from world capital to world capital, or the rosy forecasts coming from a few politicians who insist that great prosperity lies ahead.

The Bible says, "Anyone who is among the living has hope" (Ecclesiastes 9:4). The writer knew that the only real hope in a hopeless world comes from God Himself. Writing to the Corinthians, Paul said, "If only for this life we have hope in Christ, we are to be pitied more than all men" (1 Corinthians 15:19). Paul saw the Christian hope reaching across the landscape of despair to the presence of God Himself. It gave him an assurance that life is more than the hopelessness of life today.

How does a Christian have hope in a hopeless world?

First, he believes that there is hope for the present because of God's power to change the circumstances of despair. That is why writer Charles L. Allen said that the man who gives up hope slams the door in the face of God. Read the biographies of men and women such as Richard Wurmbrand and Corrie ten Boom, both of whom spent years in prisons, and you will learn that hope is born of prayer. Hope in God is not wishful thinking but is based on the sure and certain promises of God.

Secondly, a Christian has hope in an otherwise hopeless world because he is sure that death is not the end of existence. This gives meaning to life—no matter how difficult or desperate—in the world today. That is why Paul could say, "If only for this life we have hope in Christ, we are to be pitied more than all men" (1 Corinthians 15:19).

Where is your hope today? If your hope rests only in men or governments or programs—no matter how worthy—you have little hope to live for. However, if your hope is in God and you trust Him, He will be a refuge and a hiding place from the stormy tempest. Jeremiah, the prophet of old, was right when he wrote, "Blessed is the man who trusts in the LORD, and whose hope is the LORD" (Jeremiah 17:7 NKJV).

Resource reading: Jeremiah 14:19-22

When Anger Gets the Best of You

God said to Jonah, "Do you have a right to be angry about the vine?" "I do," he said. "I am angry enough to die."
JONAH 4:9

Insight: When you become angry, you cease to think rationally and begin to leave common sense behind you.

Everybody these days is subject to stress. Whether a person lives in Manila, Tokyo, or Los Angeles, we all live at a faster pace than at any other time in history. It's the traffic, the pressures and stress of life, along with the family stress, that cause us to reach the boiling point, and when that happens, we explode. We can say we are letting off steam, but any way we look at it, anger has the best of us. After our tempers get out of hand, we are embarrassed and feel disappointed because we know we have hurt others. Looking at it from a selfish viewpoint, we also hurt ourselves and our futures as well.

The apostle Paul offered some sound advice to those of us struggling with strong emotional feelings. He counseled, " 'In your anger do not sin': Do not let the sun go down while you are still angry" (Ephesians 4:26). The Phillips translation puts it like this, "If you are angry, be sure it is not out of wounded pride and bad temper. Never go to bed angry—don't give the devil that sort of foothold." Commenting on Paul's advice, one writer tells how he visited a gift shop where his attention was captivated by a large bottle cork trimmed with sequins and nestled in tissue in a plastic box. The card with it read, "For the hole in your head when you blow your top." What a clever reminder that when we blow our tops, we are the ones who get the headache.

In his book *None of These Diseases,* Dr. S.I. McMillen has a chapter on anger and how it affects you physically. He tells of a little lady, well into her eighties, who came in frequently to have her blood pressure checked. He said that it usually hovered around 200, but one day it soared to 230. Inwardly, Dr. McMillen was alarmed, but rather calmly he said, "Your blood pressure is up today." With a smile the little lady answered, "I can easily account for that. I just had an argument with another patient in your waiting room." Dr. McMillen comments, "Think of it: that cultured, intelligent woman could well have blown a cerebral 'fuse' and suffered a fatal stroke, simply because she wanted to get even verbally with a man for his provocative chatter. Her diagnosis of the spectacular rise of her blood pressure was correct."

How modern Paul's advice is—"Be angry and sin not." The apostle is not saying that all anger is sin but that anger is a poison to our souls and bodies. Paul advises us to get the anger out of our systems—and he does not mean by telling so-and-so just what we think of him! Christ demonstrated by His own life that there is a place for anger—call it righteous indignation. Christ was angry about hypocrisy and selfishness as well as more obvious sins. Our problem is usually ourselves; we are afraid someone will take advantage of us or someone else will get the praise we think we deserve.

In place of letting anger and malice breed hatred and sin, Paul says that love can be a catalyst that removes misplaced and unjustified anger. Notice his advice and apply it to your life: "Get rid of all bitterness, rage and anger, brawling and slander, along with every form of malice. Be kind and compassionate to one another, forgiving each other, just as in Christ God forgave you" (Ephesians 4:31-32).

The apostle Paul's advice provides guidelines for right living, but the best counsel in the world is useless until we follow it. His words are a spiritual prescription, but we each must make an application. If you have a ferocious, unwieldy temper, admit it. Do not hesitate to ask God's help in overcoming that temper. As you begin each day, say, "Lord, You go with me today and help me to do and say the things that reflect Your presence in my life." You can find God's power to make your life worth living.

Resource reading: Ephesians 4:29-32

Is It Bad to Get Mad?

When Saul heard their words, the Spirit of God came upon him in power, and he burned with anger.

1 Samuel 11:6

Insight: All anger is not wrong. The Bible says you should be angry for the right reason, for the right duration of time, and in the right manner.

In the days when people rode trains instead of flying on airplanes, a certain businessman gave a porter a large tip, asking him to be sure he got off the train the next morning at 5 AM in a certain town where the train stopped. He explained that he had an important appointment, and since he was a sound sleeper, he feared he would not wake up.

"Yes, sir!" replied the porter, "I'm sure I can take care of it for you."

But at 9 AM the next morning, the businessman awoke to discover he was still on the train, 200 miles past his destination. It was a very angry man who found the porter and gave him a verbal tongue-lashing, throwing in a few words he had not used since his Navy days.

"That absolutely has to be the maddest man I have ever seen," remarked the conductor, who had happened to be standing nearby.

"Boy, if you think he was mad," replied the porter, "you should have seen the man I put off the train at 5 AM this morning."

We chuckle at this, but the number of people who allow anger to get the best of them today is no laughing matter. Displays of anger and rage, both public and private, are on the increase. A generation ago when drivers failed to turn on their headlights at dusk, other drivers blinked theirs! No more! We're fearful that what we intend to be a helpful reminder may be taken as a hostile gesture. If you question whether anger is on the increase, notice what happens when somebody crowds in front of a person at the gas pump or when someone pushes another in a crowded elevator or when someone cuts in line at the grocery store. Tempers flare, and fast!

Most of us have grown up feeling displays of anger are wrong, but are they really? Is it bad to get mad?

Surprising as it is to some folks, the Bible has a great deal to say about anger or strong wrath. In the Old Testament alone, there are 455 references to anger, 375 of those references referring to God Himself. Many of those references pertain to His relationship with His own people, who refused to follow the directions of their heavenly Father. As a result, God was displeased with them—yes, even angry.

In the New Testament, there are many references to anger and how to cope with it. Jesus was angry with His disciples on several occasions because of their refusal to believe Him. He became angry with the Pharisees because of the hardness of their hearts and their hypocrisy. He said, "Woe to you, teachers of the law and Pharisees, you hypocrites! You are like whitewashed tombs, which look beautiful on the outside but on the inside are full of dead men's bones and everything unclean" (Matthew 23:27).

Of course, there is that classic illustration of making anger work for you to do a right thing, as Jesus did when He picked up a whip and drove the money changers away from the temple. The Bible makes it clear that anger, like a two-edged sword or a scalpel in the hands of a skilled surgeon, is amoral in itself; it can be harmful and wrong, or used properly, it can be a powerful motive for moral action. Temper properly used produces character and integrity. The Bible clearly differentiates between *being angry* and *remaining angry.* Paul's guideline to the Ephesians was, "Be ye angry, and sin not" (Ephesians 4:26 KJV). Therefore, how you handle anger determines whether it is wrong or right.

Let me challenge your thinking. Why is it that we are an angry, uptight generation? To make it personal, why do you allow your temper to flare on occasion? Says Yale psychiatrist James Comer,

> People have a sense that the world is closing in on them, that there are too many people around, and that they are getting ripped off. We feel powerless. All of a sudden, we are beginning to doubt that anybody can do anything about our problems, and we are angry. We explode in frustration.[4]

To find a better way, read on.

Resource reading: Romans 12

Why Are We Such an Angry Generation?

Refrain from anger and turn from wrath; do not fret—it leads only to evil.
PSALM 37:8

Insight: Most of the reasons for anger today are negative and result only in strife and conflict. Compare your reasons for anger with what made Jesus angry.

In a 1977 interview, Dr. James Comer of Yale Medical School commented, "This definitely is an 'angry age'—much more so, probably, than any time in recent history."[5] However, since then the thumbscrews of rage and anger have been torqued considerably.

What was a problem in 1977 is a far greater problem now. Why should we be an angry, uptight generation when we have so much that previous generations did not have? For a few minutes think with me about some of the factors that make up the gunpowder of emotional outbursts that explode in a flash of anger at the slightest provocation.

Factor 1: Stress. We live busier lives today than at any time in recent history, and tension is the result. Like the string of a violin that is tightened and tightened until it snaps, we load our schedules tighter and tighter until we explode in a burst of anger. Then we ask ourselves, *Why did I get so mad?* It is simple. We crowd too much into a short span of time and then feel guilty because we think spiritual people do not get angry. When we do, we dislike ourselves because of it.

Factor 2: Frustration. Failure to experience our expectations produces frustration. When there is no relief, frustration builds into anger. A friend of mine took his trail bike into the mountains to hunt. When it stopped running, he turned his .45 caliber pistol on it and shot it to pieces. (Sometimes we would all like to do that, but it is just not economically feasible.)

Factor 3: Personal affronts. Tempers flare when we hear jokes or slang terms directed toward our race or ethnic group or about our physical characteristics or other personal features.

Factor 4: Violation of personal rights. We consider being slighted an attack on our person. Especially in marriage we expect certain considerations from our spouses, and when we do not get them, we get angry. Personal rights, especially in marriage, have been vastly overstressed. We may win arguments but lose friends—even a spouse. Part of learning to love is learning to serve, and before we can be on the receiving end, we must learn how to give.

Factor 5: Situations that run counter to our values. A study of the life of Jesus indicates that most of His anger was occasioned by situations that were wrong, and He did something about them. Call it righteous indignation or whatever you like, but we need more of it.

Newspapers recently reported an incident in which a woman driving down a street saw two muggers rifling the pockets of a man with his hands in the air. She stopped, and perceiving it was a holdup, began to honk the horn of her car. This drew a blast from a 12-gauge shotgun as the robbers made their get-away. Undaunted, the woman leaned on the horn and trailed the suspects, who soon crashed into a parked car and were arrested by police. She told a reporter, "I just said to myself, *I am not going to let them get away with that!* I guess I just got mad!"

While we applaud her valor, we question the wisdom of her actions, realizing the personal risk she took. Nonetheless, we can relate to her anger. Enough is enough! And that's when we have to take action.

Resource reading: 1 Thessalonians 4:1-7

Handling Your Anger the Right Way

Do not be quickly provoked in your spirit, for anger resides in the lap of fools.
ECCLESIASTES 7:9

Insight: An angry person is never a happy person, so before you lose your temper, ask yourself, "Is this really worth it? Am I willing to give up my peace of mind for this issue?"

"You can be angry and still be good," says Dr. Neil Warren, a practicing psychologist and a born-again Christian.

Right, we think. *That's what I want to do—be mad but still be good.* Knowing how is the secret. Here are five ways to cope with anger.

Guideline 1: Avoid stressful situations. Naturally we cannot avoid all stress, but we can avoid some. Organize yourself so you eliminate stressful situations that evoke anger, like getting up too late consistently so you have to drive fast to work, or failing to leave for the airport in time, or planning your time so tightly that the slightest change of schedule really angers you. Plan ahead and eliminate some of those situations that are apt to trigger your temper.

Guideline 2: Put the situation into perspective. When you start to feel the slow burn, stop and ask yourself, *Is it really worth the emotional stress and strain to get angry?* Maybe you need to ask, *Is that person worth losing my temper over?* The problem with too many people today is that they are *temperamental*—too much *temper* and not enough *mental.* Is it worth the risk of getting fired to tell your boss off? What does your anger do to your wife and children? Put the circumstances into perspective, and you will learn to keep your temper in bounds.

Guideline 3: Learn to discipline your emotions. There are times when the kingdom of God is better served by your learning to discipline your speech and keep your temper under control. A 6-foot-9-inch basketball player by the name of Bayard Forrest discovered this when he was playing for Athletes in Action. "If I cannot control my temper out there [speaking of the basketball court]," Forrest told a reporter, "I am not going to be a great witness. I know it gets real tough under the basket and that hard, physical contact is part of the game, but I have to retain my cool if I am going to be a Christian example."

Guideline 4: Vent your emotions appropriately. Here are five practical ways:

1. Physical exercise.
2. Music. Leonard Bernstein once said, "It is a remarkably lucky thing to be able to storm your way through a Beethoven Symphony. Think of the amount of rage you get out. If you exhibited that on the streets or in an interpersonal relationship, you would be thrown in jail. Instead, you're applauded for it." He's right. Beat the keys of a piano or attack the stings of a guitar.
3. Painting.
4. Talk through emotions, preferably with the person who has angered you, but even another person can be a sounding board to vent deep emotions.
5. Pray. Joseph Scrivens writes,

> Have we trials and temptations?
> Is there trouble anywhere?
> We should never be discouraged;
> Take it to the Lord in prayer.

Guideline 5: Eliminate stressful situations when you can. Changing a job may be better than constantly doing a slow burn. Perhaps it means changing churches or buying a new car. And there are some situations that cannot be changed; we have to learn how to live with them—that's where the grace of God makes the difference.

Resource reading: Ecclesiastes 7

Controlling Your Temper

"In your anger do not sin": Do not let the sun go down while you are still angry.
EPHESIANS 4:26

Insight: Vance Havner, the pithy evangelist of the past century, used to say, "Any bulldog can whip a skunk, but it just ain't worth it." Do you agree?

Have you ever wondered how to get mad without being bad? I have the formula for you, which may change your outlook on life. As we have noted, anger is a strong emotion, but in itself it is neither good nor bad. How we handle anger puts it in the good or bad column. When we get mad, one of three things happens.

We *stay angry.* A lot of people are like that—always mad. They are like thunderclouds about to storm. Their thermostats run at 210 degrees—just under the boiling point. They retain deep-seated hostilities that may go back to childhood. Clearly such anger is harmful.

We may *rationalize anger* and never get angry when we should. What could produce moral character and integrity produces vacillation and indifference.

We learn how to *make anger work* for us. This is the right thing.

I want to share four guidelines on handling anger so it works for you.

Guideline 1: Be angry with the right person. Too often we take out our hostilities on an innocent person. A boss may be the true cause of anger, but not having the courage to confront, we get angry with our families. This aggression is misplaced and wrong. This is why Jesus instructs us in Matthew 18, when we have something against a person, we are to go to him directly and tell him his fault. Feelings are directed toward the appropriate person, and this spares the innocents.

Guideline 2: Be angry for the right cause. Part of our problem today is that we are angry over the wrong causes. What should evoke moral indignation or old-fashioned anger is met with indifference. What does stir up anger should instead be met with discipline and tact. There is a time and a place for anger. Jesus was angry when the money changers turned the temple into a den of merchandising thieves, and rightly so. This guideline is based on Paul's direction to the Ephesians: "'In your anger do not sin': Do not let the sun go down while you are still angry" (Ephesians 4:26).

Guideline 3: Be angry for the right length of time. Paul's advice is "Don't let the sun go down on your wrath." In other words, get it out of your system. Say it as kindly as possible, but get it off your chest. Do not carry it over to the next day. What happens when we fail to heed Paul's advice? Anger left to fester can produce a number of psychological problems, most of which could be avoided by this third guideline.

Guideline 4: Be angry in the right way. If anger is directed toward resolving a problem rather than at the person who has created the problem, it becomes constructive and positive. If a person puts a fist through the wall or punches an individual who owes him money, he has only created worse problems.

Jesus was angry in the right way. He did something constructive—He eliminated the money changers from the temple. Those who are wrong will back down and flee, just as Christ's adversaries did when He drove them from the temple.

There is a time and a place for everything. By following these guidelines we discover that temper—which can destroy marriages, families, friendships, careers—can work for us. With God's help, we can learn to control anger instead of allowing it to defeat us.

Resource reading: Jonah 4:1-11

Depression Stopper 1: Taking Inventory

To all who received him, to those who believed in his name, he gave the right to become children of God.

John 1:12

Insight: Understanding how important you are to your heavenly Father begins to unravel the web of depression when it ensnares you.

Whenever I address the subject of depression, I never cease to be amazed at the number of people who respond by saying, "Yes, that's a picture of me. I don't know why I'm depressed, but I am." And more times than not the letter or e-mail will have a postscript saying something like, "By the way, I'm a Christian, and I know that I shouldn't be depressed, but I am, and I feel guilty because of it."

I can't help but feel that some of our dark moments could be avoided by understanding our relationship with our heavenly Father and how important we are to Him. One gentleman wrote saying that he had struggled with bouts of depression for 30 years, but he found Christ as his personal Savior, who gave him new hope and helped him to overcome depression.

Depression stopper 1: Know who you are in relationship to your heavenly Father. John 1:12 says, "To all who received him, to those who believed in his name, he gave the right to become children of God." Our relationship with God is the same as children with their father. It is the picture of an orphan who has been adopted into a family and then becomes the heir of all the father possesses. The concept of adoption, as developed under Roman law, gave the adopted sons equal rights of inheritance with the children of natural birth.

Furthermore, under Roman law the past of the adopted individual was legally wiped out. If he had committed crimes, those crimes were absolved. When he received the name of his adoptive father, he became a new person legally, with the past forgotten.

In like manner, when God forgives us, the past is wiped out forever. Understanding that the past is forgiven and forgotten should help us deal with depression. "As far as the east is from the west," wrote the psalmist, "so far has he removed our transgressions from us" (Psalm 103:12). The east and the west never meet, so why become depressed over deeds God has forgiven and will never hold against us?

Paul in Galatians 4 further developed the concept of adoption. Here he says God sent Christ "to redeem them that were under the law, that we might receive the adoption of sons. And because ye are sons, God hath sent forth the Spirit of his Son into your hearts, crying, Abba, Father. Wherefore thou art no more a servant, but a son; and if a son, then an heir of God through Christ" (Galatians 4:5-7 KJV). The word *Abba* does not mean much to us today, but it does take on great significance when you understand that this was an Aramaic word of great affection. Perhaps the closest equivalent is the term *daddy* or *papa.* Nobody goes around calling just anyone "papa" or "daddy"; this is a term reserved for a much loved father. This term conveys the warmth and closeness of a relationship that exists when we have become God's children.

As the adopted children of God, our heavenly Father wants us to grow and mature. When we fall, He will forgive us and help us up, just as our earthly fathers did when we learned to walk. Friend, knowing who we are and what our relationship to our heavenly Father is can be a great depression stopper. It's the first step toward healing and peace of mind.

Resource reading: Galatians 4:1-11

Depression Stopper 2: There Is a God Who Cares

God has said, "Never will I leave you; never will I forsake you." So we say with confidence, "The Lord is my helper; I will not be afraid. What can man do to me?"

HEBREWS 13:5-6

Insight: When you become a believer, you are adopted into the family of God. Your past is forever wiped out. You become a new person, and God has special concern for you as His child.

When we are depressed, statistics mean nothing. Talking about causes of depression is also nearly worthless, but knowing what to do to climb out of the pit is like a breath of fresh air in a dungeon. Writers to Guidelines during the month of December often tell me that the season creates depression. Analyzing these letters helps me to realize there are some depression stoppers—simple truths that we often overlook—which can help us when we face dark times in life.

In the previous section, we saw the first great truth that turns depression to flight: We have been adopted into the family of God and therefore are heirs of the Father's wealth. This experience is the result of personally accepting Jesus Christ as Lord and Savior. It is the certainty that you have a God connection through His Son.

Depression stopper 2: God is in control of Planet Earth and our lives personally. We need not fear or worry. Do you believe that? "Well," you may answer, "I wish it were that simple. I'd like to believe it, but every time I pick up the paper, the news gives me cold chills." We believe what we read in the newspaper, in spite of the fact that even the best-intentioned reporter may have incorrect facts. So why not believe a time-proven book called the Bible? For over 2000 years people have been proving out the validity of the statements contained in Scripture.

The New Testament clearly says that God has a will and a purpose for you as His child and that He will keep you safe in the midst of the storm because you belong to Him. Underline Romans 8:28 in your Bible and memorize it, along with Ephesians 1:11, which says God "works out everything in conformity with the purpose of his will."

I am indebted to one of our listeners for the following story that illustrates this truth.

> A traveler in Norway visited a great electric power plant in one of the country's deep mountain valleys. After seeing the immense turbines in the plant, he was invited to inspect the reservoirs that controlled the flow of water to the giant turbines. These reservoirs were caverns cut into the mountainside some eight hundred feet above the power plant and were reached by means of a small cable car drawn up the side of the mountain. The car itself was perhaps four by six feet, with a plain seat at the lower end.
>
> When the visitor seated himself for what seemed to him a precarious trip up the steep mountainside, a little girl with a small basket on her arm and a happy smile on her face stepped into the car and sat down beside him. At the signal, the little car moved upward. The visitor looked down from the dizzy heights apprehensively. Turning to the child beside him, he asked solicitously, "Have you gone up here before?"
>
> "Sure, I go here every day. This is the way I go to school," she answered cheerfully.
>
> "But aren't you afraid to go up and down this steep mountain alone?" the visitor asked.
>
> "Oh no," she replied confidently. "It's not dangerous; Father is up there. He runs the machinery."

The knowledge that your heavenly Father is "running the machinery" and that life is not simply the result of fate and chance helps eliminate the fear of what might happen in the world tomorrow. When Father is at the helm, we do not need to worry or be afraid, because He has promised so beautifully, " 'Never will I leave you; never will I forsake you.' So we say with confidence, 'The Lord is my helper; I will not be afraid. What can man do to me?' " (Hebrews 13:5-6).

Resource reading: Hebrews 13:1-8

Depression Stopper 3: Prayer Can Turn Despair into Joy

This is the confidence we have in approaching God: that if we ask anything according to his will, he hears us.
1 John 5:14

Insight: Most individuals who are depressed feel estranged from God, separated from Him, and unable to touch Him. Prayer gradually breaks through that ceiling of gloom.

I have been deeply depressed," wrote a young woman in her mid-twenties as she scrawled a letter on the back of a place mat in a restaurant. "My father committed suicide, and I'm unhappily married. I don't know what to do." Hundreds of people are like her. Possibly you.

For various reasons—troubled marriages, guilt, anxiety over the future, feelings of insecurity, frustration, inadequacies, or chemical imbalances in the brain—we may succumb to a vicious cycle of concern, anxiety, self-pity, and finally depression. More nonsensical or foolish advice could never be given than "Snap out of it, friend," but it may not be necessary to have counseling or the services of a psychiatrist to overcome your depression.

In this chapter, I've been giving you depression stoppers—truths from Scripture to help you stop depression. The first is to come to grips with your identity as a believer in Jesus Christ. Who are you? You were adopted into the family of God as His own son or daughter when you became a Christian. This means you are important to God—not simply a number or a faceless individual lost among the masses, a nonentity who has only what he or she can grab. Read the fourth chapter of Galatians along with Romans 8 to have a greater understanding of your importance to our heavenly Father.

The second important truth that stops depression is the understanding that God—not fate or chance—controls the ultimate destiny of our world. When it comes to the future and the issues that tend to depress us, our response must not be worry; rather it should be to accept by faith the promises of the Word declaring that God will not leave us or forsake us in the storms of life (Hebrews 13:5). Laying hold of Him through prayer links us to the assurance that He is still in charge of the world and our lives as well.

Recently, a high-ranking government official spoke to a nucleus of individuals about the state of world affairs today, which is grim. Concluding his remarks, this knowledgeable individual said, "And what should our response be as believers who know the Word of God? It should be that of joy, for Jesus said, 'When these things begin to take place, stand up and lift up your heads, because your redemption is drawing near' (Luke 21:28)." Joy—not depression!

Few people who accept the fact that God is in control become depressed. Much of our depression centers around concern for ourselves—what will happen to us, how we look, why we are not as beautiful or as successful as someone else—yet in the family of God there is no competition.

At least three times we are told in Scripture, "There is no respect of persons with God." He will accept you and forgive you just as you are, and He will give you His Holy Spirit to help you become the person He wants you to be. Depression, on the other hand, seems to rule out the possibility of God's personal intervention. It ignores truths you know to be important: God hears and answers prayer, and He can change the circumstances that depress you.

Depression stopper 3: As God's children, we can bring our needs to Him and pour out our hearts before Him, asking His intervention. "This is the confidence we have in approaching God," wrote John. "If we ask anything according to his will, he hears us" (1 John 5:14). Appropriating this profound truth is a great depression stopper.

Resource reading: Luke 7:18-28

Depression Stopper 4: Forgiveness

God has not given us a spirit of fear, but of power and of love and of a sound mind.

2 TIMOTHY 1:7 NKJV

Insight: Ask yourself, "Have I any right not to forgive myself when God has already forgiven me?" Then let go of whatever emotional baggage you have been carrying.

Depression stopper 4: Forgive yourself. "I know that God has forgiven me, but I just can't forgive myself, and the more I think about what I have done, the more depressed I get."

Whenever I deal with the subject of depression, the number of responses we get jumps. The theme of many letters and e-mails echoes the opening sentence of this paragraph, relating depression to an event the writer cannot seem to get over. In most cases, the writer mentions he or she is a believer in Christ, but the depression continues. The memory haunts the individual and drives him or her to the despair of depression.

Let's analyze this for a moment and make it personal. If depression is related to guilt, you have to determine whether your guilt is actual—based on something yet unforgiven—or you are being depressed by false guilt feelings or a troubled conscience. There is a big difference.

I am thinking of a woman who was confident that God was punishing her children for something she had done years before. She was not only depressed but at the point of complete despair. Repeatedly she had asked God's forgiveness, and I am confident that she was sincere. On the basis of what God says in His Word, I believe God had long since forgiven her, but she could not accept His forgiveness and forgive herself. The resulting trauma left her constantly feeling guilty and depressed.

Are you like that? Are you depressed because you came to the foot of the old rugged cross and said, "God, wash away this sin"? Forgiveness never leaves you in a state of depression.

The question then becomes, "Did God forgive you?" Do you remember the promise of 1 John 1:9—"If we confess our sins, he is faithful and just and will forgive us our sins and purify us from all unrighteousness"?

All right. Did God mean it? If you confessed your wrongdoing, then God forgave you once and for all. The Bible clearly promises forgiveness to those who ask for it. If you have done this, realize your depression is not from God, but from the enemy of your soul, who defeats you spiritually by hanging a cloud of depression over your head. Remember the passage at the beginning of this section? "God has not given us a spirit of fear," wrote Paul to Timothy, "but of power and of love and of a sound mind" (2 Timothy 1:7 NKJV).

If, of course, you have never come to the fount drawn from Immanuel's veins, your depression may be linked to something you need to confess to God, something whose burden will disappear only when you come to Him and receive His forgiveness.

The second step in the process of applying this depression stopper to your life is to forgive yourself. Ask yourself, *What right have I to not forgive myself when my heavenly Father has forgiven me? Am I greater than God?* Your answer points out the foolishness of allowing yourself to live in a state of depression, which is the opposite of the kind of a life God intends. Read Galatians 5 and notice how the cluster of characteristics, or qualities, relating to the Spirit-filled life are the opposite of depression.

With the forgiveness of our heavenly Father, there can be the strength of the Holy Spirit to live above the carnal plane that drove you down initially. Depression is contrary to God's plan and purpose for your life, so realize that when God has forgiven you, you must also forgive yourself. He has provided for your victorious life. Apply the truth of His Word and begin to live and walk in His power and strength.

Only the grace of God can turn despair and depression to joy. Believe it, and see the change take place in your life.

Resource reading: Psalm 66

Depression Stopper 5: Getting Back on the Right Path

Do not be conformed to this world, but be transformed by the renewing of your mind, that you may prove what is that good and acceptable and perfect will of God.

Romans 12:2 NKJV

Insight: The will of God begins afresh every morning, so if you missed a turn in the road yesterday, simply ask, "How do I get where God wants me to go from where I am?" Then take the first step in that direction.

Depression is twice as common among women as men, contends Jessie Bernard, professor emeritus at Penn State University. She asserts that wives give their husbands far more emotional support than husbands give to their wives, which may result in periods of depression. But there is more to it than that. As one psychologist put it, "Men and women are put together with a different set of nuts and bolts." We came from the drawing board of heaven with those differences. It's the way God made us. There are emotional differences stemming from biological factors that create different levels of emotions.

Whether they are male or female, when depression strikes, people are often debilitated and may cease to be productive. They feel as if God does not care and that others do not care either.

The despair of depression can be stopped. The depression stoppers I recommend are not prescribed by a doctor. They are principles of truth from Scripture—the oldest and best-loved textbook on living. In this chapter I've mentioned discovering your spiritual identity, resting in the assurance that God is still in control, discovering that prayer can break through depression, and learning how to find forgiveness from God and how to forgive yourself. Now I'd like to go one step further. This depression stopper may be a truth you've heard before but have not applied.

Depression stopper 5: You can stop depression by realizing that, in spite of the perplexity of life and the circumstances, God can still direct your life into His perfect will.

"Dr. Sala, you don't know the mess I've made out of my life," some say. "If God had a will for my life, I've messed things up so much that there is just no hope." Feeling discouraged and abandoned, people have allowed self-recrimination to bring depression and discouragement into their lives.

In fairness to God, let's not attempt to blame Him for our failures. When we blow it, we need to admit it and also realize that forgiveness includes restoration and healing. In a real sense, God's forgiveness creates a whole new ball game and enables God to continue to work, perfecting His plan and purpose.

"Do you mean God can still do something with my life?"

Absolutely. "If we are faithless," Paul wrote to Timothy, "he will remain faithful, for he cannot disown himself" (2 Timothy 2:13). Where there is life, there is yet hope.

May I share three guidelines about God's will in relation to depression?

Guideline 1: God's will brings peace to your heart, which eliminates depression. He's no cosmic killjoy who delights in your misery. Getting back into His will brings peace of mind and joy to the soul, which drive depression away.

Guideline 2: God's will—His plan for your life—results in your personal contentment and security. His will is described as being "good and acceptable and perfect" (Romans 12:2 NKJV). We will never be more secure than when we allow our heavenly Father to put His hand on ours and guide each step we take.

Guideline 3: God's will is the only way to be fulfilled. "Thou hast made us for thyself, O God," wrote Augustine many years ago, "and our heart is restless until it finds its rest in thee." You can find and follow God's will, and doing it will break the shackles of depression every time. It's God's answer to a terrible sickness.

Resource reading: Luke 7:36-50

When Your Faith Is Weak

He who began a good work in you will carry it on to completion until the day of Christ Jesus.

PHILIPPIANS 1:6

Insight: Faith is not complex; it is simply taking God at His word and acting upon it.

Charles Spurgeon once wrote, "You may think that it is easy to define faith, and so it is, but it is easier still to confuse people with your definition." Martin Luther defined faith as "a lively, reckless confidence in God." The Quaker scholar J. Elton Trueblood said, "Faith is not belief without proof, but trust without reservation."[6] In her excellent book *The Christian's Secret of a Happy Life,* Hannah Whitall Smith wrote, "Faith is the simplest and plainest thing in the world...It is simply believing God."

All of these quotes are paraphrases of Hebrews 11:1: "Now faith is being sure of what we hope for and certain of what we do not see." The Berkeley version states it this way: "But faith forms a solid ground for what is hoped for, a conviction of unseen realities."

In analyzing what the Bible says about faith, I have come to the conclusion that real faith contains two elements: *belief,* which is intellectual and appeals to the mind; and *trust,* which is experiential and demands a response to beliefs. It is one thing to intellectually accept an assertion as fact, and it is totally something else to be so convinced of what you believe that you act upon it, realizing your life may depend on your commitment.

Years ago Charles Blondin, the great acrobat and entertainer, walked across Niagara Falls on a tight wire pushing a wheelbarrow in front of him. Having completed the harrowing journey above the churning white water of the rapids, Blondin was hailed as the crowd burst into a thunderous applause. Finally, Blondin spoke to a boy who stood in the front of the crowd: "Son, do you think that I could push you across the falls in the wheelbarrow?"

Without hesitation, the boy said, "Sure!"

"Fine," drawled the acrobat, "Now you get in, and I'll push you across"—whereupon the lad quickly pushed toward the back of the crowd and the security of his mother's apron.

When it comes to trusting God, many of us are like that boy. We believe God can get us across the angry waters of life's Niagara Falls, but we are not sure we want to take the ride. Belief? We have that. But we are short on trust, and without trust your faith is incomplete.

Many of the songs of the Christian faith have lyrics about the importance of trust. Remember the words of the refrain of the famous song? "Trust and obey, for there's no other way to be happy in Jesus than to trust and obey." George Beverly Shea sings so well of faith: "Come, every soul by sin oppressed; there's mercy with the Lord, and He will surely give you rest by trusting in His Word. Only trust Him, only trust Him."

Trust is a little puppy relaxed before the embers of the fire; trust is the hands of a little child reaching toward her mother's arms. It is the wordless look in the eyes of two lovers, the confidence an individual has in a friend, the heartfelt assurance that God—who cannot lie—will never let His child down. Trust is faith in action; it is rest from anxious striving, freedom from worry, surrender to the will of a loving heavenly Father. Trust is confidence that God is fully in control so we may rest in His protection.

"Being confident of this," wrote Paul as he described the life of trust, "that he who began a good work in you will carry it on to completion until the day of Christ Jesus" (Philippians 1:6). If you believe that, you can trust Him.

Resource reading: Philippians 1:1-11

Raw, Naked Faith

Without faith it is impossible to please God, because anyone who comes to him must believe that he exists and that he rewards those who earnestly seek him.

HEBREWS 11:6

Insight: The attitude of accepting and believing what God says in His Word is what constitutes the core of raw, naked faith.

In his book *The Bible Jesus Read,* Philip Yancey contends that the Old Testament book of Job is not about suffering any more than flour, eggs, and shortening are about cakes. He acknowledges that suffering and pain are ingredients in the book of Job, but the real message, he contends, is about faith—the kind I think of as raw, naked faith.

Job had this kind of faith, the settled kind that says, "Though he slay me, yet will I trust Him." Raw, naked faith does not have all the answers, but it does have an unswerving commitment to God that never looks back. Job's kind of faith—unlike a lot of our thinking today—does not have all the answers before it believes, nor does it hold God responsible for what we dislike or cannot change.

Strangely enough, a vast number of people today cannot seem to get beyond the brokenness of our world to see how great and good is God the Father and Creator. In one of his essays, C.S. Lewis said that ancient people approached God as an accused person approaches a judge. They approached God humbly and gently, begging for mercy. But, believed Lewis, "for the modern man the roles are reversed. He is the judge: God is in the dock...The trial may even end in God's acquittal. But the important thing is that man is on the bench and God is in the dock."[7]

Raw, naked faith is different than what I think of as *contract faith,* the kind that says, "God, let's make a deal. I know you are a gentleman, so if you give me your word that you'll do this for me, then here's what I will do for you." Contract faith is the kind advocated by scores of people today who are convinced the Bible holds the key to personal wealth, health, and prosperity and, if we keep our end of the bargain, God is going to honor His contractual obligation and pour out His blessing on our lives.

Contract faith is not new. When we read the book of Job, we realize that the basic attitude of Job's friends is, "Look, Job, you've blown it. Something is wrong with you, so take responsibility for your problems, confess your failure, and get on with your life."

During my middle twenties, I visited a man in his eighties who was in the hospital dying. Looking into my eyes, he asked, "Why does God allow me to suffer as He does? Why won't He just let me die?" I think beads of sweat must have burst out on my brow. Now five decades later, I still remember the frustration bordering on panic as I searched for an answer that had not been given during my classes.

What I have learned since is that naked, raw faith is the only kind that will take you through the dark hour when things happen that make no sense. When a baby is born who will never run and play like other children. When a woman with three children dies with cancer. When a man is struck by a truck as he changes a tire while his wife and children wait for him to finish so they can continue on the way to church.

Raw, naked faith is the kind that the writer of Hebrews wrote about, saying, "Without faith it is impossible to please God, because anyone who comes to him must believe that he exists and that he rewards those who earnestly seek him" (Hebrews 11:6).

Resource reading: Romans 10:1-17

The Eyes of Faith

"Abraham believed God, and it was credited to him as righteousness," and he was called God's friend.

JAMES 2:23

Insight: Trusting God enables you to leave behind the burden of needing to understand God's plan as you move ahead in faith.

Any tragedy—great or small—forces us to acknowledge our humanity, and often that realization leaves us depressed or immobilized. But through difficulty or disaster, many turn to God; others turn on Him, blaming Him for the difficulty, accusing Him of failing to stop the tragedy, forgetting that He loves us but never promised to protect us from all evil.

Many find strength, encouragement, and help in God. The upward look is the look of faith, and it focuses on God. It connects spiritually. As the writer of Hebrews put it, "Let us fix our eyes on Jesus, the author and perfecter of our faith, who for the joy set before him endured the cross, scorning its shame, and sat down at the right hand of the throne of God" (Hebrews 12:2).

You may say, "I can't see Him!" But *by faith* you can! Faith sees what can be seen only by your soul. The classic passage in the New Testament that describes faith is Hebrews chapter 11. Here the writer talks about men and women who believed God in the face of great difficulties and says of them, "These all died in faith, not having received the things promised, but having seen them and greeted them from afar, and having acknowledged that they were strangers and exiles on the earth" (Hebrews 11:13 ESV).

Faith means taking our eyes off our troubles, our losses, our pain, our difficulties, and redirecting our concentration and focus toward the Lord.

There are many things that faith does not know and cannot know. These are the dark questions that confront us during the night when we cannot sleep.... such as *Why? What? Where? When? How?* Those are the questions that rise from our old natures, the ones that often have no answer this side of heaven. In most cases, should God choose to answer them, we still could not really understand.

Faith knows one thing though: *Who.* In prison for his faith and suffering at the hands of the Romans, Paul wrote to a young man named Timothy: "I know whom I have believed and am convinced that he is able to guard what I have entrusted to him for that day" (2 Timothy 1:12). Sight rests upon *something;* faith rests upon *Someone.*

Many stumble through life dogged by bitterness, cynicism, and anger, feeling that God has forsaken them or does not exist at all because they cannot understand why a certain event happened. Faith does not deny the presence of evil, but it sees Him who is above and beyond the evil. Faith chooses to get on with life and to find purpose in living that comes only through a spiritual framework.

Faith is the assurance that no earthly experience lasts forever, that dawn follows the darkness, that someday we will understand the questions that plague us, that God has not singled us out for special trials, and that in our pain and difficulty we can find His comfort and help.

Faith has eyes that penetrate the darkness with spiritual night vision. Faith sees the hand of the Almighty in stronger outline than the hand of evil. It hopes in the final triumph of good over evil, and believes in the face of unbelief. Faith rests in the knowledge that God is good and puts into His strong hand what you can neither reverse nor change. It allows Him to take the night shift, and it believes that when morning comes, He will be there to welcome us and to walk with us through the long day.

Resource reading: Hebrews 11:1-16

Feeding Your Faith

This is my prayer: that your love may abound more and more in knowledge and depth of insight, so that you may be able to discern what is best and may be pure and blameless until the day of Christ.

PHILIPPIANS 1:9-10

Insight: When your head and your heart disagree, faith means you go with your heart, and you leave the manner by which God takes action to His discretion and care.

A century ago John Stockton wrote a hymn with this refrain: "Only trust Him, only trust Him, only trust Him now; He will save you, He will save you, He will save you now." Following the advice of Stockton is not always easy. It is easier to trust our resources, our skills, our doctors, our knowledge—even to gamble on the odds rather than to trust God. I would like to share three simple guidelines that will help you reach beyond the horizon of your own understanding and limitations and trust Him more. Here's how.

Guideline 1: Stretch the muscle of your faith. Has God ever answered a prayer for you—even one time? Stop and remember. I am certain you can single out at least one time when you prayed and your request happened, right? When you stop and remember, you can probably think of many times you scored a direct hit—but all of those answers are dimmed by today's needs.

For many years I kept a ledger of crises—situations that were tough—and as the result of prayer, how God answered in a definite way. Human nature is such that we tend to forget yesterday's answers—the money He sent, the way He brought healing to a sick body, the way He resolved a misunderstanding. The answers have been eclipsed by present needs, yet as we remind ourselves of yesterday's answer, it helps us believe for today's need. Do you want to trust Him more?

Guideline 2: Be encouraged by the testimonies of others. *Wait a minute,* you may be thinking. *Can I really believe God will meet me like He* *did somebody else? I'm not a spiritual giant—I'm just little old me.* Immediately Satan seizes the twinge of doubt to create a spiritual inferiority complex. Before you agree with Satan's argument, ask a few questions: Does God have favorites? Would He ignore me and favor someone else? No! Then refuse to believe your doubts and feed your faith. The testimonies of other people will build your faith and help you to trust God more.

When I was a youth, my father bought a Packard automobile, and I soon discovered the car would do things the manufacturer did not know about, such as run in low gear up to 45 miles per hour and up to 90 miles an hour in second gear. "*Ask the man who owns one!*" was their advertising gimmick. It was great advertising. So if you want to build your faith, talk to a person who has prayed and whose prayers have been answered. Do not bother with the skeptic who is sure that God cannot break out of His black box.

Guideline 3: If you want to know how to trust God more, stand on the assurance of God's Word. It cannot be broken. No matter what may happen in our world, we can count on a few things, and the promises of His Word are among them.

If you have never settled the issue of whether or not you can trust God's Word completely, you will never have great faith, for faith is generated by an understanding of the nature and character of God, who cannot lie or mislead you.

Annie Johnson Flint so beautifully wrote,

> Hitherto the Lord hath helped us, hitherto His hand hath led,
> hitherto His arm protected, hitherto His bounty fed.
> Will His love desert us wholly, will His heart our need forget,
> will His presence clean forsake us, who has never failed us yet?"

As John Stockton wrote, "Only trust Him, only trust Him now; He will save you, He will save you now." May God help us to trust Him more *today.*

Resource reading: Philippians 1:12-18

Real-World Faith

Faith comes from hearing the message, and the message is heard through the word of Christ.
ROMANS 10:17

Insight: The real world is also a world of faith—because when faith in each other, in the government, in the banking system, in sanitation, and in commerce break down, society disintegrates.

Almost all parents, at some time or another, tell their children something like "When you get out in the real world," emphasizing that the world in which they are nurtured, the environment of a loving home, is a marked contrast to the "real world." What is the real world? It's a great deal different from the protected environment many children are privileged to be born into and grow up in.

The real world is a tough one, a world of cutthroat competition, a dog-eat-dog world, where the golden rule is "He who has the gold has the rule" and the motto of the street is "Do it to the other guy before he does it to you."

The real world is a hard one. It's the world where the runner with the fastest time in the tryouts loses to another athlete whose family has connections. The real world is the one in which the immoral, carousing alcoholic gets a promotion while the worker with better skills gets passed over because his integrity makes others think he's a goody-goody. The real world is the one in which a conscientious parent with three young children loses a fight with cancer while the neighbor who sleeps around enjoys good health.

I've been thinking about our faith in relationship to the real world. We tend to feel we have to be tough to make it in the world, and that our faith, which does well in the nurtured, protected environment of a home or a church, just cannot stand the heat of the real world.

African violets or delicate orchids grow beautifully in the protected environment of a greenhouse, but put them under the scorching heat of a desert sun and they quickly wither and die. Sometimes our faith is the same way. Thinking that faith cannot stand the heat of the real world, we tend to leave it at the door of the church or at least in the parking lot adjacent to the real world. Perhaps we feel good about God and heaven at home, but at the conference table or in the marketplace where there is intense competition and only the strongest, most cunning seem to survive, we aren't sure that faith can stand the heat.

Is there such a thing as real-world faith? One that wears overalls and helps a person maintain composure when another driver runs him and his bicycle off the road? Faith that perseveres when your competition delights in destroying a salesperson's territory?

The dictionary defines the English word *real* as "genuine, authentic, without fraud, sincere." Real-world faith! Frankly, there is but one kind of faith, and it is real-world faith. It was into a real world that Jesus came long ago, and His was not a nurtured, protected kind of faith. He faced the assaults of an unbelieving, hostile world, and He did not turn and run.

Real-world faith begins with an encounter with the real Jesus, not a wimpy, namby-pamby individual who wears lace on his handkerchief and hides in the cool recesses of a cathedral. When Jesus Christ touches our lives, our lives change. That change can stand the heat of the real world.

Are you interested in strengthening your faith, taking it from the hothouse to the real world? Then pay attention to this guideline that comes from the book of Romans. Paul wrote, "Faith comes by hearing, and hearing by the word of God" (Romans 10:17 NKJV). The better you know Jesus, the living Word of God, the stronger will be your faith in Him.

Real-world faith is the only kind that can meet the needs of people today. Real-world faith works!

Resource reading: Joshua 1

Sure, I'll Be There

You yourselves are our letter, written on our hearts, known and read by everybody.
2 CORINTHIANS 3:2

Insight: When you have a problem telling the truth, your dishonesty dishonors your Father in heaven.

A certain dentist, syringe in hand, bent over a patient who was about to have a tooth extracted. "You might feel a little sting," he gently intoned, and then added, "but then, on the other hand, it might feel as though you've been kicked in the mouth by a horse." Whether the patient fled or laughed was not reported, but at least that was an honest dentist.

"I'll come by and give you an estimate on the work this Friday!" says an electrician you have called. Friday comes; he does not show up. On Monday, you call and get an answering machine. On Tuesday, you finally get him on the phone. "It was my understanding you were coming on Friday," you say with irritation, but not so much that he will refuse to do your work.

"Yeah," he says, "something came up."

King David said all men are liars (Psalm 116:11). If he had lived today, he could have said that even more truly.

What does it mean when a person gives her word when asked to participate in an event? When she says yes, does she mean, "Yes, I heard you. I understand you want me to come on Friday at seven, but I'll come when I get around to it," or "Yes, I will be there"?

Chuck Swindoll says integrity means "keeping your word." If following through with commitments is part of the fabric of integrity, it is sadly lacking. Tradesmen—contractors, electricians, carpenters—are notorious for saying they will come, because they want the work. But they do not show up when they are supposed to, and once they have started jobs, the customers are at their mercy. But they do not have a monopoly on the "I'll be there" line at all.

"The check is in the mail," a businessperson tells the bookkeeper who calls to politely inform him that his account is over 90 days delinquent.

He knows he is lying, but he does not care. He gets rid of her and pays it before she calls again.

Do Christians do a better job of keeping their word than non-Christians? Not necessarily, but non-Christians expect Christians to do a better job, and when Christians do not, they shake their heads and say, "You guys are no different from the ones who never darken the door of a church!"

When Paul wrote to Titus, he instructed that slaves be subject to their masters, being trustworthy "so that in every way they will make the teaching about God our Savior attractive" (Titus 2:10). This instruction on trustworthiness applies to all of us today.

To the Corinthians he wrote, "You yourselves are our letter, written on our hearts, known and read by everybody" (2 Corinthians 3:2). When we lead others to believe we will do something but have no intention of following through, we are both deceivers and liars—not just schmoozers who act the same as everyone else.

God expects more from His own than many of us are delivering these days. When we make good-faith commitments but cannot follow through, we can use the phone and let others know. Nobody bats a thousand, but when telling people what they want to hear becomes a lifestyle, the darkness of our culture has penetrated our hearts—bringing reproach on the name of Christ.

Most of us would prefer a dentist who gives some warning about pain rather than one who says, "This won't hurt," but leaves the patient feeling kicked in the mouth by a horse.

Think about this the next time you are tempted to say, "I'll be there Friday morning" when you really intend to start the weekend early and not show up.

Resource reading: Titus 2:1-10

We Promise to Start Telling the Truth

They will deceive every one his neighbour, and will not speak the truth: they have taught their tongue to speak lies, and weary themselves to commit iniquity.
JEREMIAH 9:5 KJV

Insight: It is truth that counts—not the perception of truth.

In 1998, Britain's Prince Andrew said that Buckingham Palace attendants would stop lying to the press. And that's the truth! For the past two decades, the prince admitted, palace attendants and royal spokesmen had routinely lied to the press. In the interview with reporters, Andrew, the second son of Queen Elizabeth II, said the royal family was trying to make relationships better by telling the way things were, not necessarily the way the palace would like them to appear. This was no small task, Prince Andrew recognized. "The difficulty," he said, "is trying to convince you. . .that what you are being told is the truth."

So it is with every parent whose child is more adept at fantasy than telling the truth.

For a long time I waited to hear a former United States president say the same thing—that he was turning over a new leaf and promising to tell the truth. The week that the former president's videotaped appearance before a grand jury was released, a book came out called *The Anatomy of a Lie,* by Dr. Diane Komp, a sharp-witted and perceptive medical doctor, then a children's cancer specialist at Yale University's School of Medicine.

In the prologue to her book, Dr. Komp quotes the Russian author Fyodor Dostoevsky, who wrote,

> When we lie to ourselves, and believe our own lies, we become unable to recognize truth, either in ourselves or in anyone else, and we end up losing respect for ourselves and for others. When we have no respect for anyone, we can no longer love, and, in order to divert ourselves, having no love in us, we yield to our impulses, indulge in the lowest forms of pleasure, and behave in the end like an animal, in satisfying our vices. And it all comes from lying—lying to others and to yourself.

What prompted a gifted and recognized oncologist to become interested in the anatomy of a lie? Dr. Komp started thinking about the whole issue when she ran across a book written by a Yankee army chaplain, H. Clay Trumbull. The chaplain found himself in a Confederate prison in the summer of 1863, at the height of the Civil War. Trumbull was a pastor who believed God said what He meant and meant what He said. He also knew that he and some of his friends could probably escape from prison, provided he would lie to his jailer and deceive him. Trumbull refused to do this.

"Why not?" chided his fellow prisoners, telling him people have no obligation to tell the truth to the enemy in times of warfare. Trumbull did not agree, stayed in prison, and eventually was freed to write about his experiences.

In analyzing her personal and professional life as well as her observations of society, Dr. Komp concluded that the problem started at the bottom and worked up. She writes,

> No wonder our world is such a mess when we reap the effect of dishonesty trickling down from exalted positions into our ordinary lives. If the facts prove that our leaders lie, how can we expect our children to value truthfulness?...
>
> Hear me out...What if the cultural trend toward lying begins the other way around? What if the trickle works from the bottom up to the top? What if my own lies make a difference to the world? What if, instead of shaking my finger at those in public life, I examined my own half-truths, puffery, and little white lies?

I'm reminded of the words of Alexander Pope:

> Vice is a monster of so frightful mien,
> As to be hated needs but to be seen;
> Yet seen too oft, familiar with her face,
> We first endure, then pity, then embrace.

Resource reading: Ephesians 5

The Truth About Lying

I was appointed a herald and
an apostle—I am telling the truth,
I am not lying—and a teacher of
the true faith to the Gentiles.
1 TIMOTHY 2:7

Insight: When you lead someone to believe something is true, but you know it is not and fail to correct the misperception, you have lied as certainly as though you purposely fabricated the truth.

Is it okay to lie when you are protecting someone? Is a lie only as bad or as wrong as the harm it may do to someone? David Blankenhorn of the Institute for American Values says, "What disturbs me is people are now trying to make distinctions between types of lies; some are pardonable, and some are not. The mere act of lying is not enough for censure."

A generation ago, I had a heated conversation with my father, who had been a loyal and avid supporter of president Richard Nixon. It was during the time of the Watergate investigation, when Nixon was suspected of departing from his Quaker upbringing and developing a major problem with telling the truth. I remember saying, "Dad, this man is lying. They've caught him red-handed." Not wanting to admit defeat, my dad conceded, "Okay, so the Republicans are liars. The Democrats are liars too—only the Republicans are better liars."

Who is the better liar today may be hard to determine. The fact is, lying has become endemic in society. It has become so prevalent that no longer do we feel any obligation to censure or condemn someone for lying. We are willing to do that only if some person is badly hurt as the result of it.

Mary McNamara, a staff writer for the *Los Angeles Times,* says,

> People lie on their résumés, their tax returns, and certainly on first dates. We lie about our age, our income, our marital status...Big ones, little ones shimmering by in deepening shades of gray. We have made lying an industry—lobbyists, diplomats, lawyers, salesmen, advertisers—those are just a few folks who, many would argue, are essentially paid to lie.[8]

Is she right? Unfortunately, it seems so. But is a lie wrong only if someone gets hurt because of it? Some would say so. In fact, the reticence of the general public to say, "This is wrong. This person is lying to us," is a reflection of a moral condition that makes people hesitant to condemn others for what they tolerate in themselves.

You know what the problem is. But what can be done about it? Few acknowledge the correlation between society's move away from its spiritual roots and the prevalence and acceptance of dishonesty today. No matter how they may differ on many issues, Judaism, Catholicism, Protestantism, and all other major religions agree: It is right to tell the unvarnished and straight truth regardless of consequences.

Flippant acknowledgment that one has been less than truthful is far short of a commitment to truth and honesty, which has been the very fabric of society. The further away we are from God and the principles of Christianity, the greater will be the moral deception and dishonesty confronting us. May God help us to go back to the drawing board and teach by example that no matter what others may do, we by God's grace and help will tell the truth, the whole truth, and nothing but the truth. Only this standard can serve as the foundation for our children, our grandchildren, and their children after them.

Resource reading: Joshua 9:1-18

Lies of Necessity

Do not lie to each other, since you have taken off your old self with its practices.
COLOSSIANS 3:9

Insight: There is no such thing as a white lie. You do not "nearly" tell the truth; you either tell the truth or you lie.

George Barna, the poll taker who registers the moral temperature of people today, says that approximately three of four adults between the ages of 18 and 25 do not believe in absolute truth. Cheating, dishonesty, and misrepresentation have become a way of life, not only to this generation but also to their parents, who developed the art of fabricating truth in the 1950s and 1960s.

This raises a question. Does God view honesty as a black-or-white situation? Would God accept our argument that situations determine whether telling the truth is the best policy? The arguments "Everybody is doing it," "You can't get into grad school without fudging on entrance exams," "You can't convince a girl that you're a macho guy unless you bend the truth," and "Your lectures will be more exciting if you add made-up narration to history" do not impress God. In simple terms, God stresses telling the truth. His integrity and character never give Him the freedom to lie, nor does He give His children that freedom either.

Whenever this subject comes up, almost invariably someone throws out two situations from the Old Testament. One involves the midwives who had been instructed by Pharaoh and his government to kill the boy babies born to Hebrew women. "They get here before we can do anything about it," lied the two women, Shiphrah and Puah. The other situation involves Rahab, who protected Joshua and Caleb when they came to spy on Jericho.

"There," say detractors of absolute morality, "are two examples from the Bible of justifying bending the truth to protect other people." Centuries later, in Nazi Germany, medical personnel were required to report any appearance of deformities or abnormalities in children, purportedly for the reason that such children were to be given special treatment. They indeed got special treatment—the kind that earmarked them for certain death.

Does God require you to keep faith or be honest with evil? Theologians are divided. Dietrich Bonhoeffer, the German theologian who resisted Hitler's regime, did not believe that God wanted men to keep faith with wickedness. He was part of a plot to overthrow the Führer that went sour, and for his involvement in the attempt, he was executed.

By and large, this is not the same issue that confronts us when we fill out a tax return or go through customs or fill out an expense report. No life is at stake, and no one stands at the door with a swastika on his armband. When we are tempted to bend the truth, it is usually to get a larger paycheck than we deserve or to appear better than we are.

"Speak the truth" is the dictum of Paul to the Ephesians, who lived in a world not unlike ours at all. "Do not lie to each other, since you have taken off your old self with its practices" is the direction that Paul gave to the Colossians (Colossians 3:9). This means the burden of truth rests on our shoulders. We have two options: to present the truth as we want it to appear (which is dishonest) or to break with the mentality of our day and choose to tell the truth in all honesty and candor, to live in such a way that we do not have to protect ourselves by dishonesty.

Of one thing I am certain: The person who lies consistently and repeatedly to himself is not sure of the difference between truth and his perception of truth, but God understands the difference clearly, very clearly indeed. Of that you can be sure.

Resource reading: Joshua 6

Pathological Liars

The cowardly, the unbelieving, the vile, the murderers, the sexually immoral, those who practice magic arts, the idolaters and all liars—their place will be in the fiery lake of burning sulfur. This is the second death.

REVELATION 21:8

Insight: Truth will make you miserable before it sets you free.

When someone is consistently dishonest or fabricates the truth, we refer to that person as a pathological liar, as though the problem is genetic. The term *pathological* gives the connotation of something wrong in a person's brain—something that she can no more help than being born with poor eyesight or contracting an infection that addles the brain. We hang a psychological term on people to relieve them of personal responsibility.

"It's pathological," we say—"he can't help doing it." Instead of labeling people as pathological liars, it might be more descriptive to call them chronic liars. Some people become very good at distorting the truth—so good, in fact, that they convince themselves of their fantasies. The chronic liar is in a different category than the professional liar—the attorney, the car or real-estate salesman, the stockbroker, the astrologist who reads tea leaves and tells fortunes.

The chronic liar (pathological, if you prefer) has made lying so much her everyday lifestyle that she has a hard time distinguishing falsehood from truth. Is such a person doomed? Is a chronic liar so biologically handicapped that she is destined to go through life confusing fact with fantasy or so insecure that she must always strive to impress, even at the cost of distorting the truth?

Such a person needs shock treatment, but not the kind where doctors attach electrodes and pass high voltage through the person's body. She needs the kind of shock treatment through which she realizes that dishonesty is absolutely intolerable. Not only does God disdain it, but the liar is also destroying her own credibility and life in the process. The first step for a chronic liar to turn a lifestyle of dishonesty around is realizing she has a problem—not an incurable one, but a persistent, devastating one.

Step 1: Acknowledge your problem in all honesty. That's the first step. This may mean going public with the acknowledgment that you realize you have had a problem. For the alcoholic, there is no hope of change until he accepts the reality he is an alcoholic. "My name is John, and I am an alcoholic," someone says at a meeting of Alcoholics Anonymous. But I have yet to hear of a group whose members confess, "My name is John, and I'm a chronic liar."

Step 2: Ask God's forgiveness and help. Do not appeal to a "higher power." Realize that *God* labels your disorder as sin. The good news is that there is forgiveness for this problem, and with God's forgiveness comes His help. Chronic dishonesty is not an irreversible malady, though it is a persistent one.

Step 3: Become accountable to someone who will ask you tough questions and keep you on target. When you blow it, confess it and strive to clarify the misrepresentation. The New Testament says, "If we confess our sins, he is faithful and just and will forgive us our sins and purify us from all unrighteousness" (1 John 1:9). Do not take the attitude, "It's okay for me to lie about this since I know God will forgive me anyway." That cheapens God's grace. It's the attitude Paul condemned when he wrote, "What shall we say, then? Shall we go on sinning so that grace may increase?" He answers his own question: "By no means."

Step 4: Keep short accounts with God. In a notebook record the day's events. Each day review what happened the previous day—a kind of running spiritual diary and checklist. Look back to see how you're doing; make confession and correction if needed.

If you believe that God's word is valid when it says in Revelation 21:8, that all liars will have their place in the lake of fire, then you need to tell the truth. It's much safer.

Resource reading: Revelation 21

What Is Life About?

David said, "What have I now done?
Is there not a cause?"
1 Samuel 17:29 KJV

Insight: Acknowledging that you have lost your way, that you are uncertain of where you are, and that you are without focus, is the most difficult part of finding purpose.

At a street meeting held by a Salvation Army group, a young drummer in the band reflected on his past life and how it had changed. "Before I was converted," he said, "I used to drink a lot, but I don't drink anymore. Before I was converted, I used to swear a lot, but I don't swear anymore. Before I was converted, I used to womanize, but I don't do that anymore." Then he added, "Since I was converted, about all I do is stand on this street corner and beat this old drum!"

A lot of people—both before and after conversion—are like the young man who felt that all he did was beat the drum. In many lives this translates into "get up, go to work, come home tired, and start all over again the next day," or "drive the carpool, shop at the store, make the kids' lunches, and start all over again the next day."

What's the purpose of your life? Simply beating the old drum day after day? Is there more?

Francis Schaeffer, an apostle to the intellectuals of the last half of the twentieth century, wrote, "Man, made in the image of God, has a purpose—to be in relationship to God, who is there. Man forgets his purpose and thus he forgets who he is and what life means." And when you forget, you begin to think your life is like a coffin with both ends kicked out, an endless, meaningless routine of drudgery and work.

The Bible says we are made in the image of God. That gives definition and purpose to life, and beyond that it asserts that God has a plan for our lives—which takes away the uncertainty of where we are going and how we might get there. Our sense of purpose was lost when sin came into the world and separated all people from God. Without God, a person is like an airplane pilot who has lost communication with the control tower, like a traveler in a storm who has lost sight of all landmarks, like an aged man with Alzheimer's who cannot remember where he lives. We are disconnected. That's why life appears to be without rhyme or reason, a ship of fools without a captain and a journey without a destination.

Your sense of purpose in life begins with a relationship with God. So how do you come into relationship with God? The first step is to acknowledge you need this relationship. The Bible says that all of us have gone astray, like sheep without a shepherd. Most of us have no trouble admitting we've missed the path to purpose and fulfillment in life, so we quickly say, "Yes, this is what I need."

The second step is to understand that God sent His Son to bring us into that relationship, to show us the way back. So when you allow Him to become your Lord and Savior, you connect with God. In responding to the questions of the disciples, Jesus explained, "Anyone who has seen me has seen the Father" (John 14:9).

The next step is to find out how God wants you to live—His blueprint, His guidelines for purpose and fulfillment. You find this in the pages of the Bible, an age-old textbook on living.

Coming home to the Father allows Him to give you purpose and guidance so you can love, live, and enjoy. It's the only way you can find your true purpose.

Resource reading: 1 Samuel 17

Live, Love, Enjoy

You do not even know what will happen tomorrow. What is your life? You are a mist that appears for a little while and then vanishes.
JAMES 4:14

Insight: The difference between the nihilist (who believes life has no purpose) and God's child is the belief that God created you for a purpose and will guide your life so you can fulfill His purpose.

Adjacent to a busy highway in Downey, California, where thousands of people pass by every day is a large billboard. Staring viewers in the face are bold letters with the message, "Live. Love. Enjoy!" Underneath this message appear smaller words: "We'd rather wait!" Who is the sponsor? Rose Hills Cemetery. I'm not quite sure what the intended message is, but the one that appears obvious is "Live, love, and enjoy life because we're going to get you in the end."

Should we live with the realization that life at its longest is short? Should we say, "Hey, we're not going to get out of this alive, so let's eat, drink, and be merry because in the end, the friendly mortician is going to win after all"?

There's nothing wrong with living life to the fullest or loving freely and passionately or enjoying every day and every step of the journey, but the issue is how to do this.

John Bernieri has been facing this issue. On the morning of September 11, 2001—a dark day deeply etched in our memories—John was soundly sleeping. In the early hours of the morning, he had left his job as dining room captain at Windows on the World, a restaurant at the top of the World Trade Center North Tower, having worked most of the night. He crawled into bed about 4 AM, only to be wakened from a sound sleep by his mother, who was shaking him and telling him in excited gasps that the World Trade Center towers had collapsed.

"Go home, Ma," he said sleepily. "You don't know what you're talking about." In the hours that followed, John learned that 81 of his friends and colleagues—his family, as he called them—were gone, their lives snuffed out in a few moments of flame and turmoil.

John is not sure why he survived or what to do with his second chance. He can still say "I love you" to his wife and daughter, as well as "It's no problem" to friends or family with whom he disagrees. He still has the chance to look up old friends and say, "I never told you what your friendship has meant to me or how grateful I have been for your help up the ladder to where I am now." In an interview, he said, "I was saved for a reason. But as for what—who knows? I'm working on it."

John will never have to be told, "Life is fragile and uncertain; you had better make the most of it." He knows that. The question he faces is one that you face as well, perhaps: *How do I find purpose in life?* Lacking purpose brings despair, despondency, and gloom, driving many to absolute desperation and destruction. Pondering what to do with his future may result in a changed career or direction for John's life. Facing near tragedy often motivates people to re-examine and redirect their lives.

Living with the reality that time is an allotment from God, an unknown commodity we use or abuse, should cause you to ask, "For what purpose did God put me on this earth? And what does He want me to accomplish with my life while I'm here?" Facing that issue led one man to close his law practice, change his lifestyle radically, and go to seminary to prepare for Christian ministry. It caused a professional woman to quit her job and apply for a position with a world mission agency.

"Live, love, enjoy!" reads the billboard…with the subscript, "We'd rather wait!" Do not worry about the mortician, who is willing to wait. Instead, remember that God will be on the other side to greet you—a certainty that allows you to connect with a life of purpose between now and then.

Resource reading: James 4

The Definition of Life

I press on to take hold of that for which Christ Jesus took hold of me.
PHILIPPIANS 3:12

Insight: Remember that the person who said, "You have plenty of good things...take life easy; eat, drink, and be merry" was called a fool by our Lord.

Scores of people spend their lives in search of happiness—the right mate, the right job, friends, good feelings about themselves, and enough money to surround themselves with anything they want.

Often their search for happiness ends in despair and cynicism. Their conclusion to the whole search is much the same as that voiced by Solomon, who had women, riches, and fame, yet cried, "Vanity of vanities! All is vanity." Whatever it is that makes life worthwhile eludes them. Yet if God's Son came for a purpose and His death was not wasted, then there has to be more to life than living, loving, and enjoying. There has to be a purpose for which you live, a reason for your existence, and an answer to the searching of your heart. To really live, love, and enjoy, you need three things—none of which can be bought with money or influence: a sense of definition, a sense of purpose, and a sense of empowerment.

Let's start with a *sense of definition.* You go to the dictionary when you want the definition of a word or term. Where do you go when you want a definition of what your life is about? Psychotherapy? Psychology? A scientific laboratory? Religion? No, even religion does not give a definition of life and what makes it worthwhile.

Go to the Bible. It alone answers the two serious questions that define life: "Who am I?" and "Why am I here?" When you have found answers to these two questions, you have defined the parameters of life and existence. The Bible says that you are not an animal, but a person, an individual, a unique being created in the image of God. Unlike an animal, you love, you think, you feel. As a person with intelligence, volition, and a soul, you will live forever. "Dust to dust and ashes to ashes" does not apply to you. Instead, you have a deep searching in your heart to know God and to know you are His child. The question of what makes life worth living is proof of a spiritual nature that wants to connect with God.

What of the question "Why am I here?" Is it important? Tremendously important. The Bible says that your birth was not an accident, an evolutionary happenstance. Neither are you a mistake, as one woman put it, adding that her mother tried to abort her because she was conceived out of wedlock. She was not wanted and should not have been born.

The Bible says that every person is important in the sight of God, that He loves each individual, and that He will respond to each heart cry. To know you are an individual of value and worth in God's sight helps you understand life. Only when you are in conscious agreement with God's purpose for your life will you find a sense of fulfillment—which allows you to live, to love, and to enjoy your world, your friends, your children, and your neighbors.

A sense of definition of what life is all about produces a *sense of purpose.* But God alone gives you the empowerment to a successful life, allowing you to look back at life's end and say with Paul, "I have fought the good fight, I have finished the race, I have kept the faith" (2 Timothy 4:7).

Resource reading: Philippians 1

Empowerment

You will receive power when the Holy Spirit comes on you; and you will be my witnesses in Jerusalem, and in all Judea and Samaria, and to the ends of the earth.

Acts 1:8

Insight: A connection with God gives you empowerment, an understanding of who you are, and leads to a plan for the future.

It's never easy to separate the myth surrounding an event from the historical facts; yet at times, whether or not a story can be corroborated, there's still some truth that comes through unscathed. Such is the story about one son of Louis XVI, who came to the throne at a time when France had been defeated in war by Great Britain. Instead of addressing the financial woes and other problems of his people, which included a desire for more influence in their government, he indulged himself, ignoring advice and counsel from knowledgeable ministers, and lived in luxury while peasants and working people suffered.

King Louis was executed in 1793. As the story goes, one of his sons was raised by a hag, a debauched woman whose purpose was to debase the life of the young prince. However, whenever the prince was urged to do something wrong, he would stamp his foot and say, "I refuse to do that. I am the son of the king."

Who knows if it really happened? One thing I do know: God has a lot of children today who need to stamp their feet and raise the defiant cry, "I refuse to be corrupted by the culture and contaminated by the world because I am the child of the King of kings."

Let's review some basics we covered earlier in this chapter. Knowing who you are gives you a sense of definition for life. It's like a frame for a painting. A relationship with God is the only thing in the world that gives you the materials you need to build a life with purpose, knowledge of the reason for your existence, and meaning for your life. Without it, people live only for the moment. They see no meaning for existence, and they take on the attitude "If I am not accountable to God, then everything is permissible." A relationship with God resolves the questions, "Who am I?" and "Why am I here?" You know who you are—God's child. Paul says that when a believer trusts Christ as Savior, he becomes God's child and is adopted into the great family of God—which unites men and women of every race, color, and ethnic background. God's children are color-blind.

This relationship with God produces a sense of definition and a sense of purpose in life, but it also gives you something else—*a sense of empowerment.* What is this all about? Simply put, when you become God's child, He comes to indwell your life. Paul used the analogy of a temple. Read 1 Corinthians 6, where he described our bodies as the temple of the Holy Spirit.

This indwelling presence of God results in an empowerment for life and service. It's the key to a successful, purposeful life. I use the term *successful* in a far broader sense than just making a lot of money, being popular, or rising to the top in your career. It means fulfillment, purpose, knowing where you are going in life, and being content in your pursuit.

No person has really succeeded in life until he writes *Enter God* as the first stage direction in life's script. When Paul tells believers they are to be filled with the Spirit, this is what he is talking about. It is something missing in the lives of many of God's children today.

Are you a child of the King? Your answer is either yes or no. If your answer is affirmative, may I follow by asking, "Do you live like one?" If you are not a child of the king, I would ask, "Why not become one?" It's the key to living, loving, and enjoying life to the fullest.

Resource reading: Galatians 5:22-23

Hammering in the Old Rusty Nails

No discipline seems pleasant at the time, but painful. Later on, however, it produces a harvest of righteousness and peace.
HEBREWS 12:11

Insight: Wake-up calls—illnesses, automobile wrecks, financial crashes—can serve to redirect your life onto a path of purpose and meaning.

In his autobiographical book, *The World Is My Home,* author James Michener recounts an incident from his life that took place when he was but five years of age. A neighboring farmer had an old apple tree that was no longer productive. Instead of cutting it down, the farmer took eight long rusty nails and drove them into the tree, four at the base and four higher up, quite evenly spaced.

That autumn a miracle took place, explained Michener. The old tree bore some of the most beautiful apples he had ever seen. "Hammerin' in rusty nails," explained the farmer, "gave it a shock to remind it that its job is to produce apples."

Michener went on to say that in his late seventies, life hammered some rusty old nails into the tree trunk of his life. A heart bypass, a hip surgery, and a bout with vertigo got his attention. Goaded by the realization he would not live forever, Michener decided he had better get at the task of writing some books that had been on his mind for some time. In the next five years he researched and wrote 11 books, including his autobiography, which is well worth reading.

Let's face it. When old rusty nails get hammered into the apple trees of our lives, we take notice immediately, and our lives may become intensely productive. The book of Hebrews speaks of these painful experiences as discipline. Rusty nails are delivered with a clear exhortation to get on with the business before us because life is short. The writer explained, "No discipline seems pleasant at the time, but painful. Later on, however, it produces a harvest of righteousness and peace for those who have been trained by it" (Hebrews 12:11).

Furthermore, the Bible explains it is the Father's love that allows the blows from the hammer, driving in the rusty nails to goad us to accomplish the full measure of His will.

A letter reached me recently from a young woman just finishing her internship in psychiatry. She reminded me that years before she had sought my counsel about her future. Coming from a poor family, she knew there were lots of reasons why she could not realize her dream to become a doctor, but she reminded me I had told her God owns the cattle on a thousand hills and she could trust Him to provide for her. She did, and He did as well.

I'm also reminded of a man who confided in me how badly he wanted to get into Christian ministry, but he was almost 40 and had a wife and children to support. "I'd just be too old," he sighed.

"How long would it take you to go to seminary and prepare for a ministry?" I asked.

"Three years," he answered.

"And how old would you be when you finished?" I asked.

"About 43 years old."

"How old will you be in three years if you don't go to seminary and realize your ambition?"

"About 43." He got the point. He went to seminary and became a minister.

What you may have considered to be rusty nails in the tree trunk of your life may simply be events that God is using to redirect you into the path of most productive service. I am convinced that at times it takes the knocks of the farmer's hammer, driving nails into the thick bark of our insensitive lives, before we hear His voice saying, "This is the way; walk in it" (Isaiah 30:21). Make a note of Hebrews 12 and see if your name might be written on that page.

Resource reading: James 4

When You Feel Like Quitting

Wait for the Lord*; be strong and take heart and wait for the* Lord*.*

Psalm 27:14

Insight: It's never a sin to be tempted to quit. Remember, spiritual giants have experienced the same thing. The sin comes in doing it!

Have you ever had one of those days when you are tired and discouraged and on top of that you do not feel well? It can happen to anybody.

Some people never recover from those low times and sometimes make decisions that destroy their futures. While nothing lasts forever, including difficulty, there are some things you can do to get back on top when you're tired and discouraged and feel like quitting.

First, remember the prophet Elijah, for his life tells us that even spiritual giants can get tired and discouraged and at times not feel well. The Bible tells of Elijah's bout with the blues in 1 Kings 19. May I refresh your memory? Scripture records Elijah's battle with 450 prophets of Baal. He stood alone—a bulwark of courage and faith. Fire fell from heaven and vindicated the faith of that mighty man of old. However, the next day Elijah did not make a good showing, for he was physically tired, and his weariness gave way to discouragement. In fact, he could not even handle one woman—the godless Jezebel. Confronted by her, the prophet ran for his life and told God he was ready to quit.

The life of Elijah shows the relationship between the physical, the spiritual, and the emotional in life. When Elijah became tired and discouraged, he forgot some important truths—just as many of us have done. He forgot how God had met him in bygone days, how God had sent ravens to feed him at Kerith Ravine, and how God had sent him to Zarephath, where he had miraculously brought the widow's son back to life. He forgot how God had consumed the false prophets with fire.

When Elijah was tired and discouraged, he ran as far as he could run and then crawled into a cave. There God found him, and the fireworks started. First came a wind and then an earthquake; lightning flashed across the sky. Finally the gentle voice of God asked, "Elijah, what are you doing?"

So the next time you feel like crawling into a cave of gloom, listen for God's voice saying, "What are you doing here?" Just like Elijah, it is possible you have forgotten some important answers to prayer in your life.

Second, when you are tired and discouraged and feel like quitting, remember Jonah, who had the bout with the great fish. Remember Jonah, for his life tells us that real happiness can be found only by doing the will of God.

There are lots of Jonahs today who walk the streets of every large city in the world—men and women to whom God says, "Give me your heart," but they turn and run as far away as they can go. Their lives are filled with games, vacations, cars, electronic gadgets, and many more such things.

These Jonahs are like the captain of a ship who asked the navigator, "Where are we headed?"

The reply came back, "I do not know, sir, but we are making very good time."

Perhaps you are one of those making good time to an unknown destination. Jonah's life tells us that real happiness comes by doing the will of God. God's promise is sure: "They that wait upon the LORD...shall mount up with wings as eagles; they shall run, and not be weary; and they shall walk, and not faint" (Isaiah 40:31 KJV).

Finally, do not despair when you are tired and discouraged and feel like quitting. We all feel like that at times. David found the answer: "Wait for the LORD; be strong and take heart and wait for the LORD " (Psalm 27:14). This is the answer when you are tired and discouraged.

Resource reading: 1 Kings 18–19

How to Deal with Discouragement

David encouraged himself in the LORD his God.

1 SAMUEL 30:6 KJV

Insight: Because you are a combination of emotional, physical, and spiritual elements, when you are down in one area, all three take a hit.

"Do you ever get discouraged?" This question was asked of Sir Malcolm Campbell, the British race-car and speedboat driver. He replied honestly, "No, I don't get discouraged, and I'll tell you why: I don't believe in it!"

That is a new angle to this human problem of discouragement, isn't it? If you do not believe in discouragement, you cannot get discouraged. A friend who knew Campbell well says, "He's telling the truth. I've never seen him discouraged."

A professional writer reports that the way he has overcome discouragement is by using a stopwatch. When he gets a manuscript rejected or suffers some other disappointment, he gives himself three minutes to feel sorry for himself. When the three minutes are up, he snaps out of his disappointment and gets busy doing something constructive.

Dr. Richard C. Halverson, chaplain of the U.S. Senate a few decades ago, asks,

> Why do we ever give way to pessimism and despair? In our saner moments, we know beyond the peradventure of a doubt that God is always the Master of all circumstances, never the victim of any. He is never taken by surprise, never thwarted, never frustrated. God is in charge! Anxiety, therefore, is a kind of mistrust, a kind of challenge to God's integrity and fidelity. Anxiety means that we believe in the circumstances more than we believe in God!

The same may be said of discouragement. It is a form of mistrust, a believing in adverse circumstances more than in a never-changing God. "I agree," you might say, "but how can I deal successfully with discouragement on a daily basis?" In answer to this question I have jotted down three guidelines, which, if put into daily use, can lift you from the swamps of despondency and put your feet on the Mount Everest of abundant living.

Guideline 1: Refuse to judge life by one situation or experience. Learn to take all things into consideration before you settle on your mood for the day. Just because something unpleasant has happened, do not ruin the rest of the day by dwelling on it. "If you must cry over spilt milk, condense it," quipped one optimist. A country farmer expressed a similar thought when he said bluntly, "Trouble with people is that we remember the smell of one skunk but forget the fragrance of a thousand flowers."

The apostle Paul realized the importance of taking everything into consideration when he wrote these famous words: "In all things God works for the good of those who love him, who have been called according to his purpose" (Romans 8:28).

Guideline 2: Do everything possible to better the situation that has caused your discouragement. If physical illness nags you, seek medical help. If it is a financial dilemma, get the counsel of a person well versed in money matters. If your problem is a marital one, go to a qualified minister or a trained marriage counselor. Never allow yourself to stay in a discouraging rut. Take action to make your life happier.

Guideline 3: Learn to encourage yourself through spiritual reflection. That is what King David did. During one of the bleakest days of his life, David "encouraged himself in the LORD his God" (1 Samuel 30:6 KJV).

May I add that this is the only reliable way to find encouragement in life's midnight hours? When the outlook is bleak and the "inlook" is discouraging, try the "uplook"—it is always encouraging!

In his book *MacArthur: His Rendezvous with History,* Courtney Whitney tells what General Douglas MacArthur did the night before the famed Inchon landing of the Korean War. At 2:30 AM the burdened general turned to his Bible and read a few verses before turning off the light. Why? He needed strength and encouragement, and he knew where to find it—in God's book, the Bible. How about opening your Bible now to find the encouragement you need?

Resource reading: 1 Samuel 30

Running the Race

Seeing we also are compassed about with so great a cloud of witnesses, let us lay aside every weight, and the sin which doth so easily beset us, and let us run with patience the race that is set before us.

HEBREWS 12:1 KJV

Insight: The athlete who triumphed in a Greek athletic contest was given a crown of laurel leaves that quickly wilted and died, but when you succeed in your Christian life, you will be given a crown of eternal life that knows no end.

Should you ever have the opportunity of visiting ancient Corinth, there is an out-of-the way, seldom-seen-by-tourists place that makes what Paul wrote to the Corinthians more meaningful. Remember Paul's comments that those who run in a race should run in such a way as to gain the prize? He was probably thinking of the place near the Corinthian canal where the Isthmian Games were held every two years. The Isthmian Games were a forerunner of the modern Olympics, and Greeks loved their athletes, who were as venerated as sports stars are today.

"Everyone who competes in the games," wrote Paul, "goes into strict training" (1 Corinthians 9:25). It's still true. The old adage "no pain, no gain" speaks in concise terms of the discipline, the long hours of training, the daily hardships—all so athletes will be ready when the day comes to compete.

Athletes still use some of the basic training techniques the ancients used. To strengthen their muscles the Greeks would often carry heavy weights or strap them on their legs, but when the day of the race came, they took off everything that was not essential.

Using the same analogy to encourage early Christians, the writer of Hebrews said, "Seeing we also are compassed about with so great a cloud of witnesses, let us lay aside every weight, and the sin which doth so easily beset us, and let us run with patience the race that is set before us" (Hebrews 12:1 KJV). The writer likens your walk with the Lord to the race run by the athlete. It has a starting point, at your conversion, and it has a terminus—when you meet the Lord face-to-face. In this contest, the writer says you are to rid yourself of two things—the weights that slow you down, and the sins that—like a heavy garment—keep you from achieving.

If every word is significant, then there is a reason why two words—*weights* and *sins*—are used. Understanding the difference provides insight for us today. The first Greek word means a weight, a burden, or an impediment—anything that keeps a person from walking with the Lord, though the object in and of itself is not wrong. But it becomes wrong when it keeps an individual from doing the will of God.

The second word means sin—"missing the mark," "falling short of a goal or target." It was the same word Jesus used when Luke recorded His comments on prayer: "Forgive us our sins, for we also forgive everyone who sins against us."

The writer of Hebrews says, "Get rid of what keeps you from being at your best, including what you clearly know is wrong—sin!" And how do we do that?

First, we decide that whatever keeps us from giving our best to the Master has to go. Jesus said we cannot serve two masters, which is what we often try to do. It does not work. We never succeed with a schizophrenic approach to Christianity. If Jesus Christ is the one He claimed to be, we must serve Him wholeheartedly.

Then we confess and forsake what the Bible calls sin. God's promise is still in effect: "If we confess our sins, he is faithful and just and will forgive us our sins and purify us from all unrighteousness" (1 John 1:9).

Staying focused, renewing your determination, and hanging in there day after day is what it takes to win. It's true when you are running a race and when you are living the Christian life.

Resource reading: 1 Corinthians 9:24-27

God Daily Bears Our Burdens

Carry each other's burdens, and in this way you will fulfill the law of Christ.
GALATIANS 6:2

Insight: God is a refuge, a shelter, a safe harbor to which you can flee when life becomes a raging storm.

The barrier that keeps us from prayer is not that we think God is not strong enough to help us, but that we are not humble enough to bow the knee and admit we need help. Many of us, however, distance ourselves from God, wondering if He is interested in us because of who we are. We know our imperfections better than we know God's strength and compassion, so we feed the nagging voice of doubt and withdraw into our caves of lonely isolation.

David, a man whose triumphs and failures cover a vast spectrum, once cried out, "Praise be to the LORD, to God our Savior, who daily bears our burdens" (Psalm 68:19). Stop and think. What exactly is a burden? It's a load we carry, whether it is physical, emotional, or spiritual. It's something that keeps us from being at our best. It can be a persistent, nagging problem or something confronting us in life that we did not choose—perhaps the care of an elderly parent, a health problem, a physical impairment.

But does God actually bear our burdens? If He does, what does that mean? First, it means that He cares. He is not indifferent to what happens to us. The book of Hebrews tells us that nothing is hidden from him and everything is seen by Him. The words *nothing* and *everything* stand in sharp contrast. Most of the time we immediately think God is noting our failures. Yes, but it also means He knows the desires of our hearts, our struggles to do right, and the sensitivity that brings us to our knees to find greater strength and forgiveness when we fall.

Only someone who has a sincere, compassionate interest in another cares enough to help us with our loads. Sometimes God works through a friend; sometimes He works through His Word; sometimes He comes alongside and touches our hearts in such a way that we walk away uplifted, joyful, and relieved of the burden.

Paul told the Galatians they were to bear one another's burdens and so fulfill the law of Christ (Galatians 6:2). The Greek word that Paul used means to bear a heavy weight or something difficult. It came from the same root word that means "to reach deep within something." Ah, that's an interesting thought. A real friend does not let you get away with an "everything's just fine" response to the question "How are you?" when worry and turmoil are written in the lines of your face. She insists you tell her about the hurts.

In another psalm David wrote, "Cast your cares [*burdens* in another translation] on the LORD and he will sustain you; he will never let the righteous fall" (Psalm 55:22). This, of course, means that you are the one who has to bow humbly and say, "Lord, I need Your help!"

Jesus said, "Come to me, all you who are weary and burdened, and I will give you rest" (Matthew 11:28). There you have the concept of laying your burden at the feet of the Shepherd of your soul.

In one of her books, Hannah Whitall Smith tells of a young man carrying a heavy load on his back as he is walking along a country road. Then a farmer passes by with an empty wagon.

"I'll give you a lift," volunteers the farmer, and the boy climbs onto the empty wagon and sits down, but he does not put down his load. "Set down your load," the farmer invites.

But the youth objects. "Oh no, sir. It is too much to expect you to carry both me and my load."

Are you carrying a heavy load? Only you can accept God's help in bearing your load every single day. Think about it.

Resource reading: Psalm 55

Going Beyond Your Trouble

Though the fig tree does not bud
and there are no grapes on the vines,
though the olive crop fails and the fields
produce no food, though there are no
sheep in the pen and no cattle in the
stalls, yet I will rejoice in the LORD,
I will be joyful in God my Savior.
HABAKKUK 3:17-18

Insight: When you have read the last chapter of a book, you know how the story turns out. Remember that God—not fate or chance—will write the last chapter of your life.

When the sky turns dark, health fails, a marriage partner walks out, or a job is lost, life gradually unravels. Paul's words—"In everything give thanks, for this is the will of God in Christ Jesus"—seem only to torment. No matter how we try to piece them together, events do not make sense.

If you feel this way, frankly, you are not the first. The Bible tells us of a man who faced the same type of distress—Habakkuk. He lived about 600 years before Christ, when the world was in possibly the greatest turmoil of pre-Christian times. World powers were hanging by threads. There appeared to be no hope for Habakkuk's nation of Israel. Doom seemed imminent. Habakkuk looked at his nation and saw corruption, confusion, and bewilderment. "Why does God not intervene?" he asked. "Why does there seem to be a lack of justice in His management of the world? Why is He silent in times of disaster? Why doesn't He hear me and help me?"

Habakkuk did find an answer. The answer was looking beyond his trouble, realizing that no matter what happened, God would still be on the throne of the universe. He is from everlasting to everlasting. Said the psalmist,

> In ages past you laid the foundations of the earth, and made the heavens with your hands! They shall perish, but you go on forever. They will grow old, like worn-out clothing, and

> you will change them like a man putting on a new shirt and throwing away the old one! But you yourself never grow old. You are forever, and your years never end. But our families will continue; generation after generation will be preserved by your protection (Psalm 102:25-28 TLB).

Habakkuk had questions in his mind, but he did the right thing about them; he brought them to God. God not only answered his questions, but also put a song in his heart. When Habakkuk looked at the circumstances around about him, he was perplexed; but when he turned to God, he found joy.

The key to knowing God in a personal way lies in knowing His Son, who said, "He who has seen me has seen the Father." All too often we forget that Jesus was not greeted with great acclaim, but He was rejected, despised, and eventually crucified at the hands of Roman soldiers.

Yes, His world unraveled, but it was so that our torn and perplexing world could eventually come together. Because Christ triumphed over death, you too can triumph over your circumstances and even thank God that through it all, He is more than able to meet you and give you deliverance.

Habakkuk went beyond his doubt, his struggle, and his uncertainty, and when he did, his problems did not matter much. Take time to read Habakkuk 3 and understand there is peace and tranquility when your world unravels, when things do not go right, and when you have become a victim of wrongdoing. When you see God as Habakkuk did, that's enough. Behind the darkest cloud is sunshine.

Resource reading: Habakkuk 3

The Desolation of Loneliness

Keep your lives free from the love of money and be content with what you have, because God has said, "Never will I leave you; never will I forsake you."
HEBREWS 13:5

Insight: When you are lonely, never forget that Jesus understands your loneliness. He tasted of the same bitter dregs in the cup you have drunk.

It is the most desolate word in all human language," says Chuck Swindoll. "It is capable of hurling the heaviest weights the heart can endure. It plays no favorites, ignores all rules of courtesy, knows neither border nor barrier, yields no mercy, refuses all bargains, and holds the clock in utter contempt." That word is *loneliness,* one of the most terrible maladies of our existence. Mother Teresa called loneliness "the hunger for human love" and described it as "the world's worst ill."

One of the strangest things about the malady is that we can be in the midst of people, yet loneliness strikes. It was an American living in France who pressed his face to the windowpane as he watched people hurrying toward the warmth of their homes and turned away to write the words, "Be it ever so humble, there's no place like home." Ask the man whose hospital room has made his existence that of a prisoner, or the elderly woman who lives by herself but goes to the store daily, mostly to see others.

Ask the celebrity who is surrounded by fans seeking autographs, and you may be surprised to learn that some of the world's most influential and well-known people are also some of the loneliest ones in the world. Take, for example, actress Doris Day, once voted the world's most popular actress. She candidly confessed that she was an extremely lonely woman and often cried herself to sleep. Speaking of the emptiness in her life, she asked, "If so many people love me, how come I'm alone?"

Not only the sick, the imprisoned, the elderly, and the talented are lonely. Ask the single parent who puts the kids to bed and doesn't dare turn off the radio or television. Ask the businessman who is burned out and fearful of letting his boss know he needs help. Ask the teenage girl who is pregnant and fearful of telling her parents.

There are two things of which you can be sure: God knows your anguish and hurt, and He cares. He cares infinitely more than we can comprehend. Do you remember the loneliness that Jesus Christ faced as the disciples turned one by one and left Him? Remember the anguish as He cried out, "My God, my God, why have you forsaken me?" (Mark 15:34). Do you recall the long hours prior to the ordeal at Calvary when He struggled in prayer in the Garden and wrestled with the anguish before Him?

Do you remember how Jesus prayed? "If it is possible, may this cup be taken from me" (Matthew 26:39). Was He afraid of dying? Fearful of the nails that would be driven through His hands and feet? No! What He was asking was to not be separated from the presence of the Father. In other words, He was praying that He might be spared that unthinkable loneliness.

Jesus is a specialist when it comes to loneliness, and that's part of the reason He provides a remedy for our hurts. Because He suffered the pain of loneliness when He was separated from the Father, we need never be separated from His presence. Take His great promise and rely on it today: "Never will I leave you; never will I forsake you."

Resource reading: Hebrews 13

A Cure for Loneliness

Though one may be overpowered, two can defend themselves. A cord of three strands is not quickly broken.
ECCLESIASTES 4:12

Insight: Finding another person who is just as lonely as you and offering encouragement to that lonely heart will free you from your own prison of loneliness.

There are more people today than ever before who know the anguish of the lonely heart. In spite of the fact that more people are alive right now than have ever died from the days of Adam and Eve to the present, there are more lonely people than ever before. It takes more than masses of people to eliminate loneliness.

Why so much loneliness today? The backdrop for much of it actually began three or four generations ago with people's increasing move to the big cities to find work in the growing factories and businesses. Behind the barren walls and locked doors, the beauty of the countryside has long been forgotten. The asphalt streets and the polluted air have caused us to lose touch with the freshness of the dew on the grass in the early morning, the crispness of a new dawn, and the feel of frost underfoot. We have forgotten what a sunset looks like—how the blazing sun can paint the western sky myriad shades of red and orange—colors never captured by an artist's palette.

We tell ourselves that this is all the price of progress, that a job—or a better job—justifies it all. But far more than where we live, it is *how* we live that produces loneliness. It is true that more of us are living longer than previous generations, and this also means that there are more elderly men and women living alone than ever before. Much of our loneliness, however, is not the result of the Lord's taking a husband or wife but of our decisions to be alone rather than in an "unhappy home." Dr. James Lynch, a psychologist, says, "There is an almost unconscious cultural conspiracy to fool people into thinking that to be alone is a virtue. The myth of independence, which one sees every day in advertising and other media, makes it appear that to admit we need each other is a sign of weakness."

Is there a cure for loneliness? Mother Teresa believed there is. She said it is love. When we reach out to someone who is hurting, and in reaching out to help someone else, we find a cure for our own loneliness. You'll find hurting people all around you—the ones barricaded in one-room apartments, the lonely men and women who eat alone in restaurants, and the ones who walk alone because there is no one to share their thoughts with.

Many lonely, hurting people have found a cure for loneliness. The alternative to loneliness is to get out and use your talents and time for the Lord. Volunteer somewhere. I don't think I have ever seen a church who had so many people volunteer to work with kids or help in various programs that they could not use a few more.

Fighting loneliness? Then unlock your door, take a long look at the beauty that God has placed around you, and go looking for someone else who is hurting and needs your help. A theater critic recently closed his column by saying, "If you're feeling blue and lonely, stop by and see a movie. It probably won't cheer you up, but at least you can feel sorry for someone else." There's a better way—the way of love, as you help someone else who hurts.

Resource reading: Ruth 1

Loneliness—Dying Every Day

A man that hath friends must shew himself friendly: and there is a friend that sticketh closer than a brother.

PROVERBS 18:24 KJV

Insight: Touching another person every day helps *restore* life, just as loneliness *diminishes* life.

In case you feel you are losing faith in humanity, let me tell you about Jean Rosenstein and what happened to her. Mrs. Rosenstein sat down at a small table in her cramped, one-bedroom apartment and painfully put her thoughts on paper. The arthritis in her fingers made the writing difficult and painful, but she continued.

The scrawled words read, "I'm so lonely I could die. So alone. I cannot write. My hands and fingers pain me...I see no human beings. My phone never rings...I'm so very old, so very lonely. I hear from no one...Way past eighty years. Should I die? Never had any kind of holidays, no kind. My birthday is this month...Sometimes I even feel sure the world ended, and I'm the only one on earth. How else can I feel? Oh, dear God, help me. Am of sound mind, so lonely, very, very much. I don't know what to do."

She put the letter in an oversized yellow envelope along with some money and six stamps and mailed it to the *Los Angeles Times* newspaper. The money was to pay for the call if someone would just call to talk to her. The stamps were for anyone who would take the time to write. In a city surrounded by millions of people, Jean Rosenstein felt alone. And what happened? First, a reporter called and said he would like to visit. Mrs. Rosenstein was delighted. She had not had a visitor for a long, long time.

She described her painfully accurate situation to the reporter: "If you are alone, you die every day...Sometimes I just dread to see myself wake up in the morning." The newspaper printed her letter along with a story. Within days thousands of letters and cards poured into the little apartment. Visitors began to stream in and out to talk to the lonely lady who had no friends. So many people called that she finally had to take the phone off the hook. Letters came from elderly people; young couples sent pictures of their children. People responded from all over the world. She said, "This will last for a lifetime."

Three cheers for everybody who brightened Mrs. Rosenstein's life. I am wondering, though, how many Mrs. Rosensteins there are in the city in which you live—some lost in vast cities, some in convalescent hospitals, some in shabby apartments, some on farms—all forgotten people, forgotten by children and former acquaintances, forgotten by people who are too busy to care. All that is necessary to destroy loneliness is one real friend.

Sometimes loneliness forces us to discover friendships that will last forever. That was the way it was with Joseph Scriven, whose lovely fiancée drowned in a Canadian lake. Feeling lost and lonely, he found the friendship of Jesus Christ—one who drives away the loneliness of separation. It was this unending friendship that Scriven wrote about when he penned the lyrics, "What a Friend we have in Jesus, all our sins and griefs to bear! What a privilege to carry everything to God in prayer! O what peace we often forfeit, O what needless pain we bear, all because we do not carry everything to God in prayer."

Yes, we need each other, and we need the friendship of One who will never leave or forsake us. I'm wondering if there is a Jean Rosenstein living near you, a person who needs your friendship as badly as you need to extend it? Take a look, friend, and reach out to that person. Your life will be enriched.

Resource reading: Ruth 2

Loneliness and Emptiness

Go and make disciples of all nations, baptizing them in the name of the Father and of the Son and of the Holy Spirit, and teaching them to obey everything I have commanded you. And surely I am with you always, to the very end of the age.

MATTHEW 28:19-20

Insight: Although you on occasion may be alone, you need never be lonely if Jesus, who stays closer than a brother, is your friend.

Alone! is the title of Admiral Richard Byrd's autobiography. It's the story of the celebrated explorer's experiences in a little hut in the Antarctic near the South Pole. Byrd tells how the isolation, day after day, began working on his mind and emotions as he spent the long winter alone, separated from friends and loved ones, even separated from friendly animals that might have offered some companionship or comfort. Alone he surely was—but a person does not have to spend a long arctic night in a little hut near the pole to know what it is to experience feelings of isolation and loneliness.

I am thinking of a young mother of four who wrote telling how her family had moved from one city to another when her husband was promised a new job. She was eight months pregnant in a city without friends or relatives when her husband disappeared, leaving a note behind that he no longer loved her and that she must make it the best she could. Could any person ever feel more alone and dejected than did this woman?

Many women today know what it is to feel alone and to be alone. Death, as well as infidelity, leaves a lot of women shrouded in loneliness. Three out of four women outlive their husbands, and they do it by an average of more than seven years. Although the average age of widows the world over is 56, one of every six women over age 21 is widowed. The word *widow* comes from a word in Sanskrit that means "empty." Loneliness is emptiness.

Logic decrees that single individuals would wrestle with loneliness, but what about those who are part of a group? Are they immune? Today there is another group battling the isolation and depression of loneliness, a group that seemingly should not. A large number of young men and women between the ages of 15 and 24 feel separated and estranged from their families and society in general.

In her day, Gertrude Stein called such young people "a generation without a cause." Today, they have become a sizable army of teens and young adults. They rub shoulders with many individuals yet have empty lives without relationships that cement them to reality. Drugs, casual sex, and the quest for meaningful experiences drive them further and further into their loneliness. Pretty pessimistic? Yes and no! Recognizing this malady of the twenty-first century is one thing; knowing how to remedy the situation is quite another. It is here that I am optimistic.

My optimism does not stem from unbridled faith or wishful thinking, but from the certainty that to be alone does not mean a person has to be lonely. Man's extremity is God's opportunity. During periods of loneliness our faith is challenged to discover the guiding hand of God and learn that Christ's presence is a reality, not simply a facet of theology. Is God real? Can I experience the actual presence of Jesus Christ in such a way that I can have active fellowship with Him? Can I learn that Christ is not just a historical reality, but a friend who stays closer than a brother? If the answer is positive—and it is—then to be alone does not have to be synonymous with loneliness.

Friend, because God's words are true—"Never will I leave you; never will I forsake you" (Hebrews 13:5)—I can be assured of His companionship in a spiritual yet very real sense. Matthew recorded the words of Jesus immediately before He returned to heaven: "I am with you always, even to the end of the age" (Matthew 28:20 NKJV). His promise brings the confidence that God cares and will never allow you to be estranged from His presence. Discovering this great truth means you need never be totally alone again—ever again.

Resource reading: Ruth 3

Loneliness and What It Can Accomplish

Ruth replied, "Don't urge me to leave you or to turn back from you. Where you go I will go, and where you stay I will stay. Your people will be my people and your God my God."
RUTH 1:16

Insight: While loneliness is usually thought of as isolation, it can be a tool in the hands of the Master to help you know both Him and yourself better.

Back when the world's population was less than 250 million, a mere fraction of what it is today, the prophet Isaiah wrote, "Woe unto them that join house to house, that lay field to field, till there be no place, that they may be placed alone in the midst of the earth!" (Isaiah 5:8 KJV). I wonder how he would feel today, when skyscrapers puncture the skyline of almost every major city on earth and the world population is over six billion, yet there is more loneliness than ever before. Strange, isn't it? You would think that with more people, there would be less estrangement and loneliness, but it just does not work that way.

A lot of factors contribute to this disease of human relations we call loneliness: the breakdown of the family unit, the mobility of families who move from place to place in unprecedented numbers, the fragmentation of human relationships as people who have been hurt by others withdraw rather than reach out to each other. The results are estrangement, separation, and ultimately loneliness—the devastating kind of loneliness that makes people question their existence and their worthiness to occupy two square feet of Planet Earth. Sooner or later, every person faces a struggle with loneliness. How you face loneliness and what you do with it can either spell your destruction or help make your life what God wants it to be.

What can loneliness do? Plenty! First, it can give you an awareness of God's presence you might never find in the rush and bother of life. Scores of people have discovered the presence of God during hours of loneliness. Moses knew loneliness as he herded sheep in the desert of the Negev. David knew its presence when he spent seven long years in the wilderness area around En Gedi, as he fled from the soldiers of King Saul. Jesus knew what loneliness was as He prayed in the Garden and watched His trusted followers fall asleep one by one. "Could you men not keep watch with me for one hour?" He chided Peter (Matthew 26:40).

No one eagerly looks forward to battling with loneliness, but when you do, friend, you will discover that God is there too and that His Son will never leave nor forsake you (Hebrews 13:5).

The second contribution that loneliness can make is to help you discover yourself (which, of course, may be alarming). It can provide the time for you to develop some of your own hobbies or interests. It can give you the time you need to become a student of the Word and devour some of those books in your library you have been thinking about reading.

A third contribution loneliness can make is to force you to bridge its estranging sea by forging new friendships with other people who need your companionship as badly as you need theirs.

If you are a Christian, you are not isolated and alone. You belong to the family of God, which means you have brothers and sisters who are vitally related to one another through Jesus Christ. We are a fellowship of believers, part of a vast company of men and women from all walks of life, from every country on Earth. "Let us not give up meeting together," wrote the author of the book of Hebrews (Hebrews 10:25). It was Christ who brought together the first body of disciples, and it is He who still binds our lives together in a fellowship that leaves no room for loneliness and isolation.

A closing word: Do not wallow in the slough of loneliness and despair. Move toward the center, and the closer you get to Jesus Christ, the closer you will find yourself to a growing body of Christians who are searching for fellowship as you are. Loneliness is a social tragedy that need not ensnare those who walk in Jesus' footsteps today.

Resource reading: Ruth 4

When Less Is More

He said to them, "Take heed and beware of covetousness, for one's life does not consist in the abundance of the things he possesses."

LUKE 12:15 NKJV

Insight: There are two ways people try to be satisfied: accumulating more or being satisfied with less.

How much is enough? Have you ever pondered the question in relationship to your own lifestyle? As the story is told, when John D. Rockefeller was asked how much money it would take for him to be satisfied, he replied, "Just a little bit more!"

"It is not the rich man only who is under the dominion of things," wrote George Macdonald, the man who greatly influenced C.S. Lewis. "They too," he contended, "are slaves who, having no money, are unhappy from it."

But back to the Rockefeller question: "How much do you need to be satisfied?" Has the media convinced us in brilliant color that we must have far more than we actually need to be satisfied, that we can never be happy unless our appetite for possessions is fully satisfied?

One of the most challenging books I have ever read is Richard Foster's *Freedom of Simplicity.* In this thought-provoking confrontation with materialism, Foster begins the first chapter by saying,

> Contemporary culture is plagued by the passion to possess. The unreasoned boast abounds that the good life is found in accumulation—that "more is better." Indeed, we often accept this notion without question, with the result that the lust for affluence in contemporary society has become psychotic: it has completely lost touch with reality.

In the last three decades a great deal of my time has been spent in Third-World cultures where people have so little compared with affluent Western cultures. I have become convinced that many people today are possessed by possessions as no other generation in history. The more complex life becomes, the more convinced we are that we need *more* to be happy. Having obtained what we think we need, we soon become unhappy again because a new model with more bells and whistles comes out, making ours obsolete. We have forgotten the simple admonition of Jesus Christ: "One's life does not consist in the abundance of the things he possesses" (Luke 12:15 NKJV). Another translation puts it a little differently: "Watch out! Be on your guard against all kinds of greed; a man's life does not consist in the abundance of his possessions."

I know one thing from my limited experience. It takes far less than we think to discover happiness—if our happiness comes from within and we break the stranglehold that things have on our lives today. After Admiral Richard Byrd lived in the Antarctic all by himself for months, he wrote these words in his journal: "I am learning...that a man can live profoundly without masses of things."

Aleksandr Solzhenitsyn discovered the same thing. In one of his books he told about being thrown into a Soviet prison. Systematically everything he held dear was taken from him—his books, his home, his friends, and his freedom—almost everything but his very life. It was then Solzhenitsyn said that he came to realize that a man is never stronger than when he has nothing but the treasures within his heart.

Both Mark and Luke tell about a young man who struggled with the issue of how much is enough. He came to Jesus Christ one day and asked, "Good master, what must I do to inherit the kingdom of God?" Jesus immediately stripped away any misconceptions about adding faith as an ornament to his already opulent life. Jesus told him, "Go, sell what you have, give to the poor, and come be My follower." Tough advice! Hardly what he expected.

Jesus was against money, right? Wrong! He was against anything that becomes a god in our lives and leaves our heavenly Father on the side. How much is enough? G.K. Chesterton answered the question by saying, "There are two ways to get enough: One is to continue to accumulate more and more. The other is to desire less and less." Jesus reminded us, "Where your treasure is, there your heart will be also" (Matthew 6:21). It's something to think about.

Resource reading: Luke 12

How Much Is Really Enough?

When you come, bring the cloak that I left with Carpus at Troas, and my scrolls, especially the parchments.
2 TIMOTHY 4:13

Insight: When God does not provide more as you requested, the reason may well be that His idea of *enough* is different from yours.

Dad, why can't we buy a new computer for our home? All the rest of the kids in my class have one." At first your reaction is, "We need a new computer like we need a third wheel on a bicycle." You begin thinking about it, however, and you do not want your child to be handicapped by developing insufficient visual-motor coordination and other learning skills. Then the salesman gives you a pitch about how youngsters without an up-to-date knowledge of computers will be left out of the job market by the time they graduate.

As you mull over this information, you begin to think how a new computer could do so much more. You flip through a magazine, impressed by the beautiful layout created by skilled advertising people, and think how your own learning skills could be enhanced. You think about the added possibilities for entertainment and business.

Here is the process. At first, an item is an unnecessary extravagance; then it becomes "nice-to-have." Next your thought process moves to another level—"I really need that." Now you are one step from the bottom line, which is, "I have to have that!" So you buy it. You did not need it, but you convinced yourself you did. You could not afford it nor do you have a place for it, but you sign up to make those 24 easy payments, ignoring the high interest you will pay.

A madness has possessed people—the madness of thinking that the good life is found in accumulation and that more is better. We have become hypnotized by the media advertising that makes extravagances appear essential. In the process, we have lost sight of the needs of anyone but ourselves. We have satiated ourselves with an endless abundance of things—most of which will be obsolete in two years and need repairs in far less time than that.

How much do we need? That is the question I have posed in this chapter, and it is a tough one—one that begins to strip away the media veneer of desire. For a Christian, the question is more important than ever before. Do we really believe we have a responsibility to not only use our resources for the glory of God, but also be directly involved with the suffering of humanity? Has God smiled upon us to satiate us with indulgences, or has He blessed us so we may bless those not as fortunate as we are?

It is a rather uncomfortable issue, but one we must face. We give token acknowledgment to the truth that Christ is Lord, but we grudgingly refuse to admit that what we have is not ours but His. Our resources and possessions are given for us to use for His glory, never to abuse in fulfilling our lusts or desires.

How much is enough? I cannot answer that question for you, but I know the Holy Spirit will clearly speak to your heart if you are willing to submit the question to our heavenly Father. I suspect He will tell you what He has been telling me in recent months: "You need far less than you think, My child." And when you say, "Yes, Lord—that's fine with me too!" you will be amazed at the freedom and joy that comes to your heart. There is freedom in simplicity, the kind that is driven by the desire to put an end to the vast accumulation of things controlling us and exhausting our resources. Think about it.

Resource reading: Psalm 1

The Sin of Greed

Put to death, therefore, whatever belongs to your earthly nature: sexual immorality, impurity, lust, evil desires and greed, which is idolatry.
COLOSSIANS 3:5

Insight: You are your brother's keeper to the degree that you can alleviate his suffering, help him clothe and feed himself, and meet the needs of his family.

It's an old story, retold many times. In the fourteenth century there was a duke named Ranald, who lived in the country we now know as Belgium. The duke was not only overweight; he was grossly indulgent. He craved food, and his appetite was never satisfied, so much so that the peasants called him *Crassus,* which in Latin means "the fat one."

In due process the overweight duke became king, but his brother, Edward, deeply resented the fact that the crown had bypassed him and gone to Ranald, so he plotted a revolt and deposed him. Instead of dispatching his brother so he would never again be a bother, Edward, in a sadistic moment of perverse compassion, had a room built around his brother, a room with a normal-sized door that was too narrow for his over-indulgent brother to pass through.

Every day, Edward, the new king, would send pastries, choice foods, and drink to his brother, who appreciated this perverse kindness. "My brother is not a prisoner," Edward would say, adding, "He can leave any time he chooses."

Ranald was in fact imprisoned by his greed, not by his brother. He was a prisoner of his appetite. Frankly, greed was not only Ranald's problem, but it is also the problem challenging everyone who aspires to better himself. It's the old issue of "How much is enough?" That question needs to be addressed by the corporation that controls the market and delights in wiping out the upstart competitor, the executive with a six- or even seven-figure salary who fights for millions more in bonuses, the wealthy nations who sap the strength of poorer nations.

Food was the commodity that made Ranald a prisoner of greed, but diamonds, gold, money, and markets control many others, creating corporate takeovers, political maneuvering and, on occasions, bloodshed and war.

But—and this is where the issue gets personal—is greed only a problem of the big guys—the bad ones over there (wherever that is)? Or can it be the problem of the little guy, perhaps even the person who lives in your house?

Greed is not only the enemy of the rich but also the poor—and everyone else. It is not an issue of how much you have but how much you want.

Surprisingly, the New Testament has twice as much to say about the issue of greed as does the Old Testament. Jesus denounced the religious leaders of His day, the Pharisees, saying that they were "full of greed and wickedness" (Luke 11:39). Jesus warned, "Watch out! Be on your guard against all kinds of greed." Then He added, "A man's life does not consist in the abundance of his possessions" (Luke 12:15).

Greed, said Paul, is one of the sins of the flesh that God's people ought to excise from their lives. "Put [it] to death" is how Paul said it should be dealt with in Colossians 3:5. The New Testament also warns that greed is one of the motives false teachers use to build their empires. Peter wrote, "In their greed these teachers will exploit you with stories they have made up. Their condemnation has long been hanging over them, and their destruction has not been sleeping" (2 Peter 2:3). Further, Peter said these false teachers are "experts in greed" (2:14).

"But among you," wrote Paul, "there must not be even a hint of sexual immorality, or of any kind of impurity, or of greed, because these are improper for God's holy people" (Ephesians 5:3). It's still true today.

Resource reading: Luke 12:1-15

Freedom in Simplicity

Foxes have holes and birds of the air have nests, but the Son of Man has no place to lay his head.
MATTHEW 8:20

Insight: There is freedom in simplicity. To rid ourselves of clutter demands we begin to think God's thoughts, putting distance between our desires and the thinking of society and peers.

The American humorist Mark Twain wrote, "Civilization is a limitless multiplication of unnecessary necessities." I wonder what Twain would have said had he been alive today. Never before has the consumer been confronted with so many choices.

An anthropologist friend of mine points out that civilizations tend to move from the simple agrarian society to the industrial, complex society, which eventually collapses under the burden of its own weight and complexity. I think it is fair to say that never before has a generation had more "things" than the present one, yet with all of the toys integrated circuits and quartz crystals have presented us—from handheld computers to digital you-name-its, we are consuming more aspirin for headaches and tranquilizers for shattered nerves than ever before. If more were better, then surely we would be on the threshold of an unprecedented utopia, but it has not worked that way.

Having less means greater simplicity, which produces greater peace of mind and happiness. Some, even in times of poverty, find riches of the soul that money cannot buy.

When a builder has a problem with a house he is constructing, he goes to the blueprint. Remember the adage "When all else fails, read the instructions"? That is part of the reason we need to think through the complexity of our lifestyles and the pressures of living. We have not read or followed God's directions. We have more of almost everything money can buy but are confronted with leanness of spirit.

Jesus Christ said, "Foxes have holes and birds of the air have nests, but the Son of Man has no place to lay his head" (Matthew 8:20). He owned no real estate, though the whole world was His. He borrowed another man's boat to row on Galilee. On occasion, when He had no boat, He simply walked on the surface of the water in the power of God the Spirit. The only thing we know He possessed was a seamless robe, which the soldiers took from Him and gambled for.

What did Jesus have that we have never had? Two things impress me: a peaceful happiness and simplicity. It has been my observation that some of the richest men in the world were some of the unhappiest and most stressed, proving that money cannot buy happiness. John Paul Getty, once the richest man in the world, said he would gladly give all of his money for a happy home; but he never took that step to experiment with the possibility. This is not to suggest that the absence of money—poverty—will produce joy, but what Jesus taught is that peace and happiness do not come from the abundance of things money can buy.

What Jesus did have, which we desperately need, is simplicity. In his book *Freedom of Simplicity,* the gifted writer Richard Foster contends that simplicity is not something you *do;* it is something you *are.* "Seek simplicity, and trust it," advises Alfred North Whitehead. Simplicity brings a contentment that puts psychiatrists out of business, along with a host of entertainers and entrepreneurs who are trying to convince us that what we have or hear or see will bring happiness. Simplicity begins to put you in tune with the divine harmony of nature (which is not to suggest that God *is* nature). You learn to be still and know that He is God; you shut out the din and noise of stressful living to hear His voice saying, "This is the way; walk in it" (Isaiah 30:21).

Yes, it is time to strip away the veneer of materialism and discover the simplicity of walking in the footsteps of Jesus Christ. Simplicity demands that we not live beyond our means—financially, emotionally, or physically. Simplicity is God's antidote to the pressures of life.

Resource reading: Matthew 5

Affluenza

Who then is the faithful and wise servant, whom the master has put in charge of the servants in his household to give them their food at the proper time?
MATTHEW 24:45

Insight: There is a vast difference between legitimate needs and the selfish wants that consume much of our income, time, and interest.

You go shopping for a casual shirt and find two. One is made of good fabric, nicely cut but plain. The second is almost identical, but it has a logo on it with a designer's name, one you quickly recognize. Everybody wears *that* brand, so you check the price tag. It's more than double the cost of the other one. So which one do you buy? How much are you willing to pay for wearing a shirt with someone's name on it? In other words, how much are you willing to pay for social acceptance?

Does answering that question make you uncomfortable? Yet haven't I described the social consciousness that confronts us today? Never before in the history of marketing have we been so challenged to conform to the social images that are thrust into our faces daily.

The problem has been described as "affluenza," a play on the word *influenza,* a disease that can be treated by aspirin and going to bed for a few days. Affluenza has been driven by a growing economy that generates more money for people to spend. Because of television, the Internet, and a growing awareness of how others dress and think, we have become engrossed with "things" and "stuff" as never before.

"Our priorities seem out of skew," says Frazier Moore, writing for the Associated Press. He adds, "More of us visit a mall each week than a house of worship. On average, we spend six hours per week shopping, yet only 40 minutes playing with our children."[9]

He points out the obvious. Thinking that we must have more, we spend more, and indebtedness grows. Credit card debts skyrocket. Thinking we will catch up with the bills next month, we are surprised when they catch up with us. Paul's direction to the Romans that we should be in debt to no man except for the debt to love one another is forgotten, and we find ourselves shackled with tremendous debt, which imprisons and destroys our families.

How do we fight back? Try these practical suggestions:

Guideline 1: Make a budget. If an item is not budgeted, refuse to buy it. And do not be like the woman who said she would live within her budget, even if she had to borrow money to do so.

Guideline 2: Pay cash for your purchases. Do plastic surgery on your credit cards—cut them up.

Guideline 3: Refuse to be a victim of media hype. Realize that the values of the world and our culture are at war with family values. Do not kid yourself. The media is on the other side, driven by the quest to sell you what they have, regardless of what you need. A paraphrase of Paul's words in Romans 12:2 says, "Don't let the world force you into its mold." Dare to be different. It's okay to be you and not a cookie-cutter copy of everybody else.

Guideline 4: Define your needs, and cater to your wants sparingly. God promised to meet your needs, not your wants. Buy quality, not brand names. And if you pay more for something that has someone's name on it, ask yourself, *Why am I doing this?*

Guideline 5: Stay out of the mall unless you need something. Some people, mostly men, like this guideline. And others, mostly women, say, "You don't understand. I just go to look, not buy." Right. Like an alcoholic who goes to a bar simply because he likes the friendly environment and the smell. People who make shopping a recreation often end up spending money they do not have, buying things they generally do not need, and impressing people they do not like. Yes, there is a cure for affluenza.

Resource reading: Daniel 6

Why Pray If You Can Fix It?

You do not have, because you do not ask God.
JAMES 4:2

Insight: Prayer is not overcoming God's reluctance, but yours! When you are willing to bend your knee in humble submission, you are in the place of blessing.

Abraham Lincoln, the American president who faced tremendous personal struggles in his life, once said, "I have been driven to my knees many times by the overwhelming conviction that I had nowhere else to go."

Prayer often takes just that—the overwhelming conviction we have nowhere else to go. There is a reason. To say, "God, I'm at the end of myself, and I have nowhere else to turn," is humiliating. It's like being absolutely broke and having to go to a friend and say, "Hey, could you give me a loan? I don't have enough money to buy bread and milk for the children."

If we can fix something by ourselves, we can then sit back and say, "Hey, look what I did! I pulled strings. I made the right connections. I'm pretty good." But when we pray, we're asking from a position of weakness. There is something about the old nature that does not like to be put in that position. That something is called pride.

I'd rather do it myself, we think, hesitant to ask God to do what we cannot. Stubborn, fierce independence always militates against prayer, yet the stark reality is there are a lot of things we cannot fix—the sorrow and pain of broken relationships, the devastating reality that we are mortal. The doctor cannot fix the cancer that has spread throughout your spouse's body. We cannot change the stock market or the rains that have devastated the region's crops, leaving many at the door of bankruptcy.

Only God can "fix" problems like these.

"Man's extremity, though, is God's opportunity," someone has said, so our poverty of spirit combined with our great needs drives us to knock on the door of the King of kings.

In his powerful book *Fresh Wind, Fresh Fire,* Jim Cymbala charges that a lot of pastors with empty pews and hearts fall into the same trap as do the people who sit in the pews—the position of not wanting to knock on heaven's door, empty-handed and at the end of themselves. Instead, they try to fix things through programs instead of the power of God. When Jim joined a broken-down church in a bad neighborhood, there were fewer than 25 people in attendance. Today, some 25 years later, more than 6000 people crowd Brooklyn Tabernacle. What was the key to the growth? Programs? No, God's power to change lives as the result of prayer.

Jim says,

> God has chosen prayer as his channel of blessing. He has spread a table for us with every kind of wisdom, grace, and strength because he knows exactly what we need. But the only way we can get it is to pull up to the table and taste and see that the Lord is good. Pulling up to that table is called the prayer of faith.

How do we overcome a position of weakness? We don't. But it helps to understand that God is not expecting us to come as equals, to drive a deal with Him by agreeing that if He bails us out of our problems, we'll do something equally helpful for Him in return.

That's where grace comes in, grace that comes from the hand of a loving, compassionate Father who delights in meeting us at our individual point of need. Only willful, misplaced, senseless pride and arrogance keep us from knocking at God's door of grace, coming with an open hand, asking Him to meet our needs.

Prayer is not overcoming God's reluctance, but yours—something you must never forget.

Resource reading: John 16:17-33

Intimacy with God

He returned to his disciples and found them sleeping. "Could you men not keep watch with me for one hour?" he asked Peter.
MATTHEW 26:40

Insight: Intimacy with God is not a spiritual technique or discipline; it is the outgrowth of a relationship, being with Him, being in His presence.

Just as intimacy in marriage takes communication, intimacy with God takes prayer. Though you may have never thought of the two in relationship to each other, what makes both meaningful is much the same. Success in both is dependent upon the quality of your relationship with the object of your affection. When you cannot communicate with your spouse—for whatever reason—your relationship rapidly disintegrates. Love grows cold. Warm memories are just that—recollections of the past, not realities in the present.

Prayer is communication, and the secret of intimacy in your spiritual life is being able to share your thoughts, your heart, and your feelings without fear of rejection. What are the enemies of intimacy? There are several, and they apply to your relationship both with your mate and with the Lord. As we ponder this, I'd like to begin by asking you to focus on your relationship with God. What hinders your intimacy with God? What keeps you from moving beyond thinking of Him as just a casual acquaintance?

Enemy 1: Busyness. This is undoubtedly the chief foe that turns our good intentions into well-worn excuses and leaves us feeling guilty. Yes, we know we ought to read the Bible and pray, but we are too busy. And what's the solution? In a word: priorities. We find time for what we consider important. In my personal life, I've found that the only way to turn intentions into forward steps is to set the clock alarm 30 minutes earlier and discipline myself to take this time with God.

"But won't that leave me tired?" To the contrary, you'll find that you have greater energy and better focus and get more accomplished than if you slept for another 30 minutes.

Enemy 2: Attitude. Whose attitude? Yours. It's quite amazing how your personal relationships with others also affect your relationship with God. Anger, bitterness, harsh feelings, and other negative feelings do not put you in the mood to bow your heart and say, "Good morning, Lord. It's me, and I'm not very happy right now." Pouring out your heart to God, telling Him how you feel, will not only change your attitude but will also create an environment in which God lets you know what your response should be to what bothers you.

Enemy 3: Distractions. "I'm burned out!" writes a friend of Guidelines. "I go to work early and get home late because of overtime work. I'm beat when I reach home, and my quiet time often becomes really quiet time because I'm dead asleep." Drowsiness is a definite distraction to prayer, but it is not the only one. If you have not discovered this, you will. It happens to everyone. As soon as you bow your head to pray, the phone rings, or the kids—the ones who play tirelessly together hour after hour—start a war. Or boom!—just like that you recall something you did not get done yesterday or a phone call (an important one) you did not return.

Is there a solution to distractions? If your mind wanders, pray out loud. If something important comes to mind, stop long enough to jot a memo to yourself, but do not give up.

In the garden of Gethsemane, Christ challenged Peter to "watch and pray so that you will not fall into temptation. The spirit is willing, but the body is weak" (Matthew 26:41). It's still true.

Intimacy with God does not come after attending church for an hour on Sunday or by flinging a prayer toward heaven, just as a basketball player hurls a ball toward the hoop, hoping to win the game in the last three seconds of play. Intimacy is based on a relationship sustained through communication. We call it prayer. Find out about prayer. It will change your life, your attitude, and your relationship with God.

Resource reading: Matthew 26:36-45

An Inside Connection

If you remain in me and my words remain in you, ask whatever you wish, and it will be given you.

JOHN 15:7

Insight: Because you are God's child, you have an inside connection with the Father—24 hours a day, 7 days a week.

When Gabriel Otero was in a government office in Argentina waiting his turn, another person, who had arrived substantially after him, was immediately processed. Gabriel protested that he had been there first, but he was told that the other person had a letter from the Pope. The government worker explained, "He has a connection we must honor!"

As Gabriel related that incident, I thought of a time when John F. Kennedy was president. Cuba had pointed its armed Russian missiles at the United States. The situation was tense; reporters were being briefed in the Oval Office. Slowly a side door opened, and a four-year-old boy walked into the room. The conference stopped because that lad had an honored connection—he was the son of the President.

Have you ever wished that you had an inside connection with God, a relationship that has to be honored? You have one, provided you have become a child of God through faith in Jesus Christ.

In the Upper Room, immediately before He faced the cross, Jesus told the disciples, "If you remain in me and my words remain in you, ask whatever you wish, and it will be given you" (John 15:7). That's a connection that must be honored!

Have you ever asked yourself why God should honor your prayers? Because you are a nice person? Because you are a good deal better than your neighbor or the people in your office? No! There is but one reason: a connection that must be honored. You are a child of God, adopted into the family as the result of faith in Jesus Christ. How do I know that? Scripture tell us this very clearly—in Galatians 4:6, Paul writes, "Because you are sons, God sent the Spirit of his Son into our hearts, the Spirit who calls out, 'Abba, Father.'" He has become your daddy or papa, and you have an inside connection!

Does God pay that much attention to the needs of His children? Do we truly have an inside connection, or is God rather indifferent to the needs of His children here on Earth? How do we explain why some people pray and nothing seems to happen?

Two options are open to us:

1. We can assume God is either uninterested or not powerful enough to meet us; or
2. We can assume we do have an inside connection, but have not taken advantage of it.

As we mature, we may come to see a third option: We can assume that God is waiting, in His perfect timing, to answer our request. But too often that third option is overlooked as we strive to solve our own problems and fail to lay them at the feet of the Father, crying out for Him to help us. Long ago, James wrote, "You want something but don't get it. You kill and covet, but you cannot have what you want. You quarrel and fight. You do not have, because you do not ask God. When you ask, you do not receive, because you ask with wrong motives" (James 4:2-3).

Friend, you have an inside connection with God as a result of what Jesus Christ did. His death makes it possible for us to come to the Father in the name of Jesus. Jesus said, "I am the way and the truth and the life. No one comes to the Father except through me" (John 14:6).

The next time you are standing in the line of doubt and concern, wondering if God really hears and answers prayer, remember, you have an inside connection with Abba Father, one that must be honored. Don't forget it.

Resource reading: John 14:15-31

The Seven Wonders of Prayer

Let us then approach the throne of grace with confidence, so that we may receive mercy and find grace to help us in our time of need.
HEBREWS 4:16

Insight: Prayer is one key to spiritual development and growth, one you should readily embrace, rather than one you should be driven to by great needs.

You have probably heard of the Seven Wonders of the Ancient World: the Great Pyramid of Giza in Egypt, built a thousand years before baby Moses floated on the Nile; the Hanging Gardens of Babylon; the great Temple of Diana in the city of Ephesus; the Statue of Jupiter on the Parthenon of Athens; the Mausoleum at Halicarnassus, on the Aegean Sea; the Colossus at Rhodes; and the great Lighthouse of Alexandria (the Pharos Lighthouse).

Many years ago, Dr. Henry Frost suggested that there are Seven Wonders of Prayer, no less outstanding than the Seven Wonders of the Ancient World. Let's look at what he identified.

Wonder 1: You as a mortal can approach this great God in prayer. Until World War 2 was over, Japanese people had never heard the voice of their emperor. They would never have considered standing and boldly speaking to him. Yet God said, "Call to me and I will answer you and tell you great and unsearchable things you do not know" (Jeremiah 33:3).

Wonder 2: You may address God with simplicity in ordinary conversation. In many languages, there are levels of intimacy and formality. To speak to your superior as you would your best friend would be insulting and demeaning, yet God's Son encourages us to come to Him saying, "Our Father who is in heaven," and to tell Him of our needs, wants, and wishes.

Wonder 3: You can pray for definite needs—without using religious verbiage when you pray. The thief on the cross knew exactly what he wanted and voiced it. "Lord," he cried, "remember me when You come into Your kingdom!" The old spiritual gives us this model: "Not my father, not my mother, but it's me, O Lord, standing in the need of prayer." In the same way, the thief voiced a specific and personal request.

Wonder 4: You can pray anywhere. Anywhere? Not just in the temple or a church or a place of religious worship? Paul wrote to Timothy and said, "I want men everywhere to lift up holy hands in prayer, without anger or disputing" (1 Timothy 2:8). Some pray in prison. Paul was in a dungeon when he prayed. Some pray in their closet, some as they drive to work, some as they do housework. Prayer knows no distance; thus, I can pray for a friend in the Philippines or in Russia as though I were by the person's side.

Wonder 5: You can pray about everything of concern to you. Paul urged the Philippians, "Do not be anxious about anything, but in everything, by prayer and petition, with thanksgiving, present your requests to God" (Philippians 4:6). Personally, this wonder greatly encourages me. *Everything* is all inclusive—little things, big things, irritations, celebrations. Whatever I do, whatever consumes my interest, is fodder for prayer.

Wonder 6: You can be in constant touch with God through prayer. That's the force of 1 Thessalonians 5:17, which says simply, "Pray continually!" You can maintain an awareness of God, the realization that He is as close as your sigh: "Lord, what do I do now?" As a friend explains it, never close the circuit by saying, "Amen!"—by which we mean, "I'll be back next Sunday, God. Until then, bye!"

Wonder 7: You may pray with boldness and confidence. Hebrews 4:16 says, "Let us then approach the throne of grace with confidence, so that we may receive mercy and find grace to help us in our time of need." The King James text says, "Let us therefore come boldly." Answered prayer is based on the relationships of children with their Father, and because of that, we may cry, "Abba, Father!"

The Seven Wonders of the Ancient World are awesome and marvelous, but of greater awe and wonder is the fact we can touch God through prayer.

Resource reading: John 17

Be Careful What You Pray For

Do not be anxious about anything, but in everything, by prayer and petition, with thanksgiving, present your requests to God.
PHILIPPIANS 4:6

Insight: Praying with the right motive—with selflessness—is one of the secrets of answered prayer.

"You had better be careful what you pray for," said Dan Plies, a man who served as a hospital chaplain for many years and in the process talked to thousands of people. Why did he say this? "Because God may well give it to you." His caution, though, did not develop from talking and praying with people at their bedsides. It came through an experience in his personal life. Chaplain Plies, who continued to pray and encourage people well into his mid-nineties, never lost his smile or positive demeanor. He was a godly man who lived what he believed. Well into his nineties, he informed me he was praying that he might know the Lord better! He was expecting a personal entrance to the eternal home Jesus prepared for him, and he wanted to get to know his host even better before he arrived there.

Paul's stated goal in life, for which we can assume he prayed intensely, was "that I may know him, and the power of his resurrection, and the fellowship of his sufferings, being made conformable unto his death" (Philippians 3:10 KJV). So what happened? After he began seeking to know the Lord better, his health began failing. Intense suffering confronted him. His world began falling apart. Yes, he got to know the Lord better, and no, he would not change his prayer for a moment.

It is amazing how some things happen only by our going through difficult times. The result is produced just as the pearl is produced from a speck of sand or an irritation in an oyster. The sweet fragrance of rose perfume results from crushing the rose, and the beauty of a sunset comes only because of the clouds in the sky.

Is it legitimate to pray about *anything?* There are two occasions when prayer just doesn't seem to work for me: when I go fishing and ask the Lord to let me catch a big one, and when I play golf and ask the Lord to let me make a difficult shot. Now, if my family were really hungry, I could pray for fish and the prayer would fall into a completely different category—that of need. I would remind the Lord that He Himself told us to pray about our daily bread. But to pray to catch a fish simply because I would like a bit of excitement—no, that does not seem to connect.

I am thinking of a businessman, a relatively new Christian, who came to me and said, "Prayer doesn't work!" Surprised, I began asking him why he felt that way. The short answer is that he had been praying for a million dollars! If God chose to answer prayer for unneeded money, a better golf or tennis game, more beauty, strength, or intelligence (without studying), every church in the world would be packed with people wanting to sign up for this "pray and get whatever you want" package.

James, the half-brother of Jesus, wrote, "When you ask, you do not receive, because you ask with wrong motives, that you may spend what you get on your pleasures" (James 4:3). From the beginning of the church, people have been confused about what to ask for. "Don't worry about anything; instead, pray about everything; tell God your needs, and don't forget to thank him for his answers," says a paraphrase of Philippians 4:6.

How should you pray? Jesus Himself gave us an example: Pray according to the will of the Father. Does this mean you will receive everything you want? Not at all. But when you delight in God and your desire is to do His will, He will delight in answering your prayer His way, which is always best. As Hudson Taylor, the missionary to China, put it, "God always gives His best to those who leave the choice to Him."

Resource reading: Philippians 4:1-9

There Is Healing Today

He was pierced for our transgressions, he was crushed for our iniquities; the punishment that brought us peace was upon him, and by his wounds we are healed.

ISAIAH 53:5

Insight: God is concerned about you, *all* of you—body, soul, and spirit—not just saving your soul so you can get into heaven.

We were in a village church in southern China that was overflowing with people—farmers, students, housewives, and small-business owners (a newly emerging class in China). "How do you account for the growth of your church?" I asked a pastor.

It started with a four-year-old girl, he related, who was in the hospital at the point of death. Doctors could not do anything to help her, and it would be merely a matter of hours until the sad wail of mourning would be heard. "I went to the parents," he told me, "and asked them if I could go to the hospital and pray for her."

"Yes, yes," they exclaimed, grasping at any straw of hope, though they were not Christians. They were involved in what he described as a kind of satanic cult.

The pastor went to the hospital and prayed for the little girl, who was immediately healed. Word spread like wildfire. This little girl, destined to die, was restored perfectly whole. The pastor further related, "Her mother and father, her grandparents, aunts and uncles, neighbors and friends, half of the people in our church came to faith in Christ as the result of what happened."

"Ah," some people might say with a bit of disbelief, "that was in China!" We live in the Western world where hospitals are equipped with gleaming stainless steel and the latest technology, and doctors are trained in the art of healing the sick, prescribing "miracle medicines," and applying the latest techniques medical science has to offer.

Has the church gone out of the healing ministry in the West and been replaced by science and technology? Many, myself included, thank God for the healing and help the medical profession has brought, yet believe that *God would do more* if we only believed Him to exercise His power. They read the Gospels and see how Jesus healed people and wonder why He cannot do it where they are if He yet manifests His power as He does in China.

The early church believed in physical and emotional healing that often worked in tandem with each other. Read through the New Testament book of James and notice that an expiration date was not placed on the biblical mandate a sick world needs:

> Is any one of you sick? He should call the elders of the church to pray over him and anoint him with oil in the name of the Lord. And the prayer offered in faith will make the sick person well; the Lord will raise him up. If he has sinned, he will be forgiven (James 5:14-15).

Why is this done so seldom today? Awkwardness and fear and unbelief? Perhaps we are concerned we will be identified with the fringe group that handles snakes and runs healing services like performers at a circus. Or, lacking the confidence that anything will really happen, we take the easy way out, talking about how God has indeed blessed us today with medical science through whom He heals humanity (which, of course, is true).

The Reformers also believed in restoration and healing. When Martin Luther's friend and associate Philipp Melanchthon was dying of an illness, Luther prayed for him and commanded, "Give no place to the spirit of sorrow, and be not your own murderer, but trust in the Lord." Melanchthon recovered within two days!

"Healing," says Charles Farr, whose ministry has touched the lives of thousands of hurting people, "is any sign of God's kingdom in a person's life—not necessarily an answer to every medical or physical need. Healing in Scripture does not refer to becoming as you were; it is becoming what you should be."[10]

Healing lives should never be the focal point of worship, but following the proclamation and teaching of the Word, healing of all kinds should take place in the lives of hurting, broken, suffering people who have been ignorant that God heals the brokenhearted. He is still the medicine for the pain and suffering inflicted by our wounds today.

Resource reading: Isaiah 53

Has God's Prescription Expired?

He himself bore our sins in his body on the tree, so that we might die to sins and live for righteousness; by his wounds you have been healed.

1 Peter 2:24

Insight: There is healing for the brokenhearted, God's grace and healing for the sick, and restoration for the shattered. It's all part of what Jesus' ministry is about.

Does God still heal people today? Are there real situations that cannot be explained in psychosomatic terms or hocus-pocus make-believe ways? Medical science is coming to understand that prayer for the sick and dying does make a difference. Several carefully documented studies now prove this, studies that include situations in which the individual who is sick does not even know people are praying for him or her.

Reacting to abuses and fearing that they may be identified with the questionable fringe, godly men who are capable preachers and teachers often avoid the restoration ministry of the gospel, which includes physical and emotional healing. Those who are physically sick are only a small regiment of the vast army of hurting people who have been wounded by the effects of sin today—all of whom need health and healing of one type or another.

The New Testament tells us we are to be holy as God is, for without holiness no man will see God (Hebrews 12:14). Our English word *holy* comes from an Anglo-Saxon word—*hal,* or *halig*—meaning "whole or complete." Jesus had far more in mind when He started His ministry than emptying the sickbeds of those who came to hear Him.

He began His ministry quoting Isaiah 61: "He has sent me to bind up the brokenhearted, to proclaim freedom for the captives and release from darkness for the prisoners" (Isaiah 61:1). And what does that include? The brokenness of our lives today includes marriages torn apart by infidelity, the pain of bad memories that haunt and create turmoil, the loss of decency and morality, the guilt and trauma of childhood abuses, and a vast number of other symptoms that need healing.

The good news of the gospel is that the great, awesome God cares about you and your peace of mind and wants to bring wholeness and healing to your mind and soul as well as your body.

There is liberation for the person held captive by drugs, sexual abuse, and pornography. There is help for the woman whose self-image is trashed because she sold her virginity for the price of a good time. There is hope for the senior who fears facing God with unresolved issues that play like movie clips in the mind when sleep is elusive.

God's healing touch is the answer to our brokenness and pain. This good news, the announcement Jesus made long ago, needs to be more widely shared: There is healing for the brokenhearted, health for the sick, and restoration for the shattered. No religion, no institution in the entire world offers all these.

Those works of healing are part of the gospel of Jesus Christ and the extension of the work He came to do, working through our hands and speaking through our mouths today. It's all part of the good news.

Resource reading: 1 Peter 2:23-25

The God Who Still Heals

News about him spread all over Syria, and people brought to him all who were ill with various diseases, those suffering severe pain, the demon-possessed, those having seizures, and the paralyzed, and he healed them.

MATTHEW 4:24

Insight: Jesus Christ is the same yesterday, today, and forever, which means He is not limited by strange-sounding diseases with names you cannot spell or difficult situations for which there seems to be no cure.

Some seven centuries before Christ ever touched a sick person or commanded a lame man to walk, Isaiah said, "He was wounded for our transgressions, He was bruised for our iniquities; the chastisement for our peace was upon Him, and by His stripes we are healed" (Isaiah 53:5 NKJV). Earlier the psalmist wrote, "He heals the brokenhearted and binds up their wounds" (Psalm 147:3).

If ever a generation needed wholeness and healing, it is ours. Broken hearts, fractured relationships, the inability to live at peace with neighbors and ourselves—all have left us hurting, estranged, and troubled. None would deny we need healing, and the good news is that God has never turned His back on the suffering world.

Healing—which may be emotional, physical, or spiritual—is all part of what Jesus Christ came to bring. He made that clear: "He has sent me to bind up the brokenhearted." He healed without considering how serious the situation was. He did not differentiate between emotional and physical sicknesses, because they are often intertwined. He never considered race, position, or social status when there was a need. The influential and wealthy were accorded no more attention than the destitute and poverty-stricken.

He spoke as one who has absolute authority over disease. In healing the man born blind, Jesus made it clear that sickness is not the result of personal failure or sin. It is the result of the curse that came when Adam turned His back on God's plan and purpose for humankind.

Healing does not mean being as you once were, but rather being able to function as you are with wholeness and wellness, being able to cope where you are. In some cases, it means the complete removal of a physical affliction. In other cases it means you taste the grace of God in such wonderful ways that you are able to function with joy and gladness.

The apostle Paul saw the miraculous in his ministry. One time he spoke late into the night. A lad by the name of Eutychus fell asleep in a third-floor window and toppled out to his death in the courtyard below. Paul threw himself on the youth, and the young man was restored completely whole. In contrast, however, God chose not to remove Paul's thorn in the flesh but gave him grace to cope with it.

I have known individuals who were so emotionally wounded that they were curled up in a fetal position, withdrawn and prepared to die, when God healed and restored them. I have also seen more than a few whose cancers disappeared and others whose blind eyes had their sight restored. These things could never have just happened. They demonstrate how God takes over when medical science is impotent.

Do we need an awakening to the realization that the same simple faith that received Jesus' touch when He was on earth is sufficient today? It is sufficient to bring the touch of His hand to those living in high-rise complexes as well as those who live in squatters' shacks with no electricity or running water.

God is still *Jehovah Rapha,* the God who heals, as the Almighty chose to reveal Himself to Moses long ago. An unchanging God still has compassion for the needs of those who hurt. He still feels your pain. You can experience His healing touch personally.

Resource reading: Matthew 4:23-25

When You Need Healing

A woman who had been subject to bleeding for twelve years came up behind him and touched the edge of his cloak. She said to herself, "If I only touch his cloak, I will be healed."

MATTHEW 9:20-21

Insight: God still takes note of your tears, your broken heart, and your sincere cry, and He is still powerful enough to save and heal.

When a man turned his face to the wall and wept bitterly, knowing that the angel of death was hovering over him, God sent Isaiah to him with the message, "I have heard your prayers and seen your tears; I will add fifteen years to your life" (Isaiah 38:5). Thus King Hezekiah did not die of his illness.

Why God chooses to heal some and allow others to suffer is something that we will never fully understand. For example, Amy Carmichael, a godly woman who dedicated her life to touching the hurting people of India, was injured in a fall and spent most of the last two decades of her life bedfast. One of her biographers wrote that she also "suffered from recurring bouts of anxiety and tension." Not a picture of a living saint but a flawed human being, much like all the rest of us.

This demonstrates a paradox. At times God chooses to show His power by healing some completely, taking away infirmity and giving relief from pain. At other times, He gives His grace; He touches people with His compassionate hand, and they learn to cope with their problems. But they may still walk with a limp, still face pain, and still battle depression.

Why? The only answer is that God is sovereign. Scores of people look for answers—from Philip Yancey who wrote *Where Is God When It Hurts?* to C.S. Lewis, who wrote *The Problem of Pain.* No answer really satisfies, yet the reality is that God does meet us at the point of our pain, whether by removing the thorn in our flesh or by giving grace to cope with it. What are the steps to healing we can follow?

Step 1: Realize your pain is not punishment. Pain is the result of living in a broken world. Accepting this fact is a major hurdle to overcome. Study the story of the man born blind in John 9 and notice that Jesus clearly taught that neither the man nor his parents had sinned. The man's blindness was allowed so God could be glorified—an insight that helps us focus on God rather than pain.

Step 2: Do not feed your suffering and pain by holding on to bitterness or anger. Years ago I began to see a pattern in the lives of a number of people I knew personally who were afflicted with diseases such as cancer or arthritis. All of them lived with hatred for someone. They had been mistreated, passed over for promotion, spurned by a mate, or not given the credit they deserved. Did the hatred and anger cause their pain? Perhaps not, but it certainly contributed to it. Jesus told us to forgive quickly. Do not hold in hurt and angry feelings so they do not affect our health.

Step 3: Follow the biblical pattern of James 5 by asking the elders of your church to pray for you. Prayer and healing should be two powerful means of restoration that churches use. "The prayer of faith shall save the sick," says James.

Step 4: Believe that God will honor the promises of His Word. Why is this important? God is bound by His honor to do what He has promised. He never promised to answer because of our goodness but because of His grace and favor.

Step 5: Pray in faith, according to the will of God. "According to your faith be it unto you," Jesus told blind Bartimaeus (Matthew 9:29 KJV). Even Jesus prayed according to the will of the Father, the highest form of faith.

Step 6: When you cannot see the Father's hand, trust His heart. Someday you will understand what appears to be a puzzle today. Thank God, we can find His presence and comfort as the Good Shepherd walks with us through the valley and up the other side.

Resource reading: Matthew 9:18-38

God in the Trenches with You

He said to me, "My grace is sufficient for you, for my power is made perfect in weakness."
2 CORINTHIANS 12:9

Insight: The sufficiency of God's grace is seen in His supernatural power and His comforting, sustaining presence, which take His children through deep waters.

How would you feel if you went to your clothes closet and found it empty and swept clean? Nothing is there to clothe you. How would you feel if you knocked on a friend's door, fully expecting him to welcome you in, but there was no response to your knock? How would you feel if you persistently called the office of your doctor but he never returned your call?

You would feel empty, spurned, and rejected, right?

Go one step further. What's your reaction when you pray about something and your prayer is earnest, even desperate, but you walk away in your pain, with no apparent answer, thinking your prayer went no further than the sound of your voice?

There is a perception today that most of us are not good enough to get through to God in the time of need. Perhaps a few special people do, but not the walking wounded who stumble, get up, cry out for help, and seem to never quite get it together. If you find yourself among that latter group, take heart, friend. Paul tells how he sought God three times and prayed earnestly for God to remove a "thorn" from his flesh, but it did not happen. And what was that thorn? Probably a physical affliction, perhaps an eye disorder. Whatever it was, it bothered him.

Paul had seen God demonstrate His power in the lives of others, and thus he cried out to God for himself. You can read about it in 2 Corinthians 12. How did God respond?

Paul reports, "He said to me, 'My grace is sufficient for you, for my power is made perfect in weakness'" (2 Corinthians 12:9). Stop! God had not closed the door or turned off the phone or gone deaf to Paul's cry. He answered; He promised grace for Paul's pain.

What is grace? The simplest, plainest explanation is that it means God's help, His intervention, His strength for your weakness. The next phrase, "is sufficient," gives a picture that explains it all. Paul conveys the idea of erecting a bulwark, a fortification, or an earthen dike a person can hide behind, which gives protection from an enemy.

Are you beginning to see how God's answer—which may be different from what we ask for—is real and personal? Paul gives a picture of God in the trenches with us as His grace becomes a barrier, a wall of protection, between us and our pain or difficulty.

God never promised to heal every disease, though He is the great healer. He did promise to walk with us, to never leave us or forsake us, to be our strength in times of weakness, and our companion in times of loneliness. "The LORD is close to the brokenhearted and saves those who are crushed in spirit" said David long ago (Psalm 34:18).

John Bunyan, immortalized by his allegory of the Christian life in *Pilgrim's Progress,* spent long years in prison for his faith. Of course he prayed for release, but he chose jail over compromise. Bunyan wrote, "He that is down, need fear no fall; he that is low, no pride; he that is humble ever shall have God to be his guide."

True, we all prefer deliverance from our pain, our suffering, our prisons of limitation. Yet a taste of God's grace stops indifference in its track and helps us understand that healing and help become more personal when we feel God's presence with us in the trenches, in our suffering, in our dark hour. How else can we learn what God told Paul: "My power is made perfect in weakness" (2 Corinthians 12:9)? It is still true today.

Resource reading: 2 Corinthians 12:1-10

Frustration

I think it is necessary to send back to you Epaphroditus, my brother, fellow worker and fellow soldier...For he longs for all of you and is distressed because you heard he was ill. Indeed he was ill, and almost died. But God had mercy on him.

PHILIPPIANS 2:25-27

Insight: Your attitude determines the altitude of your accomplishments. You can make it work for you or allow it to drag you to the ground.

Dear Mr. Sala,

I need help! I am thirty-four years old, and I have not accomplished...any of my goals. I attend college in the evening. I have done well in bringing up my grade standards, but I seem to come in contact with situations that I cannot control or have the faith to overcome. That is why I am writing. I am faithless. I thought I really believed in God, but I do not. I don't even believe in myself. I have listened to your Guidelines. Can you please send me help or suggest help that is real?

With great frustration...

Can you relate to that letter? Most of us can!

Frustration is something almost everybody has to cope with these days. A man wants certain vacation dates, but his wife cannot get time off. A woman misses her bus and has trouble finding a taxi, so she is late for work and has her pay docked. A young father thought he would get on top of things financially next month, but that was before he had to repair the car and take his sick child to the doctor.

We can all relate to the story about the little dog that was in a cage in the air-freight department of an airline. A dog lover heard the plaintive howling and demanded to know what was wrong. The clerk in charge said, "I don't know where the dog is going, he doesn't know where he is going, and he just chewed up the tag that tells where we were supposed to ship him."

Our greatest frustrations in life, however, are not usually mechanical. They are people-related. They involve our families and the people we work with. They relate to the goals we set for ourselves, goals that are elusive and leave us hurting. Frustrations are often caused by situations we have no control over, events we wish had not happened but did.

Let's focus on goals. Your goals should rest upon the will of God for your life. They ought to be an outgrowth of what you feel God wants you to do. But even then, you cannot eliminate frustration. Do not think for a moment that if you are spiritual enough or have enough faith or pray enough, you will never be frustrated. The pages of Scripture tell us that spiritual giants encountered great frustration.

Think with me for a minute about some of the frustrations Moses, the greatest Old Testament figure, faced. The 40 years during which Moses led the children of Israel were a study of frustration. In Numbers 20, Moses got so frustrated with the complaining and whining of the people that he cried, "Listen, you rebels, must we bring you water out of this rock?" He was angry and about to explode. We can picture Moses lifting the rod with both hands and bringing it down on the rock at Meribah. For doing this, he was reprimanded by the Lord and was not allowed into the Promised Land. In like manner, we get frustrated and angry when we cannot have what we want. And we pay a price, as Moses did.

There's a better way to handle frustration. It comes with the realization that God's will extends to the troublesome frustrations of life. When we recognize that the hand of God hovers over our lives in times of frustration as well as in times of blessing, we can then say, "God hasn't forsaken me—therefore, I will trust Him to show me the way out of my frustration." Your attitude makes all the difference.

Resource reading: Philippians 2:19-30

Even Spiritual Giants Get Frustrated

Those who live according to the sinful nature have their minds set on what that nature desires; but those who live in accordance with the Spirit have their minds set on what the Spirit desires.

ROMANS 8:5

Insight: Even spiritual giants get frustrated, are sometimes maligned, and are often persecuted. There's no reason why you should be exempt.

Frustrated? You know the irritation you feel when what you want to happen does not come together. But do you realize that even spiritual giants also face frustration? Remember Joseph, the man who fled from his master's wife when she wanted to have an affair? He ended up in big trouble, accused of sexual assault.

What about Daniel? Do you not think he was frustrated when he ended up in the lion's den? Don't you imagine that the devil must have said, "See, buddy, what serving God gets you into?"

As you study the life of Paul, you will see that frustration was also no stranger to him. Study Romans 7, where Paul says,

> It seems to be a fact of life that when I want to do what is right, I inevitably do what is wrong. I love to do God's will so far as my new nature is concerned; but there is something else deep within me, in my lower nature, that is at war with my mind and wins the fight and makes me a slave to the sin that is still within me. In my mind I want to be God's willing servant, but instead I find myself still enslaved to sin (Romans 7:21-25 TLB).

That is frustration. He was also frustrated by wanting to take action within the will of God but having his intentions thwarted. Remember what he wrote to the Thessalonians: "We wanted to come to you—certainly I, Paul, did, again and again—but Satan stopped us (1 Thessalonians 2:18).

How do we respond to frustration? First, we feel anger. We can fight. That was Moses' response to frustration, and it cost him, as it usually does with us. Perhaps you want to engage in certain activities you believe you ought to be able to do, but your supervisor puts you in a neat little box and says "No!" You can stay there until you retire, but you do not want to shuffle papers for the rest of your days. You are tempted to tell off your boss. Expressing anger is seldom the right solution to frustration.

Another option is flight. You can quit. You can walk out. You can pack up and go. Essentially that was what Jonah did when God said, "I want you to go to Nineveh and proclaim the gospel." Jonah did not want to go. His frustration turned to anger. He could not fight God—his arm was too short—so he ran. Walking away from our problems, running away, is not the answer.

Another negative response to frustration is to anesthetize the pain with drugs or alcohol. This only creates more pain and never eliminates the frustration.

But there is one more thing we need to realize. We tend to think we are strictly on our own, that God is either uninterested or else too busy to care about our frustrations. Nothing is further from the truth. He does know and He does care. That is good news!

Make a conscious decision to bring your frustrations to God. On occasion God changes the frustrating situation; and on occasion He changes us so we can cope with it. When we reach out to Him, we experience His grace which is the answer to our need.

Resource reading: Philippians 3:1-11

Frustration and God's Child

Forgetting what is behind and straining toward what is ahead, I press on toward the goal to win the prize for which God has called me heavenward in Christ Jesus.

PHILIPPIANS 3:13-14

Insight: When we pursue goals but can't achieve them, we have to reassess our desires or face frustration. In the midst of such times, you must determine what is God's will and what is yours.

Frustration is no stranger to the child of God. Believers live in a world of broken pieces, late buses, and unbalanced budgets, just the same as the atheist. Let's go back to the source of much of our frustration—goals that are not reached, accomplishments that are not realized, and expectations that are not met.

For the believer, goals and objectives should rest upon the will of God, what God wants us to accomplish. Bringing goals and objectives into line with the will of God can eliminate much frustration.

Guideline 1: Reassess your goals. It may be that you are trying to do something God does not want you to do, and your frustration is the result of fighting against His gentle hand that stops you. Do not expect God to block everything you try to do that is wrong. Natural laws that are violated usually result in natural consequences. Prayer will not eliminate an unwanted pregnancy the morning after or the hangover of a drinking binge. Sometimes our goals are wrong. Frustration should be a red flag that says, *Whoa! I need to reassess where I am headed.*

Guideline 2: Remove the source of your frustration if you can. Obviously, this is not possible every time. Say, for example, you have an old car that keeps breaking down and you keep thinking, *This time we will have it fixed right.* Eventually there is a breaking point, and it may be you instead of your car. The problem with this guideline is that it's difficult to apply when the source of frustration is a person. You cannot trade in your brother-in-law for a new model, so there has to be another alternative.

Guideline 3: Realize God is sovereign. At some point we need God's grace to accept what we cannot change. If you are God's child you must realize that He has the means to override your puny ambitions and give you the grace to cope with frustration. If we could see life from God's perspective, how different our understanding would be. In Ephesians 1:11 Paul says that God "works out everything in conformity with the purpose of his will." Either you believe that truth and find peace, or you struggle with frustration.

Guideline 4: Bring your frustration to the Lord and lay it at His feet. In the previous chapter we talked about Paul's thorn in the flesh and the frustration he experienced, which drove him to his knees. This is but one of numerous times in his life when his plans were thwarted. God closed a door. Paul and his friends prayed. Then frustration dissipated as another opportunity opened.

On his second missionary journey, Paul and Silas sought to go east into Bithynia, which would have taken them into what we know as Russia today. But Luke reported that the Spirit of Jesus would not allow them to go. A closed door. And the result was frustration. In the night Paul had a vision in which God redirected them to Greece. Your frustration may be the result of having goals that are at cross-purposes with His, and when that happens the only thing to do is to bring your frustration to Him and ask for His direction.

Guideline 5: Overcome your frustration by praising and trusting God in the midst of a trial or difficulty. There can be a triumph that breaks through frustration. Paul writes about it in 2 Corinthians 2:14: "Thanks be to God, who always leads us in triumphal procession in Christ." This is why Paul and Silas could sing in prison with their backs raw and bleeding from the beating they had received. It was why John could rejoice from prison and see the vision of heaven's glory. Now we see through a glass darkly. With spiritual vision we see beyond the frustration that whips so many of us. Praise is the ultimate solution.

Resource reading: Philippians 3:12-21

Remember Lot's Wife

When he hesitated, the men grasped his hand and the hands of his wife and of his two daughters and led them safely out of the city, for the LORD was merciful to them. As soon as they had brought them out, one of them said, "Flee for your lives! Don't look back."

GENESIS 19:16-17

Insight: When you are frustrated, try to remember that there is an end to every earthly circumstance—eventually. Also, remember the motto: "Don't sweat the small stuff. It's all small stuff!"

Almost every youngster who goes to Sunday school remembers that Lot's wife looked back and turned into a pillar of salt. "That's nothing," said one motivated lad, "my grandma looked back and turned into a telephone pole." Yet Jesus made a reference to this woman, whose life was taken in a judgment that leaves a lot unsaid. The context is found in a discussion Jesus had with His disciples about the end times and how God would eventually send judgment upon a world that rejected His offer of life.

He spoke but three words: "Remember Lot's wife" (Luke 17:32). He did not elaborate or go into detail. He alluded to a woman who had lived more than 2000 years earlier, yet her memory was so imbedded in the minds of those who listened that to make a point all He had to do was to say, "Remember Lot's wife."

Who was this woman? Why did the lightning of judgment strike her? What do we learn from her that relates to life in the twenty-first century?

When Moses recorded the drama, he identified her as being the wife of Abraham's nephew, whose name was Lot. This man had left Haran with Abraham and his entourage. They had walked hundreds of miles together. They were family. They sat by the campfire at night and looked up at the stars and talked and joked together. Once they entered into the land that we know as Israel today, God blessed them. Their flocks and herds grew.

Finally there was not enough pasture and water for the flocks of both Abraham and Lot. Being the peacemaker that he was, Abraham said, "Lot, take your choice. If you go left, I'll go right. I want no conflict between us."

That was when Lot looked toward the fertile Jordan Valley and chose the green pastures near Sodom, probably at the southern end of the Dead Sea. There he prospered, but there he also faced the dilemma confronting parents today: "How do you raise godly kids in a depraved, ungodly world?" Even today the name *Sodom* is tainted by the practice that derived its name from the sexual sins rampant there.

God is patient, but there is an end to His patience. Eventually, God sent two angelic messengers to command Lot and his family to leave. The message was simple: "Flee for your lives! Don't look back, and don't stop anywhere in the plain!" The record tells us that as they were fleeing, Lot's wife looked back. "Surely one last fleeting glance can't matter." But it did, and she faced the consequence of her failure—death.

What does this account teach us today? In the context of what Jesus was saying, it is a sober reminder that we must maintain a loose attachment to the things that seem so important to us here—homes, cars, jewelry, and other possessions. Relationships are more important than things.

A second lesson is that a divided heart can never please God. Remember, Jesus also said that no person can serve both God and "mammon." Corrie ten Boom used to say that we ought to hold our possessions loosely, because it hurts too much when God pries them out of our hands.

Without more space available to develop this truth, Jesus' three pungent words, "Remember Lot's wife," tell us that God means what He says. He never says, "Well, we'll forget about it this time, but next time I really mean it."

If Lot's wife could only have seen that God was preserving them and protecting them from the judgment about to fall on Sodom, she would have been focused solely on escape. The bottom line is this: Never look back. Never, never, never!

Resource reading: Genesis 19

Letting Go

One thing I do: Forgetting what is behind and straining toward what is ahead, I press on toward the goal to win the prize for which God has called me heavenward in Christ Jesus.

PHILIPPIANS 3:13-14

Insight: If you cannot let go, you can never get on with your life to discover that beyond the dark night is the rising of the sun...and to know that God will take your hand and walk with you into the unknown.

Letting go is never easy. We love the familiar, the warm and comfortable, and the known. The leap into the dark unknown, the uncertainty of what is out there that you cannot see and cannot comprehend, makes the future seem dark, foreboding, and fearful. The budding high-wire artist has to overcome fear of failure, of falling, of danger; otherwise, he or she never makes it to the big time. Picture the trapeze artist, poised and ready to take the big leap. She swings into space, but at some point, she has to let go of one bar to reach and stretch toward the other freely swinging bar.

Letting go is never easy. We sometimes feel rejection when people close to us let go and move on. Picture the mother taking the hand of her little child to school for the first day. She knows her child must go to school, but if the youngster sees other children and gladly runs laughing to the playground, the mother turns away feeling depressed and dejected. She loves the feel of that warm little hand reaching toward her larger, stronger one.

The day my eyes misted was when we saw our firstborn daughter off to college. We were delighted she had graduated valedictorian of her high school class and had been accepted to the school of her choice on a scholarship, but when she walked down the jet way to the plane, we crossed a bridge I didn't like.

Letting go is never easy. For many, the difficult time to let go is when your daughter walks down the aisle with eyes glistening, focused on a young man who has stolen her heart. You say you have gained a son, but you honestly feel like you have lost your daughter. The reality is that many parents never do let go, thereby handicapping their newly married children. Remember, God's plan is for children to leave their parents and to be joined to their spouses in such a way that two become one. Apart from the leaving, there can be no cleaving. A threesome—a bride, a groom, and a parent-in-law—never makes a successful marriage.

Letting go is never easy. One of the most difficult acts of letting go I ever witnessed was when a husband of 50 years, with misted eyes, looked longingly at the photo of his wife and said goodbye until he would join her on heaven's shore.

When a ship sails toward the horizon, the person standing on shore sees the mast slowly become shorter and shorter until it finally disappears. "There she goes," he nostalgically says. But when the person beyond the horizon looks from the other direction at the approaching ship, she says, "Here she comes!" That is why, when it comes to losing someone we love—someone anchored to Jesus Christ—we never have to say, "We lost her." Rather we can be assured that our loss has become heaven's gain.

Letting go is never easy. When Paul wrote to the Philippians, he explained that he sought "to take hold of that for which Christ Jesus took hold" of him. In other words, he believed God had a purpose for his life, a will in all the difficulties and challenges he faced. Then he said, "Forgetting what is behind and straining toward what is ahead, I press on toward the goal to win the prize for which God has called me heavenward in Christ Jesus" (Philippians 3:13-14).

Letting go is never easy, but to go on, it's got to be done.

Resource reading: Philippians 3:12-21

The Blindness of Hatred

This is to fulfill what is written in their Law: "They hated me without reason."
John 15:25

Insight: The DNA of hatred can only be broken by the grace of God, following the example of the One who cried, "Father, forgive them, for they know not what they do."

"As long as the Arabs hate us more than they love their children," said Golda Meir, "there will be war." The schoolteacher-turned-politician was a tough lady who saw plenty of hatred-driven conflict in her life. But could not an Arab living on the East Bank of the Jordan have said the same thing of the Jews? There's a deeper question, however: Was she right? Is hating your enemy more important than seeing your children grow up, marry, and have a family?

Hatred comes with a high price attached to it. There is no logic to a hatred that makes a person willing to die for a cause while bringing suffering and perhaps death to another—especially a faceless person who has done no harm to the perpetrator. The object of hatred is "guilty" only for being of a different race, religion, or political creed.

While there is a trail of blood reaching back 4000 years marking the hatred between Jews and Arabs, the reality is that this hatred goes back to the first family, when Cain killed his brother Abel. In that conflict we see the DNA of hatred, which still destroys people today.

After Adam and Eve were driven from the garden, two sons were born. Here's the story of the brothers as recorded in Genesis 4:2-9:

> Now Abel kept flocks, and Cain worked the soil. In the course of time Cain brought some of the fruits of the soil as an offering to the Lord. But Abel brought fat portions from some of the firstborn of his flock. The Lord looked with favor on Abel and his offering, but on Cain and his offering he did not look with favor. So Cain was very angry, and his face was downcast.
>
> Then the Lord said to Cain, "Why are you angry? Why

> is your face downcast? If you do what is right, will you not be accepted? But if you do not do what is right, sin is crouching at your door; it desires to have you, but you must master it."
>
> Now Cain said to his brother Abel, "Let's go out to the field." And while they were in the field, Cain attacked his brother Abel and killed him.
>
> Then the LORD said to Cain, "Where is your brother Abel?"
>
> "I don't know," he replied. "Am I my brother's keeper?"

In the paradigm of this hatred-driven murder, we see the problem of irrational hatred today. People hate people who believe differently, people who have more or better possessions, people who seem to be smarter or richer, and people who look or dress differently.

Cain's hatred for his brother, Abel, began with intense jealousy. God had accepted his brother's sacrifice and rejected Cain's sacrifice. Reading between the lines, we have to conclude it was attitude more than substance that God rejected.

God assessed the attitude of Cain's heart, saying, "Sin is crouching at your door." Jealousy turns to hatred, which comes through the door of a person's heart and takes up residence, eventually blinding the person who has left the door ajar. Whenever we allow jealousy to breed, a blindness follows that destroys logic and justice.

Eventually, Cain's jealously grew so irrational that he invited his brother to walk with him in the field and killed him there. Later, casting aside personal responsibility or accountability, Cain asked God, "Am I my brother's keeper?" The reality is that we *are* our brother's keeper. As such, tolerating hatred becomes a disease, a sin, and a blindness that must be recognized as an evil and rooted from our thinking.

Resource reading: Genesis 4

Whom Then Can I Hate?

The king of Israel answered Jehoshaphat, "There is still one man through whom we can inquire of the LORD, but I hate him because he never prophesies anything good about me, but always bad."

2 CHRONICLES 18:7

Insight: Both hatred and love are irrational to those who are on opposite sides of an issue.

In a crowded international airport, I sat next to a young couple with a baby about six months old. I smiled at the baby, and he smiled back. He babbled in a language discernable only to other six-month-old babies, God, and his mother. I made faces, and he laughed.

The atmosphere in the airport was rather tense. People looked at each other through cautious "I don't know if you can be trusted" eyes—but not the baby. This little fellow was not born with distrust or dislike in his heart for people whose race, religion, or culture is different from him and his family—yet I am amazed how quickly children learn how to dislike, even to hate.

At another time, I was on a flight that had originated in a former Soviet country. Across the aisle from me was a mother with a child about four years old. I love kids. If they could run the world for a while, it would probably be a safer place than it is now. A couple of times on the flight, I poked my head inside the newspaper, playing peek-a-boo with the little kid who laughed each time. No words were spoken. I only smiled and made the child smile.

When the flight landed and the passengers were waiting for their luggage, the little child, seeing me, broke loose from his mother and ran over to give my legs a big hug. The mother, of course, dashed after the boy, grabbing him and saying in broken English, "This is America. You can't trust people here!"

I understand we live in a world where not all strangers can be trusted. But there's a larger issue than teaching our children to be safe: I marvel at how we also endow them with our prejudices, our dislikes, and eventually our hates.

Who teaches a child to hate? Not God. Jesus, breaking with conventional wisdom, culture, and centuries of practice, said, "I tell you who hear me: Love your enemies, do good to those who hate you" (Luke 6:27). The legacy of hate passed from generation to generation is not easily broken, but it can be—one generation at a time, one child at a time.

If you are a parent, ask yourself, "Whom and what do I hate? And why do I hold these feelings?" Be completely honest. Have you judged an entire race by one bad experience with someone, perhaps during your childhood? Did you happen to grow up in a neighborhood where you hated the folks who lived across the tracks or across town, the ones who went to a different school or who attended a different house of worship than you?

An important issue to think through if you are a Christian mom or dad is this: What does God hate? In the Bible, you find the expression "I hate" 16 times, used of situations or issues God hates. The reality is that God hates sin, yet He loves the sinner.

After you answer that question, ask yourself, *Are my likes and dislikes in accord with how He feels?* Our failure is that we often hate the sinner and secretly embrace the sin, which is repugnant and wrong in God's sight.

Once you have taken inventory of your own failures, ask, "Have I taught my child to hate?" I suppose grandfathers who make fussy kids smile on a long airplane ride are safe enough, but the nationality stamps on our passports made the woman and me suspicious of each other and kept us from looking at the person behind the smile.

May God forgive us of our prejudices that our sinful natures fuel, and that feed the fire of hatred from generation to generation.

Resource reading: Psalm 45

The Curse of Hating Those We Dislike

They that hate me without a cause are more than the hairs of mine head: they that would destroy me, being mine enemies wrongfully, are mighty: then I restored that which I took not away.

PSALM 69:4 KJV

Insight: We all seem certain that what has happened to us—things from the past we cannot forget or forgive—justifies our dislikes...which are, we think, totally different from the blind prejudices we condemn in others.

I was 12 years old and in the sixth grade when I first tasted the bitter dregs of hatred. My last name is spelled S-A-L-A, and another boy in my gym class at Thatcher Elementary School was a kid named Frank whose surname was close enough to mine that he stood next to me when we lined up alphabetically for roll call in phys ed.

Now Frank was no ordinary kid. Having no mother or father, he had been placed in a state home, where kids survived by their brawn. There the meanest kid was boss. The problem was, Frank brought all of his pent-up meanness to school with him and bullied everybody in his path. In a matter of days I decided that I disliked not only this kid but everyone who shared his ethnic heritage.

I gradually began thinking, *Everybody of Frank's ethnicity must be as mean as Frank.* How foolish; yet such is the logic of hatred. I had to unlearn this thinking later as God worked in my heart.

Though some have disputed the story, it is said that a student named Adolf Hitler was walking down the street in Vienna, when a rabbi dressed in black with long side curls and reading a book bumped into him, knocking him into the muddy street. Adolf got up, cursed the rabbi, and vowed that someday he would destroy every Jew. Whether the story is true or not, it is certain that his hatred for Jews, stemming from whatever irrational cause, destroyed millions of families.

In the last century, the bitter seeds of hatred took the lives of uncounted millions. Consider the purges of Stalin, which took the lives of as many as 35 million people; the Cultural Revolution of Mao Zedong, targeting any who disagreed with his ideology; the rampage of Pol Pot in Cambodia; the "ethnic cleansing" in Bosnia; and the incessant conflict between Israel and Arabs.

Following the bombing of the World Trade Center in New York, many people were shocked at the intense feelings of hatred that had driven Osama bin Laden and his cohorts to take the lives of 3000 people, leaving perhaps 5000 children orphaned. And in the days following, some American Arabs were equally surprised at the venomous hatred they experienced simply because of their ethnic background.

It is easy to say that this problem of prejudice has always been with us and that nothing can be done about it, yet ignoring the growing epidemic of hatred only fuels the fire. It can be reversed. The madness can be stopped.

In Tromsø, Norway, I sat in the home of Maren Nilsen. This talkative, smiling woman with silver hair had been a prisoner in a Nazi concentration camp. As we sat in her home and drank rich, dark coffee and snacked on sandwiches she had made, Maren told me how she had survived as a prisoner of war by stealing potato peelings from the garbage. Surely she had every reason to hate those who took her freedom and almost her life.

"Did you hate the Germans after you were released?" I asked cautiously.

She quickly replied, "No, not at all," and then added, "but we must not forget." In Maren's life, her faith in God made the difference.

He made the difference in my life as well. Only the application of the love of God and the touch of His grace can take away hatred and help us see hurting people as individuals worthy of our respect and our love. God is love, and love is the only answer to the curse of hatred. Ask God to let love take root in your heart today.

Resource reading: Matthew 5:11-16

Ridding Your Life of Hatred

You have heard that it was said, "Love your neighbor and hate your enemy." But I tell you: Love your enemies and pray for those who persecute you.

MATTHEW 5:43-44

Insight: Hatred is an emotional poison of the soul that makes you a two-time victim.

The English word *misery* comes from a Greek word that is translated "to hate." We know what hatred is, and with all due respect to what psychologists can do, I have never met a happy person whose heart was filled with hatred for someone else. A "happy hater" is a contradiction of terms.

In the Upper Room, Jesus told His disciples He would go to the cross, fulfilling the prophecy that said He would be hated without cause (John 15:25). How did Jesus respond to the venomous hatred He encountered? Did He hate those who hated Him? That's what men had done for centuries. That was accepted dogma as defined by the rabbis of His day.

Peter wrote of Jesus that, contrary to the world's norm, "when they hurled their insults at him, he did not retaliate; when he suffered, he made no threats. Instead, he entrusted himself to him who judges justly" (1 Peter 2:23).

"Yes," we say, "but I can't do that. I meet fire with fire." Of course that means both sides get burned. So what should be our response when we find that the fire of hatred has filled our souls and poisoned our thinking?

Step 1: Be honest enough to admit it when you hate someone. That's a hard first step, but it's necessary. All hatred is not wrong. You cannot love anything without hating that which would destroy it. Hating sin, hating evil in the world, hating the bitterness that tears apart relationships and families and turns fathers against sons and mothers against daughters is different from hating the person who acts with evil intent. David asked the question, "Do I not hate those who hate you, O LORD, and abhor those who rise up against you?" (Psalm 139:21).

Step 2: Analyze the reasons you hate someone. That's easy in many cases. Someone hurt you without cause. You became his victim, so you know exactly whom you hate and why. Yet, when you find it in your heart to put that person into God's hands, knowing that vengeance belongs to Him, you release the hatred that has made you a prisoner. That makes sense.

Step 3: Ask God to deal with the offender and free you from the burden of getting even. I have known some people who have lived for years, even decades, with the sole purpose of seeking revenge. Was the taste of revenge sweet when it finally came? No, like someone whose cancer had spread extensively before being cut out, the damage had been done over the years, and it was devastating.

Step 4: Pray for the person whom you hate. Difficult at best, this step works as therapy for your soul. Why? For one reason, Jesus commanded it:

> You have heard that it was said, "Love your neighbor and hate your enemy." But I tell you: Love your enemies and pray for those who persecute you, that you may be sons of your Father in heaven. He causes his sun to rise on the evil and the good, and sends rain on the righteous and the unrighteous (Matthew 5:43-45).

When you pray for an enemy, he shrinks in size. Instead of looking like a formidable Goliath who towers over you, you begin to see him as a small, misdirected, weak person who desperately needs God.

Step 5: Release your hatred. One survivor of the Nazi Holocaust told how he made the decision to leave his hatred behind when he boarded a ship for America after World War 2. He noticed that those who got on with their lives, who set new goals, who carved out a new life were the ones who refused to dwell on the injustices and misdeeds of the past. Only then could they grow and move on with life.

Resource reading: John 15

Lining Up Your Ducks of Love and Hate

Do I not hate those who hate you, O Lord, and abhor those who rise up against you?

Psalm 139:21

Insight: Loving what God loves and hating what He hates puts you on the side of righteousness and justice.

What you love and what you hate reveal a great deal about your character. Why? Because you cannot be *for* something without being *against* its opposite. For example, when you love your family, you stand in strong opposition to anything that threatens it.

Long ago the psalmist wrote, "Do I not hate those who hate you, O Lord, and abhor those who rise up against you?" (Psalm 139:21). This man hated what God hates and loved what He loves.

Surprised to learn there are things God hates? You shouldn't be. There is an old expression: "Get your ducks lined up." I'm not sure how that translates into other languages, but it translates into real life. It means you are consistent in what you love and hate. As a result, you may find yourself in the company of the minority whose voice cries out against wrong, much like John the Baptist in the wilderness.

So the question confronts us: "What does God hate?" Actually, the list of what God hates is far longer than we can consider in this brief section, but use the following as a checklist to see if you hate what God hates.

First, Proverbs 8:13 says, "To fear the Lord is to hate evil." Immediately you find yourself standing in a rather small circle, because most people today have a passive indifference to wrongdoing and evil. "It's not my fight," they say as they see these things in the world. Why oppose evil? If you don't, it can overwhelm you. Remember the familiar words of a German pastor: He wrote that the Gestapo came for the Jews, but he did not protest because he was not a Jew. Then the Gestapo came for the politicians, but he did not oppose them because he was not a politician. He continued, "When they came for me, there was no one left to oppose them."

God says, "For I, the Lord, love justice; I hate robbery and iniquity" (Isaiah 61:8). Today, passive indifference silences many who see wrongdoing—in the school, in the neighborhood, in government, on the job. We look the other way and think, *I'm not involved.* When we hate what God hates and love what He loves, we feel compelled to speak out.

In the book of Amos, there's a shocking statement. God says He hates the people's religious feasts (Amos 5:21). Surprised? God is not a killjoy who does not like a good party. He was the one who instituted the great feasts of the Old Testament, which included dancing, drinking, and celebration. What He opposed then—and now—is turning feasts into orgies and debauchery and forgetting Him.

In light of our culture, the final item is powerful. In a poignant, forceful statement God said, " 'I hate divorce...and I hate a man's covering himself with violence as well as with his garment'...So guard yourself in your spirit, and do not break faith" (Malachi 2:16). Surprised at the intensity of that statement? God is not happy with a lot of us today, who have forgotten that He is not only a loving God but also that He hates some things—at times the very things we have grown to accept.

If you get your ducks lined up with what God loves and hates, you will find the number who stand with you may be small, but you will be in the company of the Almighty Himself. It is far better to walk in the light with God than to walk in the darkness with men who trample on truth, decency, and justice. One plus God is always a majority.

Resource reading: Judges 21

I'm Sorry—Forgive Me

Be kind and...forgiving...just as in Christ God forgave you.
EPHESIANS 4:32

Insight: The four most important words to say to people you love are also the most difficult to say: "I'm sorry—forgive me."

"I'm sorry—forgive me." What other combination of so few words can bring so much healing to the world?

"I'm sorry—forgive me." These words make the difference between the malady of broken relationships and the healing that restores fragmented lives.

Edward Herbert once said, "He that cannot forgive others breaks the bridge over which he must pass himself; for every man has need to be forgiven." It seems that our pride, our refusal to admit we may have been wrong—at least partially wrong—is what makes it so difficult to say, "I'm sorry—forgive me." When you say this, you are doing a great deal more than tendering an apology. You are really saying, "I value my relationship with you, and I want to build a bridge over the troubled waters that separate us."

Our tendency to place the blame on the other person goes back as far as the genesis of man himself. Remember when Eve took of the forbidden fruit and Adam followed her example? When God asked, "Adam, why have you done this?" Adam put the blame on his wife and on God, saying, "The woman you put here with me—she gave me some fruit from the tree, and I ate it" (Genesis 3:12).

Saying "I'm sorry—forgive me" puts the blame squarely on your shoulders and tells the other person you are willing to stand the consequences of causing the separation. Of course there are many other ways you can try to build bridges. You can say, "Let's forget it," or "Let's just not talk about it anymore." You can also say, "I suppose we are both to blame." But nothing has the same healing power as "I'm sorry—forgive me."

Trying to continue a relationship without removing the bitter feelings between two people is like trying to drive a car with a flat tire. When an apology is due, it should be made as soon as possible and with dignity. A person demonstrates the nobility of a king when he sincerely apologizes and says, "I'm sorry—forgive me." A person never reaches so high as when he humbly stoops to offer an apology.

In your heart you may be saying, *I'm not altogether to blame, you know. The other person is just as guilty as I am. Why should I apologize? It is not my fault. Why should I say, "I'm sorry—forgive me"?* Perhaps you are right. Yet, are you not genuinely sorry your relationship is hurt—that someone whose friendship or love means a great deal to you is now separated from you or avoids you? Why not tell your friend just how you feel—that you are genuinely sorry your friendship has been hurt and you would like to see it restored. That confession—made in all honesty—is the equivalent of holding out the olive branch. It may be just what is necessary for the other to admit his or her part in the problem.

Years ago, the apostle Paul penned these beautiful guidelines for restoring fractured human relations: "Be kind and compassionate to one another, forgiving each other, just as in Christ God forgave you" (Ephesians 4:32). To remember is so very human; to forgive is so very divine.

When Jesus addressed the question of forgiveness, He told the fisherman Peter that we are to forgive seventy times seven (Matthew 18:22). When you think that you cannot say, "I'm sorry—forgive me," remember the words of the forlorn figure who was crucified at the hands of the Romans: "Father, forgive them, for they do not know what they are doing" (Luke 23:34). Find God's strength to say, "I'm sorry—forgive me."

Resource reading: Genesis 50:15-26

When You Cannot Forgive

Bear with each other and forgive whatever grievances you may have against one another. Forgive as the Lord forgave you.
COLOSSIANS 3:13

Insight: Forgiveness means giving up your right to hurt someone because that person hurt you.

Before Jeffrey Dahmer, the confessed killer of 17 men and boys, was sentenced to 15 consecutive life terms in prison, relatives of the victims were allowed to make statements. They told in detail how their lives and the lives of other family members had been affected by what had happened. Every person there had been hurt unalterably by what took place.

One mother began speaking quietly and deliberately, and as she continued to speak her voice got louder; and it rose in a crescendo as she cried, "I can never forgive you for what you have done." Then raging hysterically, she had to be physically restrained by deputies of the court.

Few of us could honestly say to her, "I can understand how you feel," because we have not sustained the loss she bore. Yet contrast her attitude with another parent who does understand.

This father, visibly shaken, spoke slowly but resolutely as he talked about the life of his son, one of the young men who had been maliciously murdered. Quietly but deliberately he spoke, weighing every word carefully as he said, "I can never forget what has happened, but I must forgive you. I must go on."

Corrie ten Boom understood how difficult forgiveness can be. Though she had been interned in a German concentration camp, she still wrote, "Forgiveness is not an emotion...Forgiveness is an act of the will, and the will can function regardless of the temperature of the heart."[11]

Forgiveness—this matter of giving up our right to hurt someone because of the hurt that person caused us—is never easy. But the individual who forgives is a lot further down the road toward healing and putting life together again than the person is who refuses to forgive.

It's a psychological fact: the person who can forgive is healthier and happier than the one who chooses to live with bitterness and hatred. What happens when you cannot forgive?

Result 1: Your health is affected. There is a correlation between sound emotional and physical health and your mental attitude. Repeatedly I've noticed in people I've worked with a relationship between anger and hatred and organic problems such as cancer, ulcers, hypertension, and high blood pressure. Bitterness is a cancer of the soul that erodes the body like acid.

Result 2: You live in the past. You find yourself thinking, *What if this had not happened?* or, *If only I had done things differently.* Accepting the past, no matter how painful it may be, is one of the steps necessary to face the future.

Result 3: Your spiritual life is affected. Jesus put it even more bluntly. "If you forgive men when they sin against you, your heavenly Father will also forgive you. But if you do not forgive men their sins, your Father will not forgive your sins" (Matthew 6:14-15). "I thought God would forgive anything," you say. Not according to what Jesus taught. If you want God's forgiveness, then you had better forgive your enemies. No matter how great the wrongdoing we have experienced, our failures in the sight of God are even greater. If He forgives, then we have no alternative but to learn to do the same.

Friend, forgiveness is never easy, but God can help you. Your life will be richer and healthier for it.

Resource reading: Luke 23:26-34

Forgive Them

Jesus said, "Father, forgive them, for they do not know what they are doing." And they divided up his clothes by casting lots.

LUKE 23:34

Insight: Jesus said that if we do not forgive each other, our Father in heaven will not forgive us; so if you cannot forgive, you had better live a perfect life.

Sigmund Freud, the Viennese psychiatrist who has become the guru of the profession, once said, "One must forgive one's enemies, but not before they have been hanged."[12] I couldn't help but think of those words as I conversed with a dignified, cultured woman in her seventies. She had grown up with a strong sense of loyalty instilled in her, but when someone crossed the line and betrayed her, that person became an enemy until death.

Late in life, something happened that forced her to re-examine this whole premise. Jesus Christ became real to her, and He said, "If you forgive men when they sin against you, your heavenly Father will also forgive you. But if you do not forgive men their sins, your Father will not forgive your sins" (Matthew 6:14-15). It was this last part that really got to her. "If you don't forgive other people," says Jesus, "I won't forgive you." She reasoned, "If God won't forgive me unless I forgive my enemies, I guess I had better learn how to do it."

Forgiveness not only violates our culture, but it violates nature itself. Author Philip Yancey calls it "an unnatural act." In an article by the same title he writes, "You don't find dolphins forgiving sharks for eating their playmates. It's a dog-eat-dog world out there, not dog-forgive-dog."[13]

To hold on to bitterness and hatred is easy; to release it and to extend forgiveness to enemies is not natural—it is supernatural. It takes the grace of God, but God's grace will help you forgive.

Pondering God's forgiveness helps us to understand how illogical and unnatural this whole matter of forgiveness is. Why should God think up any reasons to forgive us—people who have shaken our fists at heaven and walked away with our backs to the cross? "Father, forgive them," said Jesus, "for they know not what they do." Adds a friend of mine, "And they don't want to know, either."

Understanding we can never summon even slightly persuasive reasons as to why God should forgive us, we are stripped of any reasons why we should not forgive others. Our debts forgiven by God are far greater than the debts we must address involving spouses, neighbors, or friends. Writing to the Ephesians, Paul teaches us the new pattern of "forgiving each other, just as in Christ God forgave you" (Ephesians 4:32).

What does forgiveness do?

1. Forgiveness breaks down the door of the prison where you have been both prisoner and jailer. Bitterness has imprisoned you, and your isolation from someone with whom you once had good relations has nailed shut the door. Life is far too short to live with anger and hatred. The physical effects of bitterness shorten your life and produce deadly enzymes in your body, contributing to cancer and a host of other harmful maladies.

2. Forgiveness restores and heals broken relationships. "I'd so much like for my brother to come to my wedding," a man told his counselor.

"Well, why don't you invite him?"

"Oh, I can't do that. We haven't spoken to each other for years."

"How come?"

There was a long pause before the man said, "You know, it seems foolish, but I can't remember. Something happened, and we just drifted apart."

That drifting apart, friend, is the natural result of an unforgiving spirit. To forgive reverses the trend and brings former enemies toward each other.

3. Forgiveness also adds years to your life and health to your soul. Is that a scientific fact? It is. Make a study of individuals who have lived beyond the fourscore (80 year) mark, and you will find people who are generally at peace with themselves and have learned to forgive their enemies.

Philip Yancey is right. Forgiveness is an unnatural act, but it is one we desperately need today.

Resource reading: Psalm 68

Joseph and Forgiveness

Love your enemies, do good to them, and lend to them without expecting to get anything back. Then your reward will be great, and you will be sons of the Most High, because he is kind to the ungrateful and wicked.
LUKE 6:35

Insight: When you cannot forgive, you become both victim and perpetrator, jailer and prisoner.

Of all the endearing and compelling qualities of the Bible, none is more striking than the fact that stories were not altered to make individuals look better than they really were. (It also confirms that the hand of God moved the writers of Scripture.) Read something in the paper today, see a documentary on television, or read a comment on the Internet, and you're not at all certain someone didn't put a spin on the story to make people look better—usually much better—than they are. Often reality is vastly different from the projected image. It's the perception of truth that is written about—not truth itself.

The Bible tells it all—the sordid details of human failure...the lust that turned gentleness into savagery...the failure of individuals who were godly but forgot their calling in moments of passion, hatred, or greed.

Scripture, in Genesis, details the account of brothers whose jealousy drove them to strive to kill one of their own—their very own brother and daddy's favorite. The boy's name was Joseph. If you recall the story, a compromise was made to not kill him but sell him to slave traders who took him—probably in his late teens—to Egypt.

About a decade passed, and through a set of circumstances more bizarre than fiction, Joseph ended up being the prime minister of Egypt, second only to Pharaoh. A major famine was parching the Middle East, and Joseph's brothers came to Egypt seeking humanitarian relief.

Eventually, the brothers faced the past. Their own brother was the Egyptian prime minister, but they did not recognize him. Ten years had changed all of them. He was clean-shaven and dressed like an Egyptian. Who in their wildest imagination would have thought the scrawny kid sold for a few shekels to a bunch of slave traders would end up running Egypt? That was Joseph, and this was his moment for revenge—the hour he had lived for, right? No! Based on the account recorded by Moses, another Hebrew exiled from Egypt, Joseph had long since forgiven them.

The story is rich in insights for those who have been victims, who have lived with wrongdoing. Joseph not only forgave his brothers, but he also did them great good instead of exacting punishment or revenge. He brought down his father's entire household and gave them some of the best land in Egypt for their flocks. Furthermore, his step of forgiveness resulted in complete restoration with his family.

Forgiveness means that I give up my right to hurt you because you hurt me. It means that I can trust Him who sees the sparrow fall to take note of the wrong that has been done to me. I can trust that God, in His own time and in His own way, will deal with the one who has wronged me. It means I refuse to exact an eye for an eye lest we both end up blind.

Forgiveness practices what Jesus taught: "I tell you who hear me: Love your enemies, do good to those who hate you, bless those who curse you, pray for those who mistreat you" (Luke 6:27-28). It is the only way to healing.

There is no loneliness as great as that which results from our imprisonment brought on by anger, hatred, and the thirst for revenge. When you cannot forgive, you are victim and perpetrator, jailer and prisoner. Learn a lesson from Joseph, who rose above revenge to live in honor and fame.

Resource reading: Genesis 42–45

No Digging Allowed

As far as the east is from the west, so far has he removed our transgressions from us.
PSALM 103:12

Insight: What God has forgiven need never again be confronted.

In her book *Hope Lives Here,* my friend Janet Bly tells about driving along a desolate section of country road in central Idaho, where she encountered a sign that warned, "No Digging Allowed!" Until that moment she had not thought about anyone wanting to dig in such an out-of-the-way place. But then she wondered, *Why was the sign posted?* Were cables buried underneath? Were artifacts or gold hidden there? Were there ancient unmarked graves?

I'd like a few of those "No Digging Allowed" signs in computer code so I could plant them in the memory banks of some people I know—a kind of red screen similar to the "You have a virus" warning a software program occasionally flashes on my screen. Believe me, if I've been dozing, the red warnings bring me to immediate attention.

Why would I like some "No Digging Allowed" signs? Plenty of reasons. I'm thinking of the young pastor whose wife confided to him that she had been sexually involved with another man before she married him and before she had become a believer in Jesus Christ. Instead of closing the door on the past, he kept digging to know more. With tears she said, "I've told him everything there is to tell him, and it's ruining our marriage."

I know some folks who made bad business decisions years ago. On paper they had a lot of money, but then the stock price fell, and they rode it to the bottom. When things leveled off, they had nothing. They keep reliving the "if-only" game.

Wives dig at their husbands, and sometimes husbands use the shovel and hit back. "No Digging Allowed" is a good principle.

I know hundreds of people who live with failure complexes. They made a mistake; they failed. They took a wrong turn in life and went the wrong way. Their failures keep them from moving ahead. "As long as the present is at war with the past," said Winston Churchill after the terrible conflict we know as World War 2, "there is no hope for the future."

At some point you have to put an R.I.P. sign (envision the "Rest In Peace" headstone you see over the villain's grave in an old Western movie) on the burial place of yesterday's failure and then post a "No Digging Allowed" sign. Let go of your past.

In Micah 7:18, the prophet asks a question of God: "Who is a God like you, who pardons sin and forgives the transgression of the remnant of his inheritance?" Then he adds, "You do not stay angry forever but delight to show mercy. You will again have compassion on us; you will tread our sins underfoot and hurl all our iniquities into the depths of the sea" (Micah 7:18-19).

That's good news, friend. When God forgives your failures, He buries them and puts a "No Digging Allowed" sign over them. He hurls all your iniquities into the deepest sea and puts out a "No Fishing" sign. Can you do less?

I don't know if Janet Bly ever found out why the sign had been posted on that isolated Idaho highway, but I do know that when God says, "No Digging Allowed," it is not to pique your curiosity but to give you stern warning that what lies beneath, buried in the sands of forgiveness, should never again see sunlight. That's good news.

Resource reading: Micah 7

Remember, You Were a Slave in Egypt

Remember that you were slaves in Egypt, and follow carefully these decrees.
DEUTERONOMY 16:12

Insight: Only those who remember where they have come from can appreciate where they are going.

"Remember that you were slaves in Egypt," Moses instructed the Hebrew people as he came to the end of his life. But did the sons of Abraham need to be reminded? Had they not sat around campfires listening to the stories of parents and grandparents? Had they not seen the scars on their wrists and ankles and the marks on their backs that they would carry to their deaths?

"Remember that you were slaves in Egypt." Some might have thought, *Hey, Moses, you don't have to remind us of this. That's all behind us. We need to think positive thoughts, not negative ones. We need to focus on the good things ahead, not reflect on the past difficulties and troubles.*

"Remember that you were slaves in Egypt." Moses knew what he was doing. Why look back? You are reminded of your humble roots and resist the temptation to say, "Look what I've done. I raised myself from poverty to success." Remembering that you were a slave in Egypt eliminates the temptation to be arrogant and prideful. Slaves had no rights of their own. They were chattel. If a slave displeased his owner, he could be beaten, thrown into prison, or killed. Slaves came with certificates of ownership, not warranties with rights and privileges guaranteed.

In remembering that they were slaves in Egypt, the Israelites acknowledged that it was not their resources or clever negotiations that secured their release. It was the God of Abraham, Isaac, and Jacob who sent the plagues that finally convinced Pharaoh that it was in his best interest to cooperate with this 80-year-old sheepherder-turned-deliverer. Remembering was a tacit acknowledgment that God had led them forth by His mighty hand.

In remembering that they had been slaves in Egypt, they would treat others with compassion, fairness, and kindness. God instructed Israel to be kind to the stranger, reminding them that they too had been strangers. He commanded safeguards against the abuses that had been inflicted on them.

A few years ago, a landlord whose financial statement listed millions in assets was convicted of imposing terrible conditions on the poor people who lived in his rat-infested, cockroach-laden buildings. The strange quirk to the story is that he himself had survived Nazi concentration camps and had experienced terrible conditions. He forgot that he had been "a slave in Egypt." He had become a taskmaster of the worst kind, without conscience or heart. His conscience became hardened to the very things he once hated. A judge sentenced him to live in one of his rundown apartments in the hope that his conscience might be awakened. Who knows?

But you may be thinking, *I've never been a slave in Egypt.* Remember, if you would, that Egypt in the Bible is a "type," or a representation, of the world. Millions have been slaves of different kinds—slaves of habit, of temper, of arrogance and pride, of alcohol, drugs, or sex. Do not forget that you too, were a slave in Egypt.

It is possible you are still a slave in Egypt, that more than anything in all the world you would like to be free, to be delivered from the demon that enslaves you. There's good news. The God who delivered the Hebrew slaves out of Egypt is still seeking and saving those who will take the hand of His Son and follow Him through the wilderness to Canaan's fair land.

Only those who have never tasted the honey and wine of Canaan would choose to remain a slave in Egypt. It's time to celebrate the Passover and pack your bags to travel. Remember that you were a slave in Egypt.

Resource reading: Deuteronomy 16

Passion

Brothers, I do not consider myself yet to have taken hold of it. But one thing I do: Forgetting what is behind and straining toward what is ahead, I press on toward the goal to win the prize for which God has called me heavenward in Christ Jesus.

PHILIPPIANS 3:13-14

Insight: Passion is necessary for success.

What do you have a passion for? Nobody succeeds at anything for which they do not have passion. What is your passion? Whether it is art, collecting butterflies, painting ceramics, football, basketball, old books, history, or seeking God, without passion you dawdle through life, much as someone who goes through a smorgasbord, sampling little bits of many things without having anything that completely satisfies.

I never cease to be amazed at the wide diversity of things for which people have passion, interests that have consumed lifetimes and large portions of economic resources, but that are of little interest to me.

Being passionate about someone—a spouse, a friend, a child—is not quite the same thing as having a passion or a strong desire for something. Jesus was challenged by a man who was sent by the Pharisees to test Him by asking what the greatest command in the Law was. Jesus replied, "Love the Lord your God with all your heart and with all your soul and with all your mind" (Matthew 22:37). Eugene Peterson paraphrases His words, saying, "Love the Lord your God with all your passion and prayer and intelligence" (MSG).

In thinking about your priorities and your passions, the things that drive you, how great is your passion for God? This question may create some concern in your heart because we often think of individuals who have a passion for God as being somewhat quaint and eccentric. *Yes,* we think, *passion is okay for mystics and aesthetics who enter monasteries and convents and shut themselves away from the world. That's how people with a passion for God should be treated.*

What of the businessman who has a passion for knowing God, who also believes that what drives him to know God also energizes him to do what he believes God wants him to do? That passion for God is the outworking of his work ethic, which makes him succeed where others fail. He remembers Paul's admonition, "Whatever you do, work at it with all your heart, as working for the Lord, not for men" (Colossians 3:23).

What of the single mother whose husband walked out on her, leaving her with three children to raise without much support? Did passion leave when her husband packed up and walked out? Not necessarily. I have known single women who experienced the resources of God by throwing themselves completely on Him. These women loved God with passion and experienced His provision in ways they never thought possible.

Loving God with passion means you have made Him Lord of all your life. He is not an appendage tacked on to your other tasks and responsibilities. Passion means making God a priority, not a possibility, and taking time to nourish a relationship with Him day in and day out.

Having passion for God does not replace or displace passion in your personal life or passion for what God has called you to do. To the contrary, it means you do a better job of whatever you have been called to. Along with Paul, you have laid hold of that for which God laid hold of you, and with passion you do His will.

Without passion to drive your life, you will never succeed at anything. When you make knowing Him a priority, learn that He is a good God, and grow to love Him, you will discover that a passion for Him is a flame that cannot be extinguished, a light that cannot be dimmed, and a love that will never be disappointed.

Thank God that a passion for Him is merely our human response to the far greater compassion He demonstrated for us when He sent His Son to Earth long ago.

Resource reading: Genesis 5

Handling the Stress of Your Life

A heart at peace gives life to the body.

PROVERBS 14:30

Insight: Living without stress is impossible. The secret is learning to cope with stress, knowing how much is beneficial and at what point it becomes counterproductive to your goals and life.

Tension itself is not necessarily a bad thing. A violin's beautiful tone results from tension applied to the strings, but too much tension snaps the strings.

There are three basic responses to the stress of life today. The first is to try to ignore it. There is no help if you ignore stress and the accompanying signs of crossness and irritability that signal trouble. Many try to ignore tension as though their systems thrive on abuse. They are the ones who startle when you walk up behind them, and they tell you, "You shouldn't frighten me like that!"

Some try to avoid tension. There is wisdom in learning to say no when you realize that to accept more responsibility will only subject you to added tension by involving you in activities that take your mind away from other priorities.

The last and best response is learning to deal with tension. I would like to give you three guidelines to help you deal with tension effectively.

Guideline 1: Deal with your tensions by putting life in perspective. Is the problem worth the stress you are taking? Ask yourself, *What difference will it make a hundred years from now? Ten years from now?* Chances are, you are overrating the importance of your concern. Whenever I am privileged to walk through the ruins of ancient Rome or Athens or in the shadow of the Egyptian pyramids, I always pause and reflect on the problems that have so concerned me. In the stillness of those ancient ruins, my soul cries, *It is not worth killing myself over this problem.*

Guideline 2: Deal with your tension by getting proper exercise. Lack of physical exercise is one of our greatest modern shortcomings. If you sit at a desk or work without moving more than a couple dozen steps every hour, your muscles grow a little tighter. Tension is the normal response. Even a few minutes of physical exercise will relax you, and your mind will be much clearer. In most situations, exercise has a therapeutic effect that far exceeds the helpfulness of any tranquilizer.

Guideline 3: Deal with your tensions by trusting God with your difficulties and leaving the problems in His hand. This last guideline is the tough one, and it is at this point that we so often fail. We say we believe in the power of prayer, and yet we worry ourselves into tense bundles of nerves. Stomach ulcers, heart trouble, and hypertension become the badges of our faith. Have you come to grips with the greatness of God? Or is God only a concept that has never invaded your heart and life? If you are a Christian, learn to accept these words of Scripture: God "works out everthing in conformity with the purpose of his will" (Ephesians 1:11). "And we know that in all things God works for the good of those who love him, who have been called according to his purpose" (Romans 8:28).

Learning that we can trust God to be God breaks the tension habit. When you are tense, get away from the lights of the city and sit down to look at the stars. They are known by the same names today that they had centuries ago. The words of Psalm 147:4 tell us that God calls the stars by name, by the greatness of His might. Now tell yourself, *If God can control our world, if He can stretch out the heavens, then He surely can help me with my problems.* You can break the tension habit before it breaks you.

Resource reading: Psalm 46

Southpaws Are Okay Too

I praise you because I am fearfully and wonderfully made; your works are wonderful, I know that full well.
PSALM 139:14

Insight: Body language, including that of your hands, speaks far louder than your words.

What physical trait do the following people have in common: Leonardo da Vinci, Charlie Chaplin, Bobby Fischer, Bill Gates, Albert Einstein, and Bill Clinton? Furthermore, one out of every nine people who walk down the street share that same trait. We who share this common trait often feel a bit of discrimination, and we are aware of the us-versus-them syndrome. So what is it? We are left-handed. I'm included in that group, which includes people from all nationalities and walks of life.

The ancient Romans thought that something was wrong with left-handed people, and the Latin word *sinstra* (from which we take the English word *sinister*) described them. To them, being left-handed meant being insincere, double-faced, or hypocritical—much more than just the way someone held an eating utensil.

When I was a child beginning to write, I was bribed with a gold watch if I would write with my right hand. I did. Since then, no one, myself included, has been able to read my writing. In China, children are still forced to switch. Going through a factory there where ceramics were painted, I noticed that not a single artist painted with his left hand. When I asked why, I was told that Chinese characters cannot be painted well with the left hand. I'm still dubious.

Thirty-five muscles control the twenty-seven bones in your hand, making it one of the most versatile, efficient tools ever created. Whether or not you have thought much about it, your hands are a vital part of your body language and express the emotions of your heart. When you are angry, your fists clench. Your raised hand, palm facing outward, conveys the desire for peace. Split index and middle fingers stand for *victory,* a symbol used long before Winston Churchill made it famous. Even before the days when gladiators fought in the coliseum, a thumb pointed up meant *okay* or *life* and one pointed down meant *death*.

During the period of the judges, before Saul was crowned king, certain left-handed folks were mentioned. Israel's judge Ehud came to Eglon, the king of Moab, and said, "I have a message from God for you." Reaching into his clothing with his left hand, he pulled out a dagger strapped to his right thigh and delivered God's cutting message.

Among the men from the tribe of Benjamin was a contingent of 700 chosen men who were left-handed, "each of whom could sling a stone at a hair and not miss" (Judges 20:16).

Over 100 times the Bible mentions hands. "Make it your ambition to lead a quiet life," says Paul, "to mind your own business and to work with your hands, just as we told you" (1 Thessalonians 4:11). Three times "clean hands" are used to express innocence. Paul also directed "men everywhere to lift up holy hands in prayer, without anger or disputing" (1 Timothy 2:8).

A business executive tells how he often scrutinizes the hands of people he interviews. Why? Hands tell a lot. They indicate nervousness, strength, or softness. They reveal whether you like the outdoors, whether your work is hard, or whether you pamper your hands by hiring others to do the hard work.

I applaud those who have invented artificial limbs, enabling those who have lost hands to have the ability to grasp and pick up objects. I also know that most of us take our hands for granted. We seldom if ever think about their marvelous design until we injure a thumb or finger and then realize what a great job God did in designing our appendages. Thank God for your hands.

Resource reading: Psalm 139

To Be Completely You

Do not think of yourself more highly than you ought, but rather think of yourself with sober judgment.
ROMANS 12:3

Insight: Understanding that you are a person of value and worth in the sight of God leads, not to arrogance or pride, but to gratitude to the Lord, who enables you to be all that He has planned.

If I could write a prescription for the women of the world," wrote psychologist Dr. James Dobson, "it would provide each of them with a healthy dose of self-esteem and personal worth. I have no doubt that this is their greatest need." Is the same need present for men? I believe it is. What most people need today is a good dose of self-esteem. And that is a great deal different from ego or pride.

You may consider the distinction academic, but I believe there is a big difference between self-love and the love of self. Self-love is the knowledge you have that you are a person of value and worth. Without this you cannot function adequately. This is totally different from the love of self—pride—that Jesus condemned.

People who frequently make self-deprecating remarks usually are as good as most people. They are unhappy people who do not function well.

Knowing who you are—understanding your strengths and weaknesses—allows you to maximize your effectiveness and realize your potential. This is God's intent for your life. It is what Paul was driving at when he wrote, "Do not think of yourself more highly than you ought, but rather think of yourself with sober judgment" (Romans 12:3). Knowing who you are allows you to let God work through your life and gives you the freedom to be yourself.

In His ministry Jesus recognized the value of the individual when He said that you ought to love your neighbor as yourself. He never went around saying, "I'm not baptizing nearly as many people as John is." Nor did He suggest the woman at the well find a good counselor to break through her obsessive–compulsive behavior. He treated people as individuals of value and worth, which is part of what changed their lives. On occasion, Jesus walked long distances to talk with only one person, usually someone society would consider to be unimportant or even contemptible.

We've got to learn that many of the expectations that are thrust upon us today are society's, not God's. The woman who is constantly comparing herself to others, saying, "I'm not as beautiful or as lovely as so and so," has not recognized that God made her an individual, a unique person different from the other 3.5 billion women in the world.

No one in all the world sees with your eyes or feels with your emotions or experiences what you do. You're one of a kind, an original without duplication.

To be the person you can be, you've got to rid yourself of feelings that you do not measure up to someone else's expectations or your culture's expectations. You need to say, "God, I want to be all *You* want me to be, nothing more, nothing less, so here I am. Fill me with Yourself and let me be the person You want me to be."

That, friend, gives you the liberty to be completely you. Shortly before his death, the poet E.E. Cummings wrote to a high school student, "To be nobody-but-myself—in a world which is doing its best, night and day, to make you everybody else—means the hardest battle any human being can fight, and never stop fighting."[14]

It's time to turn our backs on the images that bombard us on television, in newsstand publications, and in society and turn to reality and genuineness. When you are at peace with yourself, you can make peace with those who trouble you.

Resource reading: Exodus 3:7-22

Commitment to Excellence

Whatever your hand finds to do, do it with all your might, for in the grave, where you are going, there is neither working nor planning nor knowledge nor wisdom.

ECCLESIASTES 9:10

Insight: Doing your best glorifies God and makes your Father in heaven proud of you.

William Wadsworth Longfellow once wrote,

> Lives of great men all remind us
> We can make our lives sublime,
> And, departing, leave behind us
> Footprints on the sands of time.

Today, however, most of us are not interested in leaving footprints on the sands of time, not even minuscule tracks. We want the easiest shortcut, the least demanding job, and the fastest way to success that requires the least effort.

The commitment to excellence is gone. The commitment to mediocrity is in. Ask any high-school guidance counselor how many students she knows who have brains but do not use them. Ask how many teens could do outstanding work, but fearing the comments of their peers, they sink to C-level work.

I've been thinking about the contribution of Jerome, a little-known scholar who lived for 30 years in obscurity in the city of Bethlehem but gave to the world the text of the Latin Vulgate—which became the standard Bible for the Christian world for a thousand years.

At Christmas I listen to the strains of George Frideric Handel's *Messiah* and ask myself, *Will there ever be another piece of music so great?* Will we ever see another Beethoven or Bach or Tchaikovsky?

I walk through art galleries, marveling at works of the masters and ask, *Will the world ever again see masterpieces that will rival these—or even come close to them?*

Is it possible that today's problem—the curse of mediocrity—is the reason why the lines of excellence are not connecting one generation to the next? I refuse to accept the conjecture that all the great art, literature, and music that fill our libraries and museums were products of an age that has been supplanted by science and technology, which says we had better preserve the past because there is no future.

These thoughts raise another question: What motivated the artists, the authors, and the scholars of the past? Certainly not fame or fortune, because many of them struggled with poverty, surviving on a few crumbs of support from the crown or a wealthy patron. For every name that has survived, thousands of scholars, artists, and musicians lived in ignominy and obscurity. Their names never made even the dictionary's short biographical section.

My hypothesis is that they were compelled to excellence by the thinking that God requires our best—and to do less than the best is not only a sin against God but also a shame to the family and the family name. Some have called the Puritan work ethic a prime example of this attitude.

Paul put it this way: "Whatever you do, work at it with all your heart, as working for the Lord, not for men" (Colossians 3:23).

Here we are in the twenty-first century, an age of satellite communication and other technology that we had previously not thought possible. Where do we go from here?

Make the question personal. Where are you headed? Are you content with getting by, or are you determined to do your best, whether you drive a bus, head a corporation, teach school, or dig weeds and cut lawns?

Longfellow concluded the poem "A Psalm of Life" in this way:

> Let us, then, be up and doing,
> With a heart for any fate;
> Still achieving, still pursuing,
> Learn to labor and to wait.

Good advice for today. Unless you do your best, you will never know what you might have accomplished. Indeed, who knows?

Resource reading: Colossians 3

Your Best

Do your best to present yourself to God as one approved, a workman who does not need to be ashamed and who correctly handles the word of truth.
2 Timothy 2:15

Insight: To someday hear, "Well done, faithful servant!" demands only one thing—your best.

The greatest accomplishments in life are made, not by the smartest people in the world, but by those who did not know enough to quit. They were the ones who kept plodding, who kept practicing, who kept investigating until they stumbled onto success.

This fact was driven home to me when I was studying in the university. There were two men in my classes who were geniuses. Their IQs were above almost everyone else. At the end of a class, they slapped their books shut and did not open them. They were just plain smart.

I was among those who dug it out. Some people thought I was gifted. Not so—but I knew how to work and study. My parents spent hard-earned money and sent me to school to study, not party. I knew why I was there and made the most of my opportunity.

Learning to apply myself was something I happened to grow up with. Not everybody has a dad who cuts off the broom handles to make them short enough for a boy to use or who works alongside his son.

But we can learn to work. We can develop self-discipline. We can set goals and eventually reach them.

One of my heroes is a New Zealander, the late Sir Edmund Hillary, who with his Sherpa guide, Tensing Norgay, crested Mount Everest for the first time in history. It was an awesome achievement, and he did it before there was a lot of the high-tech gear climbers use today. When asked how he accomplished the climb when others had failed, he replied that when he was tempted to turn back, he took just one more step.

William Carey, the father of modern missions, said that his greatest ability was to plod on in the face of adversity.

After Thomas Edison had tried 10,000 ways to produce an incandescent globe and had not succeeded, he was still confident he would eventually find one that would work. He did!

I have sometimes wondered how many determined, stubborn individuals we have today.

The foundation of our modern achievements was laid by thousands of unknown individuals who lived in obscurity and died unknown, who faithfully contributed to what has enabled us to send men to the moon, circle the globe with communication, and accomplish other great and mighty works. They laid the foundation we have built upon through research, hard work, and trial and error. Their strength and energy, like a gradually falling barometer, were meted out in hard work, years of often-unrecognized service, and blood, sweat, and tears. But they did not quit. They did not look for something with less work but more money.

I have been told that in a European cathedral, high in the rafters where no one ever goes, are some intricate carvings of exquisite beauty, done by a master craftsman whose name has long since been lost to posterity. Why did he take time to do some of his finest work on an abutment that will never be seen by the public? He valued excellence. He took seriously the admonition of the Bible: "Whatever your hand finds to do, do it with all your might, for in the grave, where you are going, there is neither working nor planning nor knowledge nor wisdom" (Ecclesiastes 9:10).

Cultivate excellence. Make it a passion. Refuse to let the world and our culture shove you into the mold of mediocrity. Whether or not you reach the top, you are building a foundation, and upon your shoulders, someday, someone will reach the top. Thank God for teachers who inspire excellence, for mothers who bring out the best in their children, for dads who have the patience to find tools their small children have left lying around and show their children how to use them. Indeed, aim high!

Resource reading: Ecclesiastes 9:1-10

Why Bother?

Whatever you do, work at it with all your heart, as working for the Lord, not for men.
COLOSSIANS 3:23

Insight: Doing your best allows you to reach your potential, to be all you can be, to be all God intends you to be.

For 30 years a certain foreman worked for an employer who treated him honestly and fairly but never paid the man what he wanted. The foreman griped and complained, "He always wants my best work, and he's never satisfied." One day the owner of the company called in the foreman and said, "I'm going to retire next year, and I want you to build one more house for me. Give it your best effort! Use the finest materials and craftsmen, and when it's done, I'm retiring and going out of business."

The foreman thought, *Hey, if this is his last house, there is no way I'm going to put the best materials into it. Furthermore, why bother, if I'll be looking for a new job this time next year?* So the foreman built the house, cutting corners where he could, charging to the job materials he actually sold on the side, pocketing the money.

When the house was completed, the owner called him into the office and handed him the keys to the front door. "Here," he said, "I wanted this to be your best work because I'm giving it to you as a reward for these many years of service." He signed over the papers and handed the keys to the foreman.

For the rest of his life, that man lived with the reality that the poorly built house was his. Had he only known, he would have done his best job.

When you are assigned a task, how much effort do you put into it? Just enough to get by? Sufficient to satisfy your boss, get the work signed off, and keep your job? If you are a student, is your goal to do well enough to pass the course, or do you give it your best?

"How long have you been working here?" a supervisor asked a factory worker. "Ever since my boss threatened to fire me if I didn't start producing," replied the employee with a smile on his face.

Why bother anyway? If people can get by with minimal effort, why go all out? That's the question many people are asking. They have the mentality that it is stupid to exert themselves if they can cheat or squeeze by with minimal effort. What has happened to our commitment to excellence?

Let's go beyond the motive of reward to another issue—what God, not your employer, expects. The Bible says that God demands our best, not just enough to get by. Paul instructed slaves in Colosse, "Whatever you do, work at it with all your heart, as working for the Lord, not for men" (Colossians 3:23).

Why does God care whether we do our best or just enough to get by? What's the connection between our effort and His will? God's desire is for us to become all we can be. What we are is God's gift to us; what we become is our gift to Him.

God gave you tremendous talents and abilities, and doing your best, no matter what it may be, is what it takes to realize your potential. Doing your best profits you, not your employer.

A closing thought: A commitment to excellence is different from being a perfectionist who is never satisfied with what he does. A commitment to excellence means at the day's end, you turn out the lights, tired but fulfilled, knowing you gave your best and have nothing to be ashamed of.

You may someday have to live in the house you build. Who knows?

Resource reading: 2 Corinthians 4:7-11

Looking Back

He said to them all: "If anyone would come after me, he must deny himself and take up his cross daily and follow me."
LUKE 9:23

Insight: You cannot see the path that leads to the future when failures from the past obscure your vision.

It isn't how you start that counts, but rather how you finish! This is what Jesus had in mind when He said, "No one who puts his hand to the plow and looks back is fit for service in the kingdom of God" (Luke 9:62).

Rarely does the long-distance runner who sprints first out of the starting blocks with a burst of speed break the tape, winning the race.

You cannot drive by looking in the rearview mirror. Neither can you accomplish God's purpose in your life by vacillating, compromising, wondering whether you should commit yourself to the task before you.

Jesus' comment about looking back after you have put your hand to the plow was the linchpin of a conversation He had with several people as He challenged them to follow Him. One had an excuse that he first had to go bury his father, and then he would come and follow Jesus. Another said, "I will follow You, Lord; but first let me go back and say goodbye to my family."

I've never plowed a furrow, but my father did—plenty of them when he was a boy. He explained that to plow a straight furrow, you've got to fix your eyes on a distant point of reference—a tree, a fence post, a landmark of some kind—and keep moving straight toward that point. Looking back while trying to move ahead means you veer from one side to the other, uncertain, indefinite, and unsuccessful.

As long as you look back, wondering if you married the right person, hesitating to fully commit yourself to your mate, your marriage will not improve. I've never seen a drug addict who had the strength to walk away from the habit as long as he dabbled in drugs—even a little bit. On more than one occasion great generals have burned their ships when their troops hit the beach so there was no possibility of going back. Burn your bridges behind you.

We cannot find the victory, the joy, and the power to live as God intends us to live until we make the decision, unconditional and without reservation, to walk with God. We can never say, "No, Lord," because when we say no, we deny that He is Lord.

There is strength and power in the decision to move forward, to refuse to look back, to go for it, no matter what happens. In the early 1950s, everyone assumed running a four-minute mile was impossible. Then two athletes did it—an Australian, John Landy, and a British runner from Oxford, Roger Bannister. Later, the two were matched against each other in a historic race to determine which of the two was faster.

They met on a track in Vancouver and, say observers, Landy was leading as they turned toward the finish line. Then he made a mistake. He looked back to see how close his competitor was. As he looked back, he momentarily broke his stride, and Bannister seized the moment, surging ahead to win the contest.

Friend, when you turn back or even look back, you stumble over the future and what you might have been, what you might have accomplished, what God might have done through you.

Forget Egypt. Put your eyes on the Promised Land. Forget the past and build for the future. Remember what Jesus said: "No one who puts his hand to the plow and looks back is fit for service in the kingdom of God" (Luke 10:62). Paul got it right when he wrote that we are to forget the things that are past and press forward to receive all that God has for us. It's the only way to the finish line.

Resource reading: Exodus 14:10-28

Excess Baggage

With you there is forgiveness; therefore you are feared.
PSALM 130:4

Insight: Excess baggage is annoying when you travel but devastating when it is emotional.

Never will I forget the first time I was charged for excess baggage. I was in Africa on a missionary jaunt, and I had the feeling that the agent looked me over and said to himself, *This guy is good for some extra money!* He did not show a gun, but it was a situation over which I had no control. Either empty out the suitcase or pay the piper. I paid.

Since then, I've paid for excess or overweight luggage a few times. The solution to an expensive problem: Travel light. The right number of pounds and no more will get you home without extra charges.

Traveling light is good business in life as well. The more you carry with you, the more difficult it is to get through life without stumbling over people. What do people carry with them that they should get rid of?

Item 1: Get rid of fear. Back in the 1970s, a man named Leonard was sure the bomb was going to be dropped, and the only way to handle that fear, so he thought, was to dig a bomb shelter in his backyard. He told his friends that when they got torched, he and the gophers would come out of their holes unscathed. But it was not a nuclear blast that got him. His friends found him in the bottom of his hole, dead of a heart attack. Whatever you fear becomes your master, and it's a heavy burden to live with.

Item 2: Get rid of your malice toward others. After I moved to the Philippines in 1974, a fellow who listened to Guidelines over the radio service of the Far East Broadcasting Company visited me. Under his arm was a file about four inches thick. As he sat and talked, he grew angry and agitated. Ten years before he had been terminated at work. The file contained the running dialogue of suits and accusations. Instead of getting on with his life, he gunnysacked his hatred and anger. He was the loser. Today it's a proven fact that when you have malice and hatred in your heart, it affects your health. It's heavy excess baggage.

Item 3: Get rid of your resentments. When Jim's dad passed away, Jim expected to get his share of the inheritance and also some personal items his dad had promised to him. Before anything was distributed, however, some of the other family members arrived at the home, and what Jim thought was his went out the door. Sure, he was angry. For years he did not even speak to some of his brothers. "If that's how they want it, then I will have nothing to do with them," he declared. The trivial items his dad had promised were sentimental but not of much value. For more than a decade, he lived with the bitterness. Eventually he forgave his relatives, but it cost him a decade of isolation. Resentment is excess baggage you cannot afford. There's a high charge in the currency of your health when you keep resentments.

Item 4: There is one more item of excess baggage you need to shed: your guilt. To attempt to leave guilt behind without understanding that only God's forgiveness can take it away is akin to making yourself think you are warm when you are freezing. The good news is that God can and does forgive, but you've got to ask Him to remove your guilt and sin. David, who knew guilt, said, "With you there is forgiveness; therefore you are feared" (Psalm 130:4).

I've never liked the thought of paying for excess baggage at either the airport or the bar of God's justice. Travel light. It's the only way to go.

Resource reading: Hebrews 12:1-2

What Is It Like to Die?

Hard choice! The desire to break camp here and be with Christ is powerful. Some days I can think of nothing better. But most days, because of what you are going through, I am sure that it's better for me to stick it out here.

PHILIPPIANS 1:23-24 MSG

Insight: Death and taxes are as certain as the rising and setting of the sun.

Some time ago newspapers reported on an eight-year-old boy with a troubled background who wrote a letter to God, addressed it to "Heaven," put a stamp on it, and mailed it. As you probably know, letters with insufficient addresses are sent to the dead-letter office, where they are usually disposed of; however, this letter was opened. The message read, "Dear God, what is it like to die? I just want to know. I don't want to do it. Your friend, Michael."

Michael's troubled cry is a commentary on the violence that makes life today fragile and uncertain: drive-by shootings, gangs, and terrorism to name a few. Life is cheap—which causes some to live life to the hilt, often throwing care to the wind because one never knows what a day may hold; and which moves others to live in fear, wondering whether someone's knife or bullet has their name on it.

This is the world in which eight-year-olds ask the sobering question, "What is it like to die?" We know eight-year-olds should be thinking about life, not death, yet the reality is that both are part of life. Knowing that God sent His Son to take away the fear of death makes a difference in how you live.

Because he knew death is merely a transition into the presence of the Lord for God's children, Paul could cry out, "Where, O death, is your victory?" (1 Corinthians 15:55). But anything we have never experienced or do not understand can be frightening—whether we are eight or eighty.

When Paul wrote his second letter to the Corinthians, he used the analogy of living on earth and pitching a tent, as you do when you camp out. He spoke from his own experience, because he was a tentmaker. He said that when our earthly tent, or body, wears out—beaten by wind and weather of adversity, with torn seams that can no longer be repaired—God will have a new eternal home prepared for us. Here's how he put it: "Now we know that if the earthly tent we live in is destroyed, we have a building from God, an eternal house in heaven, not built by human hands" (2 Corinthians 5:1).

In His last week with the disciples, Jesus comforted His followers by telling them He was going to prepare a place for them so that "they may be with me where I am." This, of course, personalizes heaven and makes it real, not simply a nebulous "out-there-somewhere" concept. Heaven is a home, and for those who have been homeless or who have wandered as refugees, knowing they will be secure and will never lack is good news indeed.

When I am going to some part of the world I have never seen before, I start reading and investigating to find out what it is like. I browse through travel books in a bookstore. I go on the Internet to find what I can learn there, and when it's possible, I talk with someone who can tell me what it is like from personal experience. No other book in all the world can tell me what the Bible tells about heaven, and only one person has ever been there who can tell us what it is like. His name is Jesus Christ.

At the end of C.S. Lewis's Chronicles of Narnia, all the characters die. Lewis concludes with these words,

> But the things that began to happen after that were so beautiful that I cannot write them. And for us this is the end of all the stories, but for them it was only the beginning of the real story.

That is the truth and the real answer to Michael's question about dying.

A closing thought. Michael signed his letter to God with the words "your friend." How would *you* sign a letter to God? Is He your friend or a long-distant acquaintance? Is He possibly even an unknown entity? Get to know Him. He sent His Son to show you the way to heaven.

Resource reading: 1 Corinthians 15:52-58

Death and Dying

Enoch walked with God; then he was no more, because God took him away.
GENESIS 5:24

Insight: When you are God's child, He is present in all seasons of your life, and going home is as natural as birth.

When he was asked his thoughts on death, comedian Woody Allen said, "I'm not afraid of dying—I just don't want to be there when it happens." Allen is not alone. A century before him, Mark Twain reportedly said that he wished he knew where he was going to die because he would never go near the place.

I wish I did not have to believe in cancer, hunger, infidelity, and the evils of a society that is out of control, along with death and dying, but they exist just the same. Knowing about something, believing in its reality, makes me want to prepare for it and not to be caught unaware and wishing I had thought about it beforehand.

It is strange, isn't it, how little thought we give the issue of what lies beyond our last heartbeat, almost as though by ignoring the whole issue we can make it cease to exist? I am encouraged that the issue of dying, called "the last taboo" by Bill and Judith Moyers, is beginning to get more attention. The Moyerses extensively interviewed people about death and dying, and through their writings, they have attempted to bring people into confrontation with the choices that ultimately have to be made—either by themselves or by someone else. The issues cannot be avoided forever.

I, for one, am glad that we have begun to talk more openly about the issue. My parents' generation refused to talk about their mortality. After spending a week in Colorado with my dad prior to his death and several more days there following his funeral, I returned home. My wife's parents, who lived near us, were wonderful, godly people. As a pastor, Guy Duffield, my father-in-law, had stood over the caskets of scores of people, but in the days that followed, never once was there a mention of my dad's death or what we were going through. Finally, my wife asked, "Why haven't we been able to talk about this?" Her parents' fear was that talking about it would make us feel worse.

Talking about troublesome issues is therapy! It allows you to ventilate your thoughts, your fears, your frustrations. It lessens the sting. Avoiding the subject does not lessen the pain; it compounds it.

Seldom do people have a game plan when it comes to death and dying. Possibly they have a will, but chances are it is one drawn up years before. Knowing where you are going and where you will be five minutes after you die can give you freedom to talk about death and heaven, your new home. The freedom to share will be a blessing to the generation left behind as well as to the one taking the journey. Following the death of a loved one, people often frantically turn pages of a Bible saying, "I know there's something in this book about heaven. I just don't know where." Find out ahead of time. Study the Word together. Talk about the past, the present, and the future.

Decide ahead of time who will make decisions if you are unable to. This includes advising the hospital of your wishes about being resuscitated should your heart fail. What are your wishes regarding being connected to a life-support system? What kind of medical treatment do you want or not want? Your failure to decide means that medical personnel will make the decision at the time, and once a procedure is undertaken, it is difficult and emotionally painful for your family to reverse it. Plan your memorial service with the realization that it is to bring comfort and strength to those you leave behind. You need to make these decisions now.

"Precious in the sight of the Lord is the death of his saints," says Psalm 116:15. If it is precious to God, it should be meaningful to us as His children. While the home-going of God's children is filled with mystery and awe, it is also a spiritual experience of great dimensions.

Death is as much a part of life as birth and the events that take place in between.

Resource reading: 1 Thessalonians 5

Life's Darkest Hour

I sought the Lord, *and he answered me;*
he delivered me from all my fears.
Psalm 34:4

Insight: Sunrise always follows the darkness of night.

In the closing years of the nineteenth century, Dwight Lyman Moody was as well known as Billy Graham was at the end of the twentieth. All over the English-speaking world, people had been affected by this forceful, energetic evangelist. In the fall of 1892, Moody boarded a ship from Southampton, England, headed toward New York. Three days into the journey, disaster struck. In his memoirs, Moody told how he was lying on his bunk reflecting on his good fortune in life and how he had never been involved in an accident of a serious nature. At the very moment he was thinking about it, he was startled by a loud noise, and the vessel began to shudder as though it had been driven onto a rock.

It was serious, very serious. The large shaft that drove the propeller had broken and smashed through the side of the ship. Water began pouring in, and soon it became apparent that the ship could sink.

D.L. Moody was no stranger to dangerous situations. In the American Civil War, he had been shot at, but the bullets had missed him. He was in Chicago during the great cholera epidemic and went with doctors to visit the sick and dying, but the sickness spared him. Moody wrote, "I remember a case of smallpox where the sufferer's condition was beyond description, yet I went to the bedside of that poor sufferer again and again...In all this I had no fear of death. But on the sinking ship it was different."[15]

Moody had never before known the cold, gnawing reality of fear. By his own testimony, "I had thought myself superior to the fear of death," but this time it was different: "I could not endure it." Keep in mind this was a man who had preached to hundreds of thousands. In his day he spoke to more people than any other man alive. Moody went to his cabin and on his knees poured his heart out to God in prayer. What happened? Moody said, "God heard my cry, and enabled me to say, from the depths of my soul, 'Thy will be done!' "

Moody touched God through prayer, and his fear left him. He went to bed and fell asleep almost immediately. He said, "I...never slept any more soundly in all my life. I can no more doubt that God gave answer to my prayer for relief than I can doubt my own existence."

At three in the morning, Moody's son awakened him with the good news that a steamer had heard their distress signals. Seven days later, they were towed into safe harbor.

Moody said it was the darkest hour of his life not because he feared dying, but because he feared leaving behind his family and the friends whom he loved.

May I share you with two thoughts? First, no one is immune from the dark hours of despair, when fear gnaws at his innermost being. Even spiritual giants are susceptible. "Elijah was a man just like us," writes James.

Second, dark hours of our lives must yield to prayer, for it is this that reminds the Father we are His children and He has promised to keep us. Moody said, "Out of the depths I cried unto my Lord, and He heard me and delivered me from all my fears," echoing the words of David in Psalm 34:4.

Scores of men and women can testify to the fact that at the darkest hour of their lives, God broke through, giving them peace and courage to say, as did Moody, "Thy will be done!"

Are you in the midst of the darkest hour of your life? As you say, "Thy will be done!" you will sense His presence and find His deliverance.

Resource reading: Jonah 1

Wake-up Calls

Just as man is destined to die once, and after that to face judgment, so Christ was sacrificed once to take away the sins of many people; and he will appear a second time, not to bear sin, but to bring salvation to those who are waiting for him.

HEBREWS 9:27-28

Insight: You are wise when you sense your humanity and live for eternity.

Wake-up calls cause us to re-evaluate our lives. Perhaps we have experienced a near-fatal car crash, a heart attack, the hijacking of a plane, a house burning, or some other event that lets us know death has been stalking us but we have not fallen prey to its grasp.

A call came in to a pilot flying a military jet over Greenland. The air was crisp and clear and very cold that day. A glance at the radar screen showed nothing of concern. Then the pilot happened to look through his narrow slit of a windshield straight ahead and saw a wall of ice that the radar unit was not detecting. He jerked back on the controls, banked the plane severely, and barely missed the iceberg immediately in front of him.

My wife got a call as she drove to the airport to pick up our son. It was raining. Whenever it has not rained for a while, a thin film of oil exhaust from thousands and thousands of automobiles can turn a wet freeway into a demolition derby. The traffic stopped ahead, and as she touched her brakes, her little car began to slide, and then it rolled over and over, coming to rest upside down on the freeway divider.

Does a wake-up call truly cause you to wake up, to acknowledge that life is short and death is certain, and to change the way you live? Does it cause you to be more loving, to take time to play with the kids, to be more interested in spiritual things? Or do you walk away saying, "Whew! That was sure close," as you wipe your brow and forget you were only a moment away from certain death?

You are wise beyond words if you live with the certainty that life at its longest is brief, and that standing on the other side of life in this world is a loving God who sent His Son to show you the way to heaven.

Haddon Robinson tells about an order of Trappist monks that has a monastery with a graveyard adjacent to it. Each day the monks solemnly proceed to the graveyard and stand for a few moments before an open grave—a solemn reminder that life is short and to make every day count. When one of their number dies, he's put in the empty grave, and a new one is dug.

In an article entitled "The Grim Shepherd" Robinson writes,

> There is a way in which the king is like the lion, the dowager is like the dog, the Mafia boss is like the pit bull, and the farmer like the cow: They all die. They have that in common. But if the dowager, Mafia boss, or farmer dies with no more understanding than animals, then they are no better than the beasts of the field.[16]

In closing, your good deeds, your money and power, and good luck or beauty cannot keep death at bay when God says, "It's time." The important thing is knowing you have made peace with Him so that when you stand in His presence, you will hear Him say, "Well done, thou good and faithful servant."

Jesus said, "I am the way and the truth and the life. No one comes to the Father except through me" (John 14:6). Knowing Him as the shepherd of your soul and your Lord and Savior takes the fear of death out of your life. Wake-up calls—near encounters with death—are worthwhile if you learn the right lesson through them.

Resource reading: John 11

No More Death or Dying

Since the children have flesh and blood, he too shared in their humanity so that by his death he might destroy him who holds the power of death—that is, the devil—and free those who all their lives were held in slavery by their fear of death.

HEBREWS 2:14-15

Insight: Some things are just too good for earth, and heaven is one of them. Who cares that equal numbers of birth and death certificates are issued? It's the "born-again certificate" that won't be negated by a corresponding equivalent.

Someone pointed out that every birth certificate comes with a death certificate attached. In a typical bureau of vital statistics, there are corresponding numbers of birth and death certificates for every century. Though we prefer not to think of it—too depressing!—the reality is that everyone eventually meets the undertaker.

But—and this is good news—there is coming a day when no more death certificates will be issued. Who says? God does. The prophet Isaiah, the most respected and eloquent of all the Old Testament spokesmen for God, records the claim. He boldly wrote that God "will destroy the shroud that enfolds all peoples, the sheet that covers all nations; he will swallow up death forever. The Sovereign LORD will wipe away the tears from all faces...The LORD has spoken" (Isaiah 25:7-8).

Did you catch those two phrases that describe death—"the shroud that enfolds all peoples" and "the sheet that covers all nations"? The poetry of it somewhat masks the bitter reality. I have logged a lot of air miles going to remote corners of the world, including China, Burma, Thailand, Taiwan, and more barrios in the Philippines than most Filipinos have seen. I've traveled in Russia, Belarus, Ukraine, Poland, Africa, Latin America, and the Middle East. It does not matter whether it is in a little Egyptian village, a mountain hut in the Andes, or the home of a wealthy family in Hong Kong, when someone you love is taken from you, your heart is wrenched in pain.

But God says, "Enough is enough! One day, I'm putting a stop to all of this!" The prophet says that He will swallow up death forever and put an end to our tears. Here's a beautiful picture. God doesn't just say, "Hey, don't cry over this!" He tenderly says, "I will wipe away your tears!" There is nothing more comforting to children than for their parents to hold them in their arms, tenderly wiping away those big tears that trickle down their cheeks. One day your heavenly Father will do that for you.

The good news is that there are no tears in heaven. For most of us the only thing that is more difficult than saying goodbye is watching someone you love suffer and not be able to do anything about it. At times I hear of the strange irony of specialists—the finest doctors in the world—seeing ones they love waste away, afflicted with the very disease they have specialized in curing. But Isaiah, in looking ahead, also says that in that day, "No one living in Zion will say, 'I am ill'" (Isaiah 33:24).

No wonder the songwriter rejoiced, "There's a glad day comin,' a glad day comin' by and by." I feel sorry for those who have no hope of heaven, no comfort that one day all believers in Christ will be united in the presence of the Lord, and no assurance that they will live forever in the presence of the Lord.

"In my Father's house are many rooms," said Jesus not long before He went back to heaven. "If it were not so, I would have told you. I am going there to prepare a place for you. And if I go and prepare a place for you, I will come back and take you to be with me that you also may be where I am" (John 14:2-3).

Resource reading: 1 Thessalonians 4:13-18

Epilogue

Long ago the writer of Ecclesiastes wrote, "There is a time for everything, and a season for every activity under heaven: a time to be born and a time to die." And he could have included, "a time to write the closing chapter of a book so the reader can eventually close the cover."

But before I do that, I want to finish the story I began in the preface of the book, telling you about the conversation that took place between a young man in college and his father. Clark Poling came home because of an urgent need in his personal life. His father knew God, but Clark was not sure of his relationship with God. He had to know for himself, so he put the question to his father: "What do you know about God?"

Daniel Poling, the father, thought for a few moments and then opened his heart. He spoke of difficult times in his own life and how he had trusted God, who had taken him through the dark nights of life. He told his son that God would never let him down, that he could always count on His faithfulness. He spoke with quiet assurance. He had experienced God.

That you can count on God has been the testimony of untold numbers of people who, like Clark, have faced dark hours and found the help of God. During a time of trouble, Jeremiah wrote, "Because of the LORD's great love we are not consumed, for his compassions never fail. They are new every morning; great is your faithfulness" (Lamentation 3:22-23).

There are seasons to life—some joyful, some perfunctory, some pensive, and some difficult, yet the abiding promise of Jesus Christ—that He will never leave us or forsake us—carries us through the spring, summer, fall, and winter of life.

In the first chapter I wrote about having a personal relationship with God through His Son, Jesus Christ, which gives us confidence to face the difficult times. In the last book of the New Testament we find the comforting words of Jesus, who said, "I stand at the door and knock. If anyone hears my voice and opens the door, I will come in and eat with him, and he with me" (Revelation 3:20).

The invitation has your name on it, so reach out and take His hand. Walk with Him day by day. If I can help you find peace with God, I would be happy to hear from you. May God's best be yours no matter what the season of your life!

In the United States write to

Dr. Harold J. Sala
Box G
Laguna Hills, CA 92654
E-mail: guidelines@guidelines.org

In Asia write to

Dr. Harold J. Sala
Box 4000
Makati, Metro Manila
Philippines
E-mail: Box4000@guidelines.org

Notes

1. "What Does the Average Davis Student Think of Jesus?" *The California Aggie,* 25 April, 1969, 3.
2. A.W. Tozer, *The Pursuit of God* (Camp Hill, PA: Christian Publications, 1993), 7.
3. "Death Be Not Proud," Economist.com, 1 May 2008, www.economist.com/world/asia/displaystory.cfm?story_id=11294805.
4. James Comer, "How to Control Your Anger," *U.S. News & World Report,* 10 October 1977, 53.
5. Comer, 53.
6. David Elton, quoted in Gordon Lewis, "Does Christianity Need Defense?" *Decision,* November 1976, 6.
7. C.S. Lewis, quoted in Philip Yancey, *The Bible Jesus Read* (Grand Rapids, MI: Zondervan, 1999), 53.
8. Mary McNamara, "The Truth About Lying," *Los Angeles Times,* 27 August 1998, E-6.
9. Frazier Moore, "Gimme, Gimme, Gimme," *Orange County Register,* 15 September 1997, Show, 14.
10. Charles Farr, "An Eternal Touch for Earthly Pain," *Leadership,* Spring Quarter 1985, 13.
11. Corrie ten Boom, *Tramp for the Lord* (Fort Washington, PA: Christian Literature Crusade, 1974), 88.
12. Sigmund Freud, quoted in Philip Yancey, "An Unnatural Act," *Christianity Today,* 8 April 1991, 36.
13. Yancey, 36.
14. E.E. Cummings, quoted in "Doing Your Own Thing," *The Royal Bank of Canada Monthly Newsletter,* April 1978, 1.
15. William R. Moody, *The Life of Dwight L. Moody* (New York: Revell, 1900), 400-407.
16. Haddon Robinson, "The Grim Shepherd," *Christianity Today,* 23 October 2000, 115.

About the Author

Dr. Harold J. Sala is an internationally known radio personality, author, Bible teacher, lecturer, husband, and grandfather. His radio program, *Guidelines—A Five-Minute Commentary on Living,* is heard on more than 1000 stations in 17 languages and reaches into more than 100 countries; in the USA, it reaches 49 of the 50 states. It has been the recipient of the Catholic Mass Media Award for Moral Excellence in Broadcasting.

Dr. Sala holds a Ph.D. in English Bible from Bob Jones University with proficiencies in Hebrew and Greek. His further graduate studies have been at the University of Southern California, California Baptist Seminary, Fuller Theological Seminary, and Denver Seminary.

More than 40 books and hundred of publications have been authored by Dr. Sala, focusing on marriage, parenting, singles, counseling, and daily devotionals. His book *Heroes—People Who Have Changed the World* received the prestigious Angel Award for moral excellence in the media in the U.S. Dr. Sala has also been honored by CASA with the Heritage of Faithfulness Award. He serves on the boards of the Far East Broadcasting Company and the Friends of Donetsk Christian University, and he is chairman of the board of Joy Partners, a ministry to China.

His warm, personal style of sharing wisdom and insight from God's Word has brought hope to many. Dr. Sala is a frequent guest lecturer and teacher at many churches, schools, and international conferences, such as the Asian Theological Seminary in Manila and Donetsk Christian University in Ukraine, and the Ukrainian Institute for Artificial Intelligence.

His hobbies include golf, photography, and people—the driving focus of his life and ministry. Residing in California, Dr. Sala and his wife, Darlene, have three adult children and eight well-loved grandchildren.

Jesus 365

Experiencing the Four Gospels as One Single Story

ED STEWART

"A very fine way...to understand more clearly the life of Christ."

JOSH MCDOWELL

This vivid chronological walk through the events of Jesus' time on earth weaves together the four Gospels into a single, flowing narrative. The 365 compact readings confront you with the total impact of Christ's life and message, heightened by

- up-to-date, natural language that brings the story alive
- the presence of everything recorded by the Gospel authors, with nothing added or omitted
- sidebars, maps, and notes providing cultural and historical insights

Take a fresh look at Jesus—deepen your insight into what He came to say and do, and what it means to you.

God's Best for My Life

A Classic Daily Devotional

LLOYD JOHN OGILVIE

—The bestselling daily guide to companionship with God—

As you meet with God day-by-day, His supernatural life will become real to you and in you. He will grant you His best for your life...

- friendship with Him that overcomes loneliness
- courage and endurance for life's challenges and adventures
- guidance when you're uncertain
- real love and affection for people—even those you have a tough time with
- inner peace that comes from the assurance He's always there

These 365 profoundly personal devotions invite you to discover, explore, and enjoy the incalculable blessing and love that wait for you when you spend time with the Father.

To read a sample chapter of this or another Harvest House book, go to www.harvesthousepublishers.com